Danny Gallagher
Author of 10 books about Nos Amours

Explosion

Genesis to relocation, 1994 saga, contraction,
revelations about the dying days,
Moises, Lenny, Schneids and the Expos

Foreword by Andre Dawson

SPECIAL COMMEMORATIVE EDITION

Scoop Press
Toronto, 2024

Explosion

Copyright @ 2024, Danny Gallagher

Published by Scoop Press. For information, please call 1-365-881-2389.

All rights reserved. No part of this book may be reproduced, stored in a retrieval system or transmitted in any form by any means – electronic, photocopy, recording or any other – except for brief quotations in print reviews without prior permission from Scoop Press and the author. Every reasonable effort has been made to ensure that all material is correct in the book. Information enabling the author to rectify any reference or credit in future printings would be appreciated.

Cover design and formatting by Dawna Dearing, First Wave Grafix.

Front cover photo of Moises Alou was taken by Joe Gromelski, the Lenny Webster photo is from the Canadian Baseball Hall of Fame collection, the image of Brian Schneider is courtesy of Topps. The back cover image of Tom Brady comes courtesy of Fanatics and Topps.

ISBN: 978-1-777-413-255

To: Charles Bronfman, John McHale and Jim Fanning.

Table of Contents

Foreword by Andre Dawson

Introduction

1 The positive side of Gene Mauch 1
2 20-game losing streak 10
3 Radatz ran out of gas 12
4 Floyd Wicker and Larry Jaster 15
5 McGinn big part of trivia in early days 19
6 McSween was a southpaw with promise 22
7 Joe Sparma and Paul Warfield 29
8 Strohmayer outduelled Nolan Ryan 34
9 Woods was a solid, part-time player 38
10 Ron was better than Fairly good 43
11 Gebhard tutored some good pitchers 49
12 Blair was a whiz-kid prospect 55
13 Jose Morales was the Hit Man and Yip Yaw 66
14 Granger played amateur and pro ball in Québec 76
15 Stanhouse was Full Pack and Stan the Man Unusual 79
16 Garrett only Expo to hit grand slam vs..Seaver 91
17 Playing a prank on Cromartie 94
18 Chris Smith part of Staub trade 97
19 Dan Norman and A Boy and His Dog 101
20 The Pete Incaviglia saga 105
21 Buck Rodgers was a popular manager 109
22 McGaffigan was an unsung hero 112
23 Hesketh's debut featured a balk 118
24 Santovenia shuts down Coleman's 50-game streak 122
25 Fitzgerald's love for diving for lobsters 124

26 Wainhouse only Canadian picked in first round of draft .. 127
27 Perms, masks and The Cy Young Catcher 141
28 Gardner threw no-hitter through nine innings 147
29 Duquette had his eyes on McGriff in 1993 150
30 Various roles got Boucher into Canadian hall.................. 153
31 Financial concerns about the team in 1993 156
32 Forkball made Rojas a star 158
33 Moises was the best Alou of all.. 163
34 Grissom sure had a lot of talent 172
35 Webster played his heart out.. 176
36 Remembering Tom Brady again... 182
37 The good and bad of Grudzielanek 187
38 Segui scion of fine royalty 194
39 Terry Francona, Stan Hough and Milton Bradley............. 198
40 The sneaky John Patterson narrative 201
41 Ad in Baseball Weekly paper stoked DeHart 206
42 The ups and downs of Hideki Irabu................................. 212
43 Schneider was a leader in many ways 221
44 Chavez solid in 2003 and 2004 227
45 Livan Hernandez delivered the goods 230
46 The drama behind the last home game........................... 234
47 Bob DuPuy, contraction, Loria's sale and the end 242
48 Who from the Blue Jays voted to contract the Expos? 247
49 Olympic Stadium bullshit 250
50 Tribute to coaches the last three years........................... 253
51 Robbie Hart's 'biblical' documentary 256
Epilogue 260
Appreciation to individuals and organizations 261
Interviews 261
Terry (Aislin) Mosher cartoons 262

Expos stuff missed

Valderi, Valdera
The Happy Wanderer
Jean-Guy Black firing peanuts on target
Sound of b-i-e-r-e f-r-o-i-d-e! cold beer!
Calling main office 514-253-3434
Logging onto montrealexpos.com

Guy blowing a bullhorn
Jonesville
Fernand Lapierre at the organ
Dave Van Horne's Up, Up and Away call
PA announcer Claude Mouton
Call of John Bocc-a-belllll-a

Chickens clucking on the scoreboard on opposition pickoff throws to first
Jean-Pierre Roy's "Let's have another O'Keefe and get back to the game"

Players engaged in pepper in front of the dugout
Pie-IX (Pee Noof) subway stop at stadium
Waft of hot dogs entering stadium
Steamed hot dogs with coleslaw
Scheduled doubleheaders
Afternoon home openers
Carlsberg Oom-Pah-pah band
Clack-clack of the hard, plastic seats
Smell of popcorn
Smell of minor grease fire coming into the game
Sundaes in little helmets
The Dancer at Jarry Park

Jarry Park swimming pool
Cold, aluminum seats at Jarry Park
Duke Snider's stories
Sound of Chien chaude — hot dog!
Smoked meat sandwiches
Jacques Doucet and Rodger Brulotte
Youppi
Oh Henry chocolate bar craze
The press boxes
Scoreboard magic
Home and visitors clubhouses

Compiled by Danny Gallagher with help from followers on Twitter (X) and Facebook

Foreword

In the early summer of 1975, I was contacted by the late Mel Didier, regarding my interest in participating in a pre-draft workout in West Palm Beach, Florida.

I had been scouted by Bill Adair, a regional scout, while playing at Florida A&M University during my junior year of college. Occasionally, there were additional scouts, with Buck O'Neil being one of the most notable. However, I wasn't aware of who they were when they were present. It was later brought to my attention the presence of these scouts by my head coach at the time, Costa Kittles.

After attending the workout in West Palm Beach along with high-school phenom Clint Hurdle, I was asked by Mr. Didier if any other scouts had reached out to me regarding the pending MLB draft which was a week or so away. I informed Mr. Didier that I hadn't spoken with anyone. He immediately gave me his business card and requested I get in touch with him immediately if someone did.

No one contacted me, and about a week or so later, I was drafted in the 11th round of the MLB Draft by the Montreal Expos. Not knowing much about Montreal other than it was located in Canada and very cold, my first thought being a boy from Florida was, "how in the world do you play baseball in 30 and 40 degree temperatures?"

I didn't have an agent, and I didn't have any idea about the process. I ultimately agreed to a $2,000 signing bonus. At the time, I was just excited about the opportunity to sign a professional baseball contract, contrary to the wishes of my grandmother who stressed the importance of education and obtaining a college degree.

My grandmother was suffering from early Alzheimer's, and I couldn't talk to her about the decision I'd made to leave school to follow my dream of playing baseball professionally. Fortunately, I was able to speak with two of my uncles who were mentors, and they gave me their blessings.

I reported to Lethbridge, Alberta to start my professional career, where I wound up being the Pioneer League Player of the Year after the 2-month season. During my second season, I started out playing Double-A with Québec City for two months before advancing to Triple-A Denver, where I would finish the season winning the American Association Championship.

My second season capped off with a call up to the big-league club. I joined the team in Pittsburgh where I was inserted into the lineup upon arrival, and the experience was exhilarating

Courtesy Terry (Aislin) Mosher
Andre Dawson was known as Hawk

What had once been merely as aspirational childhood dream of mine became a reality. All at only 21 years of age.

"Welcome to the big leagues, son," Larry Doby told me.

My tenure with the Expos which lasted 10 years had its moments of jubilation through experiences with teammates and gradual team success through the years, but it also had its moments of disappointment with management. Upon realizing the business aspect of the game would always be what management felt would be in the best interest of the organization, I quickly learned all I could do was give my best effort at all times and leave any distractions in the rearview mirror.

The difficult adjustments from playing on artificial turf, to learning new customs, formalities and language barriers were challenging at times. Nonetheless, they provided me with unique experiences within a different culture. My goal was to wear one uniform for the entirety of my professional career regardless of how long it may have lasted. Still, I was aware the business aspect of my profession would not allow for that to come to fruition.

My greatest disappointment was with how my free agency was handled, and ultimately, being forced to move on from 10 years of professional experience. I was grateful for the 10 opportunistic years of experience, but I was also disheartened by the reaction of fans when I left Montreal, as I presumed they weren't fully knowledgeable of the collusion process and its impact on players at the time.

The teams in the late seventies and the early eighties would eventually deliver first-hand success unforeseen for the first time for the Montreal Expos organization. "Close but no cigar," would be the unfortunate outcome of each season, but the consensus was always that we were not that far away.

A quality signing of a marquee free agent or two was something difficult to manifest as would-be superstars weren't willing to commit to crossing the border to play the game. The young players who were developed and brought up through the minor-league system pretty much just had to hold their own.

After 10+ years of service, 1986 would serve as my last year playing as an Expo. Being tagged with free-agent status for the first time in my career placed me amongst a litany of trade rumors, but also, the first of two chance meetings with front-office personnel to work out a new contract.

One meeting was with Charles Bronfman, a principal owner, and the other was with general manager John McHale. After having no success moving toward reaching an agreeable contract, I was informed Mr. Bronfman had cumulated the funds necessary for him to be able to re-sign me, but he was told by other front office officials it would not take that to sign me.

Disappointed that their best and final offer called for a $200,000 cut in my pay, I deemed it time to move on. The last comment my agent made was that 'Andre Dawson would file for free agency, and all I ask is that you people don't fuck him.'

As for the future of baseball in Montreal, Canada should have two teams as the setup was before, with one in the American League and one in the National League, and I do think the fans are starved and patiently awaiting the return of that setup.

Successfully establishing two teams in Canada will definitely be a huge hurdle to cross, but it would not be out of the realm of possibility. Without the right people in play, it will be even more difficult to manifest.

Andre Dawson, October 2023

Introduction

This is a special book, sad in many ways, so, get ready for some interesting reading.

2024 is the 20th anniversary of the Expos being shunted off to Washington in time for the 2005 season.

2024 is the 30th anniversary of that wonderful 1994 Expos team that was doomed by the strike and cancellation of the season.

It's also the 55th anniversary of the franchise's opening season in 1969.

This is the fifth in a series of books I have written about the Expos in the last five years. This series began in 2020 with Always Remembered, a series that features vignettes about players, executives and special events throughout the 36-season history of the Expos.

You will read about stars and you will read about part-time players, who were just as important to a lineup as the big guys. In all of my books, I attempt to humanize the part-timers. There is a fondness in my heart for them.

This is my 10th book about the Expos and 14th overall since 1997.

Thanks to all those who graciously accepted follow-up phone calls, text messages and emails. Among those are Canadian David Wainhouse, Don Stanhouse, Rick DeHart, Bob Gebhard and Dennis Blair, the latter of whom made his major-league debut 50 years ago in 1974.

Special thanks to freelance photographer Joe Gromelski, who volunteered to give me permission to use some of his terrific shots. He wanted no money, just a photo credit on each picture – and a copy of the book.

Kudos to my editor Philippe Grenier and graphic designer Dawna Dearing for their excellent work.

Enjoy.

Danny Gallagher

Chapter 1

The positive side of Gene Mauch

On the field, Gene Mauch knew the rule book inside out. That's why some people called him a thinking man's manager.

He employed all the tricks needed to win a game. He proved that bad teams could be victorious through the basic use of fundamentals.

He was a reserve player during his career and while on the bench watching games, he saw how important it was to rely on fundamentals, a scenario that prolonged his career but also a scenario that he promoted heavily as a manager.

He loved small ball more than the home run. Who the hell uses small ball these days in the majors? Small ball isn't glamorous but it gets the job done. High-octane offence such as home runs may cause fans to erupt and cheer more.

Mauch, which is a German name, used the hit and run, he would bunt, he would have runners stealing bases. He would have batters use the squeeze play or drag a bunt to get on base for a single.

With poor teams in Montreal's first years out of the gate with expansion, Mauch needed every kind of way to win games. It was a horror show in 1969 when the team won only 52 of 162 games. Not even Tom Seaver or Steve Carlton could have saved him in 1969, when, according to Baseball Almanac, Mauch used 42 players.

While managing the 1964 Phillies, he used that veteran policy to utilize veterans Chris Short and Jim Bunning on two days rest late in the season and it all backfired when Philly blew a 6½ game lead. Ouch.

In the succeeding five seasons following 1969, Mauch's teams won at least 70 games, with Mauch even predicting/promising that the team would win 70 in '70 after that terrible expansion season.

He would argue constantly with umpires. With the help of numerous Marlboro cigarettes and sips from a Seagram 83 rye whiskey bottle he stashed under his desk, he tried to calm his jitters and ease the pressure of being a big-league manager.

He traditionally used veteran players at the expense of younger ones because he was trying to win as many games as possible even if his teams were terrible.

"Look at the players who revived their careers in Montreal under Mauch," said Maxwell Kates of Toronto, a quasi-authority on many matters Expos. "Ron Hunt found a new way to get on base as a leadoff hitter – by getting smacked in the elbow."

Yes, all Hunt had to do was choke up so high on the back that you

Exposion

Gene Mauch in a reflection during an interview

Antoine Desilets photo

The positive side of Gene Mauch

wondered how he could get the ball out of the infield. But instead of trying to get many hits, he merely stuck his head out over the plate and many times, he got nailed.

"Mike Marshall had been turfed by four different organizations before developing into a star when Mauch allowed him to throw his screwball," Kates opined. "He turned a triple play on one pitch against San Diego. Mauch knew how to get the most out of his bench and his bullpen."

Kates also observed that Mike Jorgensen thrived under Mauch after the first baseman was acquired along with Ken Singleton and Tim Foli in the Rusty Staub trade made in late 1971. Jorgensen won a Gold Glove in 1974 as part of a solid, four-season tenure with Mauch at the helm.

"Gene Mauch really liked Tim Foli," said Bob Scotti, a clubhouse attendant with the Expos from 1970-80.

And vice-versa, Foli really admired Mauch.

Mauch overused young pitchers like Balor Moore and Don DeMola, telling/ordering them to report to winter-league duty when they had already thrown several hundred innings during the course of one season in North America.

But this chapter in Mauch's life is not about criticizing him. It's about giving him some credit for this time with the Expos. Let's face it: management kept him for seven seasons. He must have done something right.

Mauch had been fired by the Phillies on June 16, 1968 and within days, from what I was told, Expos president John McHale had Mauch secretly working for the Expos as an advance scout before he was named manager Sept. 8.

Mauch was seen in the stands at least once – on Aug. 5, scouting Jack Billingham, who was pitching then for the Dodgers.

Billingham told me a few years ago he was likely claimed in the 1968 expansion draft by the Expos because of Mauch's presence at that game.

"Gene was my first manager," Larry Parrish, ever the philosopher full of eloquence, told me in an interview April 4, 2023. "It's like your first girlfriend – he's always got a very special place in

Russ Hansen photo
Larry Parrish

your heart to obviously give me a chance at a very young age to start for the Expos.

"I can remember I got off to a slow start that year."

And then Parrish launched into a neat story that somewhat explained his slow start.

"A lot of the times, the kids back then were a bit different than today. We grew up watching those same guys, seeing them in the World Series and then you're playing against them. You sort of idolized anybody who

Exposion

Canadian Baseball Hall of Fame
Gene Mauch

was a professional player. It was sort of intimidating a bit."

So the intimidation part, he suggested, was a reason for his slow start. Anyway, the story continued.

"I remember Gene invited me to eat in Chicago," Parrish said. "We played that day at Wrigley Field and we would meet after the game. I thought this was a nice way of sending me to Triple-A because I was struggling with the bat. Gene talked. He had been around the game a lot."

And then Mauch surprised Parrish by saying between gulps of food and drinks: "You're definitely a major-league ball player and start

The positive side of Gene Mauch

thinking that way."

"I wasn't going anywhere and I was not going to be sent down. From that point on, I could play there. I ended up hitting .270 (.274) for the year," Parrish said.

Along with 10 homers, 65 RBI and 32 doubles in 570 at-bats following a 25-game stint as a September call-up inauguration of his career in 1974.

"Anybody who has been around Gene Mauch didn't realize, you know, how prepared he was or how hard he studied the game," Parrish was saying. "Every day before games, he would tell the bench guys, according to the team we were playing, what inning that night they might be used as a pinch hitter, if there was somebody pitching in the seventh, eighth – it was amazing how he could sort of manage his own club the way it would go.

"He was anticipating what the other manager was going to do. He was way ahead of computer time. With his research and studying, he was pretty much ahead of the game on that day.

"He had the ability to take an also-ran club or mediocre club, or whatever you want to call it, and pick them up a notch and make then very competitive. Gene had a club, the '64 Phillies going into the season, they were not favourites to win that year. So who knows, the water seeks its own level. They played above their heads most of the season and below their heads near the end in the way they were supposed to be."

The Phillies lost their remaining 10 games to blow the NL pennant. Later as a manager of the Angels, Mauch had teams come close again twice but lost out, the most notable yellow sticky note when they blew a 3-1 lead to the Boston Red Sox in the 1986 league championship series.

"He was a super intelligent guy, the way he thought. He would fit into today's game easily, I think," Parrish said. "He might not have put up with a general manager calling down to tell him how to run the game (analytics), using the computer for the best matchups. All the good managers. they did what separated them – it was their memory. You use the brain instead of a laptop and have the same knowledge.

"Those guys stood out back then because they had the ability. Their brain was so advanced and so sharp. Gene was always yelling at the other clubs, the other pitcher. A lot of old managers, they were also-rans as players, they made their clubs in the 40s and 50s by being a good bench jockey getting under the skin of the other players. Dick Williams was like that, too. They would try to disrupt the other team, to give their team the best chance of winning.

"I remember Nate Colbert came over from San Diego in 1975 and he was saying how he didn't like playing against Mauch, how much he hated him because he had always tried to irritate the other club. Nate said, 'I'm so happy to be here to be around this guy who is way ahead of the other guy about what is going on in the game.' Gene had a feisty attitude. You were dealing with a very intelligent man, who knew the game better than most.

"I think the only thing with me was that he had an Achilles heel. He

Exposion

sort of grew up in an era where you played a lot of times for a run – sacrifice bunting, it's gone by the wayside now, where the computer has sort of changed the game. In fact, some games are won by one big inning, instead of bunting here and there. It might have been the way he was as a player (small ball).

"Mauch loved Tim Foli, who was the scrappy, hit-and-run kind of guy, rather than a guy that could hit the ball out of the park. I sorted of managed that way. I didn't bunt very much but what I did was hit and run. I enjoyed putting a runner in motion, instead of bunting, especially with anybody at the top or middle of the order. Bunting is not used as much as it once was. Late in the game, one run can win a game. Gene bunted from the first inning on. When he was with Anaheim, Rod Wilfong, it was his job to bunt the guy over."

While some players weren't enamoured with Mauch, Parrish likes to look at him more in a positive way.

"I think he was very intelligent. He dedicated his life to the game. He shouldn't go down in a bad light," LP said.

When Dennis Blair played for Mauch in 1974-75, he also saw the savviness in Mauch alluded to by Parrish and Colbert and many others.

Canadian Baseball Hall of Fame
Gene Mauch spent seven seasons as Expos manager

"What I remember about Gene Mauch is that he was absolutely brilliant. I think had he not gone on in his baseball career, he could have done anything he wanted to do, anything. He was that smart, I'm sure his IQ was off the charts," Blair said. "I read something in the papers where he was interviewed and one of the reporters asked him what he liked to read (a book maybe). He said, 'I like to read the boxscore.'

"Gene was unbelievable. I saw this (ESPN) documentary on Gene. He was special. He played in the minor leagues and acted in movies. They were able to get him on set and he'd get a part in some movies. He was born the same year as my mom. I remember Walt Hriniak, one of our Montreal coaches, talking about Gene. When he was named manager of the Phillies, the sports writers would say Gene would recount the entire game when it was over. Heck, I couldn't remember who I pitched to two batters earlier.

"When I got to Montreal, I was 19 going on 20. Gene was a strict disciplinarian. There was a certain way to wear the uniform. There was no deviation. No errors of admission or omission. He came across as a cold, distant person. When he saw someone without a hat, he hated that.

"But in 1987, I saw a different side of Gene. The Angels were playing at home against the White Sox. I had a friend who called Angels man-

The positive side of Gene Mauch

ager Doug Rader to see if we could get two tickets. I told Doug one of the tickets was for a friend of mine and the other was my oldest son Justin, who was 9 years old.

"We went into the visitors' clubhouse and then we go outside and Gene is sitting on the bench. Doug takes my friend and Justin over to Gene. Doug said, 'Remember Dennis Blair? This is his son Justin.' I thought Gene was going to say, 'I remember him. He couldn't get the ball over the plate.' But he pops up the steps and gives Justin a big hug. I was really surprised. I would never expect that out of Gene to show that kind of emotion."

Mauch led the surprising Expos to a pennant run in 1973 and was voted National League manager of the year. But after a seven-season run, Mauch was let go Oct. 1, 1975 after the Expos went 75-87 in 1975.

Montreal Star reporter Bob Dunn wrote, "When called to be told he was gone, Mauch was playing golf near his home at Palm Springs, California. He returned the call, received the message, talked to the people involved, and went back on the golf course for another 18."

Mauch's first wife, Nina, once jokingly said, "There's no doubt in my mind that if Gene were single, he'd sleep at the park."

Talking of his wife, Nina Lee Taylor and Gene were sweethearts from Berendo junior high school in California and were married for 37 years until she died way too soon of melanoma on July 15, 1983.

When he was 35, Mauch and Nina were married Dec. 15, 1945.

"He was only 13 years old when he met my mom. He came home and told his mom he had met the girl he was going to marry," his daughter Lee Anne Simons told me.

Sure enough, Mauch and Nina did get married.

The Mauchs had enjoyed their life in the off-season at their home on the 9th hole at the Sunrise Country Club in Rancho Mirage near Palm Springs.

Her death devastated Mauch for several years.

"My mom's melanoma was diagnosed in March of that year and she died within three months," Simons said. "I was scared to death. I thought I was going to lose my dad, too. My dad said one of the reasons he survived was that (Angels owner) Gene Autry was very good to him. It was a very tough time for him. I don't know, living in the sun – she was a sun worshipper. I remember President Kennedy's nephew (Edward Jr.) had melanoma (osteosarcoma) on his (right) leg and lost his leg. My mother read about that and she was scared to death. Sure enough, she got it (10 years later). It was bad.

"I have to say my mother was pretty special. She handled baseball pretty rough. It's not an easy career to handle. He relied on her. After the game, in the front seat of the car, he talked through the game, telling my mom everything about that game, stories about certain players like Richie Allen."

Following Nina's death, Mauch stayed away from baseball until he got the itch to manage the Angels a second time. A few years later, Mauch fell in love again – this time with Jodie Mannas, who had lived in the Canadian city of Grande Prairie, Alberta for 30 years. She had split

Exposion

with oilman Tex Mannas after 28 years of marriage in 1983.

The Mannas clan had moved from Texas to Grande Prairie in 1962 when Tex accepted a job with Arrow. Tex later became VP with Cantex Drilling in Calgary and was co-founder and president of Jomax Drilling.

When Jodie split with Tex, she decided to move to Rancho Mirage where the Mannas couple had spent many winters. It was in Rancho Mirage, where Mauch met her.

In my research in April of 2023, I stumbled upon Jodie's death notice which stated she lived in Grande Prairie for about three decades. As a Canadian, this Mauch connection to Alberta intrigued me.

"Tex Mannas was a very wealthy man. They separated and ultimately divorced. She moved and lived in Palm Springs. My dad told me he had met someone. Somebody introduced them. They had some neutral friends," Simons said. "She had become a citizen of Canada. When her marriage ended, she went back to Palm Springs and she went back to her American citizenship. She had grown up in Oklahoma. My dad and her got married several years later. They dated for quite a while. She took care of him. Her family wasn't very nice to me. That was a tough time."

Although the date of Mauch's marriage to Jodie is unknown, Simons believes it was in the 1990s.

In the early 2000s, Mauch himself was diagnosed with lung cancer and died Jan. 25, 2005. Oh no.

"He didn't take care of himself," his daughter said. "He didn't want to tell anyone he had cancer. He thought he would live forever. He smoked a lot and he drank a lot. After golf, they'd play bridge. He drank a little too much. I don't say this in a bad way. He could have done a little bit better. He smoked Marlboros and when he was younger, unfiltered Parliament cigarettes. When he was with the Expos, Seagram would send cases of liquor to the house.

"Reggie Jackson and Rod Carew literally came to the hospital when he was sick. Dad really admired Rod Carew. Early in Rod's career, Dad said, 'That boy will go to the hall of fame.' "

And he did. Carew had played for Mauch with the Twins and Angels and was one of the most definitive bunters in the game's history. No wonder Mauch liked him. Carew played Mauch's small ball to a T.

"I remember seeing pictures of Dad when they came out of the depression. They were dressed to the nines. He really did like to dress well," Simons said.

Yes, the good looking Mauch did inspire many of his players such as Jerry White to improve their clothing habits.

"He was so handsome," his daughter said. "I don't think looks mattered to him. It was presentation. He didn't want anyone to think he had a conceited bone in his body. He wanted to be respectful.

"My dad moved to California from Kansas when he was 12," Simons told me in April of 2023. "He was very active in Kansas. He'd take a bat and ball and meet the guys at the park or wherever.

"His father George wanted to take him to California for a baseball opportunity. It was Depression time and my grandfather was out of work and nothing much was happening in Kansas. Entering the state of California, my dad thought he was in heaven with the palm tries, the skies and the sunshine."

Mauch's daughter said her dad went straight into the Air Force out of high school at the earliest opportunity to get his service time at boot camp in Atlanta so he could pursue baseball. He served time at the Marana Air Field in Arizona and even learned how to fly a plane.

Simons said Mauch once wrote a letter to his parents, telling them he had signed with the Dodgers.

"He said in the letter he was in competition with that young shortstop Pee Wee Reese," Simons said. "He was told Pee Wee was going to be assigned to that position. In another letter, he said he had lost the position to Pee Wee Reese. My dad got a letter from Branch Rickey of the Dodgers. It was beautifully written. I have the letter somewhere. That was pretty precious."

In that letter, Rickey apologized or at least told Mauch that "he hated to make this deal", which saw Mauch dealt to the Pirates in a multi-player trade in June 1946.

Mauch was soon given the job as manager of the Atlanta Crackers Triple-A team in 1953 and although he reverted back to playing full-time briefly, he later got the itch to manage later on.

"Growing up, my dad was recognized for his baseball strategy and brilliance," his daughter said. "He could have been successful in anything. He had a very high IQ in intelligence. He was just amazing. He had wonderful grades in school. He put his nose to the grindstone.

"He didn't like players, who had bad reputations and were into carousing. He had so much respect for the game. He went to Atlanta. He was too young. He was 28."

It was in Atlanta where Mauch started getting into arguments with umpires and that fighting spirit stayed with him throughout his managerial career.

"He just didn't like the umpires. They were always wrong," his daughter said, chuckling.

Simons talked about the time her dad took over the Expos, an expansion team, when he usually had managed some good teams elsewhere.

"I was 18. My mom would talk about financing. We were in another country, Canada, where the pay cheque was in Canadian funds," Simons said. "I was at the first game in Montreal. I remember they talked about the world's fair being there in 1967. I didn't love Montreal. My favourite years were in Philadelphia. I was 13. What happened in 1964, that was a sore spot. It just didn't work out.

"I don't remember my dad's departure from Montreal. Every time he signed a contract, he said it was possible he would be somewhere else in a few years. It's a gamble. He just loved the game. He took over an expansion team. He managed great teams that were established teams like the Phillies and Angels. It was really sad when they couldn't do it with the Angels (1986)."

Gene Mauch, never to be forgotten.

Chapter 2

20-game losing streak

The Expos' maiden voyage in 1969 was beset with misery. Who would have thought, though, it would be so turbulent on the high seas of their inaugural season.

It was not unexpected for an expansion franchise. They won only 52 games and lost 110. One can't imagine president John McHale, general manager Jim Fanning and manager Gene Mauch ever assuming the season would be that atrocious.

After winning their first-ever game April 10 in New York against the Mets, the Expos never played over .500 that season. That's true. The only time they were at .500 was when they lost their second game of the season, evening their record at 1-1. From there on, it was downhill – below .500.

Over the course of the season, the Expos' misery was epitomized by a 20-game losing streak that started May 13 and concluded June 7. It was disheartening. Never in any of the Expos' succeeding 35 seasons of operations did they endure such a long losing streak.

At the conclusion of the losing streak, the Expos were 11-37.

On June 8, the losing streak ended in a day game at Dodger Stadium when they beat the Dodgers 4-3. Jerry Robertson, an absolute workhorse that season with 179 innings of work, got the win. Robertson had pitched in the team's first game, an 11-10 victory over the Mets at Shea Stadium.

Robertson worked into the ninth inning in L.A. before he got into trouble, allowing successive singles to Andy Kosco and Tom Haller. With two on and nobody out, Mauch summoned ElRoy Face.

Jim Lefebvre grounded out, moving up the runners. Then Ron Fairly, who would be acquired by the Expos just days later, singled to score a run before being replaced by pinch-runner Bill Grabarkewitz. Bill Sudakis drew a base on balls to load the bases.

Former Cardinals great Kenny Boyer, looking out of place in a Dodgers uniform in the twilight of his career, was the next batter. Face did

Canadian Baseball Hall of Fame
Jerry Robertson

something wrong and balked in a run. That made the score 4-3 with only one out with runners on second and third.

Face got out of the jam, though. Boyer popped up to third and Willie Crawford flied to right. Game over.

The win was Robertson's first of the season. He pitched in six or more innings in 17 of his 27 starts but never got much support. In his 16 losses, the Expos scored only 20 runs. He enjoyed the best ERA at 3.96 amongst the four main starters of the 1969 edition of the Expos.

What a warrior Robertson was. Teams nowadays would love to have guys like him.

Robertson picked up his only save at the MLB level on Sept. 13. What was his reward for a decent season despite the circumstances? He was traded to the Tigers on Dec. 3, 1969 for Joe Sparma and pitched his last MLB game June 7, 1970.

Robertson was inducted into the Washburn University Athletics Hall of Fame in Kansas in 1982. He played at Washburn U from 1962-65 before being drafted by the St. Louis Cardinals. He was the director of athletics at Washburn from 1982-88 and prior to that, he had worked for 10 years for the YMCA in Topeka, Kansas.

Robertson died at 52 as a result of an automobile accident in Burlington, Kansas on March 24, 1996.

Courtesy Topps

Jerry Robertson

Chapter 3

Radatz ran out of gas

The Expos held out hope Dick Radatz might still have some gas or pop left in his bulging arm. He was only 32.

The Expos took a flyer on Radatz, hoping he might have some zing left in him like he had with the Red Sox earlier that decade. At his elitist, the imposing, 6-foot-6 Radatz could bring it, firing 95 m.p.h. heat. No wonder he was called The Monster.

So on June 15, 1969, the Expos purchased Radatz's contract from the Detroit Tigers, who had employed him for several months that season. It appeared Radatz had regained some of his former prowess in Tiger Town after he had spent the entire 1968 season in Triple-A with the Toledo Mud Hens, Detroit's Triple-A squad.

Courtesy Topps
Dick Radatz

It was the Expos' inaugural season and management had been trying a lot of retreads from other teams and Radatz was one of them. There was also another underlying scenario attached to this acquisition.

The Expos, specifically president John McHale, had a deep connection to the Tigers. McHale was born in Detroit and was a former GM of the Tigers in the 1950s. So that was a big reason why Radatz was obtained. McHale was dealing with his old Tigers buddy, GM Jim Campbell.

Radatz was 3.38 ERA in 11 games with Detroit, his hometown team, in 1969 but Radatz's time with the Expos was not successful. He was 0-4 with an ERA of 5.71 in 34.2 innings. He allowed 24 earned runs. Radatz never pitched in the majors again. It turns out Radatz's career, period, was ephemeral.

"I could never really figure out why," Radatz told a reporter one time about the decision by Detroit to let him go on waivers.

With the Expos, he did strike out 32 in 34.2 innings of work and saved three games.

Radatz ran out of gas

Ironically, Radatz's last game in the big leagues was Aug. 15, 1969, which was also the last game in which his older teammate Elroy Face pitched. Strange but true. Face gave up two runs in two innings and he was followed by Radatz, who also threw two innings, giving up a run while fanning two.

Face, 41, was released following the completion of the game when manager Gene Mauch called him into his office. Face, too, was linked to the Tigers-Expos lovefest. The Tigers had let him go in early April, 1969 and the Expos decided to sign him as a free agent April 27.

"Was he there?" Face asked me in 2022 about Radatz in Montreal. "I pitched in over 800 games so I can't remember (some things). I had my car up there. A friend of mine and the kids drove home (to Pennsylvania from Montreal) through the Pocono Mountains. We stopped and played some golf and the kids went fishing. Mauch asked me if I wanted to retire or be released. I told them to release me so I would get an extra month's pay."

Radatz's Baseball Almanac Transactions online say he was released on Aug. 26. But that is not true, according to Québecer Claude Raymond, who became the first Canadian to join the Expos that season after his contract was purchased from the Atlanta Braves, who had employed McHale for years. That Raymond deal was confirmed by an Associated Press story I saw that appeared in Canada's Saskatoon Star-Phoenix.

"When I joined the Expos on Aug. 19, 1969, Dick Radatz was released by the Expos. I was to replace him on the roster," Raymond told me in an interview several years ago. "I had to wait for him to empty his locker so I could get dressed for that night's game against the Padres. When he left his locker, he shook my hand and wished me good luck.

"He was one of the best relievers in the game for a long time but the end had arrived. He was mean on the mound and besides his very heavy fastball, he had an outstanding slider. He was the type that everybody on his team was happy to have him aboard."

Radatz burst onto the major-league scene in 1962 with the Red Sox, going 9-6 with a 2.24 ERA, a National League-leading 24 saves and an impressive 144 Ks. He just got better the following two seasons. In 1963, he was 15-6 with a 1.97 ERA and 162 strikeouts. Those strikeouts totals included 10 in one game in relief and 11 two days later.

In 1964, he reached the peak of his career. He threw 157 innings with an unheard of 181 strikeouts, a major-league record to this day for a reliever. He was

Antoine Desilets photo
Claude Raymond replaced Dick Radatz in the bullpen

Exposion

16-9 with a MLB-leading 29 saves and a 2.29 ERA. He threw aspirins at hitters and was the talk of baseball.

"Dick and I were good friends," said Bill Lee, one of his Boston teammates. "He was the godfather of one of my children."

From there on, though, he started to fade into oblivion. Arm fatigue set in. By June of 1966, Radatz was traded by the Red Sox to the Cubs. They had given up on him. After his stint with the Expos, he never appeared in another MLB game. Weird. He'd gone from the penthouse to the outhouse. At one point, Radatz had even engaged the services of a Detroit psychiatrist to undergo hypnosis in an attempt to help him gain his control on the mound.

There was speculation excessive work doomed Radatz following his three-season success with Boston but he would later say he got stale because he was underused. He reasoned that he wasn't as effective and lost his edge when he wasn't used much.

Radatz was accustomed to throwing upward of three innings or more per game and he seemed to thrive on it.

When Moose was in decline with the Red Sox in the mid-1960s, the team used film to study and improve his delivery. Radatz also put on weight far too easily. Some reports say he weighed 275-300 pounds, compared to his listed 230. He gained weight easily so that may have affected his pitching. He would get help from a doctor, Warren Guild, and Red Sox trainer Jack Fadden. More often than not, Radatz would take up running to try and lose weight.

During and following the end of his career, Radatz was employed by a copying machine company, sold industrial lumber, had his own weekly radio show, sold insurance for Penn Mutual, worked for a corrugated packing firm and was the pitching coach for an independent team in Lynn, Mass. called the North Shore Spirit.

Radatz spent the last years of his life near Boston, where he died tragically on March 16, 2005 when he fell down a flight of stairs and struck his head on a carpet-covered concrete floor. The official cause of death was severe head trauma.

Gosh, what a sad ending.

Chapter 4

Floyd Wicker and Larry Jaster

It was a friendship that began more than 60 years ago and it's still thriving.

Pitcher Larry Jaster and infielder Floyd Wicker were brought together in Winnipeg, Manitoba in 1963 as members of the St. Louis Cardinals organization and then six years later, they were teammates again with another Canadian team, the Expos.

Even when they went on to play for other teams or when their playing careers ended, they remained glued as friends.

Just like Cliff Floyd and Rondell White, Ken Singleton and Mike Torrez, Sean Berry and Jeff Fassero, Bill Lee and Rodney Scott, Bryn Smith and Bob McClure, Brian Schneider and Brad Wilkerson, Lenny Webster and Marquis Grissom – and others.

"Larry and I are good friends. We keep in touch quite a bit," Wicker was saying in an interview.

"Talking about Floyd, he's like a brother to me. We've kept in touch. It's been one of my best friendships over the years," Jaster was telling me in early 2023. "We met in Winnipeg in 1963 and right away, we got along real well. We were roommates. It's been a good friendship. We have a lot in common, even though he was living in the south and I was in the north. We try to meet somewhere."

And there's always the phone to keep abreast of things.

"I remember in Winnipeg, in the summer time, the weather was good. At 11 or 12 at night, there was still light," Jaster said, marveling at what he saw. "We got snowed out for about a week in 1963. We worked out in an auditorium. We'd play catch and see what we could do. There were no indoor cages."

From Winnipeg, Wicker and Jaster parted ways to other teams before becoming teammates again briefly

Canadian Baseball Hall of Fame
Larry Jaster

Exposion

in 1968 with St. Louis. Wicker appeared in five games and Jaster was a mainstay of the stellar pitching staff. Bob Gibson was 22-9, Nelson Briles went 19-11, Ray Washurn was 14-8, Steve Carlton came in at 13-11 and Jaster, the smooth-throwing fifth man in the rotation, was next at 9-13.

Gibson worked 302.1 innings, almost double the 150 innings thrown by Jaster, who admitted he didn't have a productive season overall, especially in the second half and didn't get to pitch much in that year's World Series.

In that 1968 World Series against his home state Tigers, Jaster gave up a grand slam to Jim Northrup in Game 6 as the Tigers won 13-1. Detroit won it all in Game 7.

"He hit a fastball. I was behind in the count. He was waiting for a fastball. He was more of a fastball hitter. It wasn't a pleasant moment because I grew up there two hours away," Jaster said. "I was hurt part of the 1968 season. I hurt my throwing shoulder. I was not effective in the last part of 1968. I was 1-9 in the second half of 1968. I hadn't pitched consistently."

Yes, Jaster grew up near Detroit in Midland, Michigan so that grand slam hurt. He got a lot of exposure playing junior and high school ball and was discovered by the Cardinals at a game in 1961 against a group of high school recruits.

"The St. Louis scout, Chief Bender, showed up. I think I threw five scoreless innings," Jaster recalled. "Next year, when it came time to sign, football scouts at Michigan State were looking at me but I decided to play baseball."

On Jan. 1, 1962, Jaster signed with St. Louis. One of his greatest claims to fame was in 1966 when he threw five shutouts – and they were all against the Dodgers. Imagine.

Jaster was a lefty-firing quarterback and defensive back, who almost committed to a scholarship at Michigan State before accepting what he called a "$60,000 total package" that included a "$40,000 signing bonus" with the Cardinals, who threw in money for him to go to school as part of the overall deal.

Lefty quarterback? I've always been fascinated by southpaw signal callers such as Kenny Stabler, Jim Zorn, Steve Young and Boomer Esiason. I even love southpaw guitar players and of course, southpaw baseball players, especially first basemen.

In the 1968 National League expansion draft to accommodate the Expos and Padres, Jaster was snagged by the Expos to help stock their team for 1969.

"I wasn't that surprised when I was selected in the expansion draft," Jaster told me. "In my first two and a half years from 1966-68, I won something like 30 games. At spring training in 1969, Gene Mauch said I deserved to throw the first pitch at the first game in Montreal. I had a pretty good spring training.

"I remember the first game in Montreal. It was a pretty cool day. They were still blowers at both ends of the dugout. We made a few errors and things didn't go well and I was taken out of the game.

"I had an erratic season (1-6, 24 starts, 6.85 ERA). I had a wart on my release finger, the left index finger. At the release point, it kept splitting on me. It was not a good season. I decided to pitch in winter ball."

Jaster's tenure with Montreal ended on Dec. 2 of that year when he was traded to the Braves for Jim Britton and Dan Johnson. 1970 would be Jaster's last season in the majors.

Years later, Jaster didn't forget Atlanta. He got a bachelor's degree from Georgia State University and a master's degree in biomechanics of pitching movement. How about that, eh? Jaster also worked for a number of years for different organizations, including Atlanta – before "I was retired by Baltimore in 2012."

Wicker spent some time in Winnipeg like Jaster did and remembers the wintry-like conditions.

"It was cold," he said, chuckling, "and the infield was terrible. It was gravel-like stuff and hard to handle. It wasn't very good."

Courtesy Topps
Larry Jaster

Wicker was taken by the Expos in the Rule V draft on Dec. 2, 1968 from the Cardinals so he got to spend all of the 1969 season with his buddy Jaster.

What was very remarkable is that Wicker stayed with the Expos all season and got into very few games, only 41. I'm probably close to being right when I say Wicker is the Expo with the least amount of playing time for a position player who was on the roster the entire season – through the franchise's 36 seasons of operation.

According to my research on Baseball Reference, Wicker started only one game, in centre field on May 13 in Montreal, when he went 1-for-3.

In those 41 games, he amassed only 41 plate appearances, 39 at-bats, two walks, 0 homers, two RBI. In total, he appeared in 11 games in the outfield, seven in centre field. You have to give credit to Mauch for at least keeping Wicker in games after he had pinch hit. His total amount of innings in the outfield totaled 24.2.

Wicker didn't play much but you got to admire someone like him who prevailed and persevered in the face of adversity but trying to be as patient as he could while spending most of the season's 162 games on the bench.

1969 was the only season Wicker was on a team roster all season long. He was able to experience the joy of travelling to all away games, fancy hotels and nice meals.

"It was very hard," Wicker said of being typecast mostly as a pinch hitter. "Gene Mauch was an older manager. He liked experienced players. I thought he was a smart manager. I was a Rule V player and they still tried to send me out (to the minors)," Wicker said.

"I had a game-winning pinch hit in Atlanta. We were on national TV, the NBC Game of the Week."

The date was May 6 and Wicker pinch hit for Bill Stoneman in the seventh inning and delivered two runs on a single off Ron Reed, who was an 18-game winner that season for the Braves.

Behind 3-1, the Expos came back against the Braves when Mack Jones hit a solo homer to cut the deficit to 3-2. Wicker's hit gave the Expos a 4-3 win.

"I was thrilled to be in the major leagues," Wicker said. "I loved Jarry Park. It was a great fan base. I was honoured to be there. I tell people I played for four different teams in the majors."

Wicker also suited up for the Cardinals, Giants and Brewers.

Shortly after the 1969 season ended, Wicker was sent to the Milwaukee Brewers on Oct. 9 to complete the trade in which the Seattle Pilots (forerunner of the Brewers) traded Marv Staehle to the Expos for a PTBNL.

Following his exit from baseball, Wicker raised chickens for many years and worked close to 35 years as a delivery man for the United States Postal Service. He gets a nice pension from the USPS, gets his U.S. Social Security pension and he receives a non-vested cheque each February from MLB because he didn't qualify for a pension.

Canadian Baseball HOF
Floyd Wicker

"They picked me up about eight years ago," Wicker said of the small annual stipend from MLB. "Thankful that they did that."

Wicker gets a net cheque of about $4,500 a year. He was put on the non-vested payroll pretty late in his life at about age 72 but at least he's getting something.

Baseball activist Doug Gladstone has been trying to convince MLB and the MLBPA for years to add these non-vested players into the regular stream of pensioners and that way, they would get a cheque each month with much higher intake, not one cheque a year.

As a result of talks for a new Collecting Bargaining Agreement, these non-vested retirees received a 15% increase in their cheque, effective February of 2022.

Those players who appeared in games prior to 1980 aren't included in the pension group because they didn't accumulate the required four seasons of MLB service. Wicker's service time amounts to about two years. That one year with Montreal sure helped.

Chapter 5

McGinn big part of trivia in early days

Dan McGinn hit the first home run in Expos' history and was prominent in two opening-day games, one on the road, the other at home, as a pitcher for the team in their inaugural season in 1969.

McGinn is being remembered fondly with the sad news he passed away March 1, 2023. He was 79. He had fought mouth cancer for 17 years.

McGinn was claimed by the Expos in the 1968 expansion draft from the Cincinnati Reds and pitched for Montreal from 1969 to 1971.

"Dan will definitely be one of our top bullpen men. Our scouts have been tremendously impressed with his potential as a relief pitcher," Expos general manager Jim Fanning told reporters at the time. "We expect big things of him."

In the franchise's first game in New York April 8, McGinn homered to lay claim as the first Montreal player to hit a home run, a solo blast off the great Tom Seaver of the Mets.

McGinn didn't realize he had gone yard until he saw the second-base umpire make the signal.

"Even then, I wasn't sure until I looked back at Seaver. He was standing there with his hands on his hips, glaring at me," McGinn said later. "The next day, both of us were running in the outfield and I apologized. I told him, 'I'm as surprised as you.'"

Why would McGinn wanted to apologize?

In that same game, McGinn became the first relief pitcher in Montreal's history, taking over from starter Mudcat Grant as the Expos squeaked out an 11-10 win.

Canadian Baseball Hall of Fame
Dan McGinn

In the Expos' home opener at Jarry Park on April 14, McGinn spun 5 1/3 innings of scoreless relief to get the win as Montreal topped St. Louis 8-7.

"He was the winning pitcher in the first MLB game played outside the U.S. I was the losing pitcher," recalled Gary Waslewski, who became McGinn's teammate two months later following a trade.

"McGinn got the single to drive in Coco Laboy from second base in

Exposion

Courtesy Pro Stars Publications
Dan McGinn

the seventh inning, the only run I gave up in four innings of relief."

McGinn's obituary also states he was the first Expos' pitcher to "pick off a baserunner." That notation prompted me to go searching on Retrosheet. Sure enough, in that very first game at Shea, McGinn eliminated a runner at second

Tommy Agee had socked a three-run double off Mudcat Grant, prompting manager Gene Mauch to bring in McGinn. Almost as soon as

McGinn big part of trivia in early days

he was finished with his warm-up pitches, McGinn wheeled and threw to shortstop Maury Wills, who tagged Agee wandering off second.

McGinn caught Agee "leaning the wrong way", as baseball jargon goes. Agee was caught up in a moment of glory after his bases-clearing hit.

McGinn produced identical 7-10 records for the Montreal in 1969 and 1970 and then slipped to 1-4 in 1971. His six saves in 1969 led the team and ElRoy Face followed with five. During such a terrible inaugural season, there were few save opportunities.

McGinn was born and raised in Omaha, Nebraska, and was a multi-sport athlete at both Cathedral high school in Omaha and the University of Notre Dame in Indiana, where he enjoyed a "full-ride scholarship", according to his obituary.

McGinn played for Notre Dame as a baseball player and was a fifth-string quarterback with Notre Dame for awhile but then worked his way into the lineup as the team's regular punter.

To this day, McGinn still holds the Notre Dame record for most strikeouts per nine innings at 12.66, which he established during his junior year in 1965, while fanning 105 batters in only 74 innings of work.

After his days as a baseball player ended, McGinn was a National Account Manager for AT&T for 24 years. After retiring, he became a scout for the Philadelphia Phillies for a number of years.

McGinn was also a pitching coach at an Omaha-area school for 15 years.

A clubhouse attendant's flashback

"Woodie Fryman was one of the nicest guys for us. He would talk with us all the time. He would never change his uniform when he came in after batting practice. He always kept the same uniform for the game. Dave Van Horne was really nice. I saw what happened between Chris Speier, Charlie Fox and Steve Rogers (July 20, 1978). Charlie Fox was after Speier. Rogers stepped in. Charlie said, 'Mind your own business'. They tried to shove each other. Sometimes, Mike Jorgensen would be taken out of the game in the fourth inning and he'd come into the clubhouse and start drinking all the beer. I told him to keep some for the guys. He understood. Gene Mauch, the manager, would keep a bottle of Seagram 83 under his desk. The team belonged to Charles Bronfman, who owned the Seagram's company. Duke Snider would come in and see Gene a lot. They both loved to golf. Pepe Frias was poor and only had one T-shirt. Gary Carter had all kinds of T-shirts. He would never give one to Pepe. Carter was stingy. Bill Stoneman was a nice man. He'd fill up the garbage cans with ice for beer." – **1970s Expos clubhouse attendant Bob Scotti.**

Chapter 6

McSween was a southpaw with promise

When I was in Montreal as an Expos beat writer in the late 1980s and part of the 1990s, I would often by-pass Salaberry-de-Valleyfield, Québec on my way to see my folks in Douglas, Ontario northwest of Ottawa.

On the 20-Ouest located about an hour southeast of Montreal near Valleyfield, you could either follow the right arrow to Ottawa for Highway 417 or the left arrow to Highway 401 and Toronto.

Valleyfield is where Denis McSween was born and raised. Specifically, it was Sainte-Timothée, which amalgamated with Valleyfield in 2002.

After starring for many years in his hometown, McSween ventured out of Valleyfield to play in Montreal's Métropolitaine junior league to get more baseball exposure. He had the potential, he had the arm, he had the arsenal and he was a left-hander.

That's where the Expos noticed him, when he was pitching for the Kiwanis-Maisonneuve team. The Expos had seen him play, they had heard about him and saw the press clippings extolling his virtues.

It was late May of 1969, just several months after the Expos had begun play in the National League as an expansion team.

Expos general manager Jim Fanning and scouting director Mel Didier had also heard what McSween had accomplished years earlier in the age 11-12 bracket for Valleyfield in the Canadian Little League championship and the Little World Series in Williamsport, Pennsylvania.

"When I signed with the Expos. I was only 18. God damn it. Pretty young, eh?" McSween said in an interview with me in early 2023. "I signed for $5,000. It was not much but I thought it was good at the time. I could study in any university in the States (baseball scholarship), and I did not, and that was the only thing I regret.

"My fastball was around 95. At the time, it was pretty good. I had three pitches: a fastball, a changeup and curve. I had a two-seam fastball and a four-seam fastball."

McSween signed his contract on May 29, 1969 in the company of Fanning and Michel Dostaler of Montreal, who also signed a deal. Fanning had been watching McSween for several weeks before the club decided to sign him.

Jacques Beauchamp of Montreal Matin reported that the signing took place 90 minutes before the Expos game against the Dodgers at Jarry Park. In his story, Beauchamp said the first Québec amateur to sign with the Expos was Gaetan Groleau of Montreal, who in very quick order abandoned the organization.

McSween was a southpaw with promise

Pierre McCann photo/La Presse Archives
**Expos GM Jim Fanning with Denis McSween
a week before the Expos signed the kid**

So, McSween was the first Québec player signed by the Expos to be of any substance in pro ball. Let's put it that way.

The news prompted a long-long feature on McSween in the Toronto Star's Saturday supplement magazine The Star Weekly. McSween was big news because he was a Canadian – from Québec – a rarity in the Expos' organization.

"The first year, after I signed my contract, I was assigned to Bradenton in the Florida rookie league," McSween said.

Exposion

McSween played briefly – six innings – in 1969 in Bradenton and pitched a little more – 32.1 innings – in 1970, also in Bradenton.

By 1971, he was pitching a lot more, the whole season with Jamestown in the New York-Penn league, where he worked 99 innings, going 5-5 with a sterling 3.38 ERA. He was showing the Expos what he was made of.

McSween really emerged in 1972 when he spent the entire season with the Double-A Québec City Carnavals of the Eastern league. He was 9-8 with a 3.38 ERA. He was getting better and better.

All through his time in the minor leagues, he was known as Mac McSween, as I noticed in his Baseball Reference statistics online. One of his 1972 teammates was the great Steve Rogers.

"When I pitched in Québec City, there were 5,000-6000 people watching me pitch," McSween said. "When I didn't pitch, there were maybe 700 or 800 people there."

Such was the power and allure of a Canadian from Québec with a Québec pro team. The French love their sports heroes so they would come out in droves to see McSween.

For some reason, the Expos befuddled McSween, his family, his friends and the media in 1973 by having him back in Class A in West Palm Beach while getting some work in Québec City. He was 7-2 in West Palm in 86 innings of work and he only pitched 21 innings in Québec City. Strange. Those kind of mind games didn't sit well with McSween.

1974 saw McSween back for an entire season with the Carnavals. He was 6-6 in 114 innings of work. His ERA was 1.89. What more did he have to do to get promoted to Triple-A with the Peninsula Whips or even all the way to Montreal?

"I pitched a couple of no-hitters," McSween said. "I remember in spring training one year, I pitched against Hank Aaron, when he was still playing. I pitched five innings, gave up no runs and they sent me down to Double-A."

Hrmmph. So when he reported to spring training in 1975 and got in a few weeks of work, he was demoted to Québec again. Oh no. Shit.

"I had pitched in Double-A for three years and maybe three and a half. I wanted something more than that," McSween told me, speaking dejectedly. "(Expos manager) Gene Mauch didn't like me, oh for sure. That's a true story."

Mauch had seen him pitch in spring training and for some reason, he didn't like him? McSween headed home to Valleyfield. He was only 22. The Expos asked him to come back. He didn't reply in the affirmative.

"I said no way. That's it, buddy," he said. "I had enough of Double-A and bus riding. When we were in Québec City, it wasn't too far to Trois-Rivieres and Sherbrooke but when we'd make trips into the U.S., the bus trips sometimes would be 12 hours long.

"I played for Karl Kuehl in Québec. He was a captain in the U.S. Army. He was taught to do the same thing (discipline) in the major leagues but that's not the case. My next manager in Québec was Lance Nichols. He was a nice guy, tough but fair. He never yelled at anybody. He'd call me in to his office. And very slowly, he would talk to me. That's what I liked

McSween was a southpaw with promise

René Picard photo/La Presse Archives
Denis McSween at spring training

about him.

"Ellis Valentine and Warren Cromartie were my best friends, all black people (1974). Ellis was one of the best players ever for the Expos. Ellis

Exposion

was the best of all. He took me under his wing. We'd get into trouble during the night," McSween quipped.

McSween played with many other household names in Québec – Gary Carter, Barry Foote, Jerry White, Balor Moore, Dale Murray, Walt Hriniak, to name a few.

Toughest hitter he faced in the Eastern league while he was with Québec City? There wasn't much hesitation.

"Ken Griffey Sr.," McSween he said. "He was with Trois-Rivieres. His son, Ken. Jr., had a bat in his hand. I remember when he was around. That was 50+ years ago."

Can you imagine what McSween would have drawn for crowds at Jarry Park if Mauch, Fanning, John McHale had their druthers and promoted him to the majors? Did the braintrust not think McSween would be a swoon for the organization the way he was each time he pitched for the Carnavals before thousands of people at home or at important Little League games in Valleyfield?

McSween was no publicity stunt for the Expos. He could pitch.

"The Expos were unfair with him, even more so because he was a local kid," commented Alain Usereau, a French-language broadcaster at RDS in Montreal and an expert on the Expos' minor-league system. "They should have at least promoted him to Triple-A after he led the Eastern league in ERA.

"The main prospects on the mound at the time were Chip Lang and Joe Keener. Thing is, Mel Didier had a plan and never budged from it. Mel was looking into football-type athletes. He was targeting big athletes. He was looking to build around position players and then pitchers."

Shortly after saying no to the Expos and no returning to pro ball, McSween got involved in sales with the Molson beer company in Québec, peddling Export, Canadian, Golden and other brands such as Coors Light, Miller Light and other iconic names when Molson and Coors merged in 2005.

"I was with them 32 years. I was a salesman until 2008. I'd check in with restaurants, hotels, golf clubs, grocery stores. Everyone's got a licence to sell beer in Québec," he laughed.

McSween turned 71 in May of 2023 and is in good health, although he admits he was "very sick" in 2018. In 2023, he was honoured by his hometown by having a baseball field named after him.

"They phoned me. I was pretty surprised. It wasn't something I expected," McSween said.

McSween was also feted in 2022 when provincial-parliament members in Québec bestowed him with the Medal of the National Assembly of Québec, which is awarded in recognition of individuals who have followed an "extraordinary path in their lives."

At a party organized by Guy Bourassa to honour him recently, he received an Expos' sweater with his name and No. 14 on the back – 14 was the digit he wore all through his minor-league days. 14 was also on the front.

McSween most certainly would be one of the most famous names to come out of Valleyfield.

McSween was a southpaw with promise

Courtesy Southwest Voice
Denis McSween with Expos top

In a lifetime of wonderful moments, McSween won't forget two events in the fall of 1963, scenarios that will stay with him forever.

McSween was at 1600 Pennsylvania Avenue in downtown Washington, D.C. in late August of 1963 with his Canadian Little League teammates from Valleyfield.

The Valleyfield team had won the Canadian Little League championship at home and then went to Williamsport and was eliminated after losing its first two games: 5-1 to Connecticut and 4-3 to Mexico.

But McSween and his teammates were advised they were being feted with a dinner at the White House by you know who: President John F. Kennedy. The Valleyfield boys had driven all the way to Williamsport from Valleyfield with their parents or their coaches so, when they were finished in Williamsport, they drove to the White House located about four hours away.

"I was with the coach Roland Boyer," McSween said. "At most two days after the tournament, we went to the White House.

"You know what? You won't believe me. President Kennedy came down with a helicopter. We had dinner with him in a big, big room at the White House. I don't remember the name of the room. I found that all very interesting.

"Oh yeah, it was something big for us. Mmm," McSween emphasized. "We were happy to do that. President Kennedy shook hands with us. We were there at least two hours. Just us players and coaches. No other teams. I was 11 years old at the time. The trip home to Valleyfield

Exposion

was about 12 hours maybe."

Then more than six weeks later, McSween, like many around the world, were saddened to find out Kennedy was assassinated in Dallas Nov. 22.

"It was in November. That is what I remember the most," McSween said.

McSween was a star like no other from Valleyfield. He played Little League from 1962-64 and Valleyfield won the Canadian championship all three years he played. In 1963, Valleyfield lost a heart-breaking game to Japan 1-0 in Williamsport.

"I only gave up one hit, on a bunt. That's what I really remember," McSween said.

McSween recalled that prior to one tournament game in Williamsport in one of those years, he had Mother Nature calling because of the anxiety, the pressure associated with pitching in such an illustrious event.

"In Williamsport the first year during the national anthem, I waved to my coach and said, 'I want to pee. I have to pee.' "

In the Canadian final in 1964, the great left-hander engineered a narrow 1-0 victory in the final, recording the shutout on the mound and hitting a resounding home run to produce the only run of the game played at Parc Delpha-Sauvé, a neat facility located on Rue Victoria on the magnificent bay of Lac Saint-Francois.

"I was pretty nervous. There were at least 6,000 people at the stadium in Valleyfield," he said.

Your story is really heart-warming, Denis.

Chapter 7

Joe Sparma and Paul Warfield

One-time Expo Joe Sparma excelled in both football and baseball at Massillon Washington high school in Ohio.

He had some kind of ability as a pitcher. He was so good that he accepted a deal to play both sports at Ohio State University in Columbus, just down the road from where he was born. He had a full-ride scholarship in football.

"I was 15, he was 16," said his future wife Connie. "He was a year ahead of me in high school. I approached him through one of my best friends. I fell in love with him. He had that handsome kind of look about him. That was pretty much the way it was. We were married Aug. 17, 1962.

"Joe was my high school sweetheart. He was a football and baseball star athlete at Massillon. He went to Ohio State on a full football scholarship but could have gone to any Big Ten schools including Notre Dame. He was inducted into the Stark County Football Hall of Fame in 2011 in Canton, Ohio."

Sparma joined the Buckeyes as a freshman in 1960 but didn't play on the varsity squad. In 1961, Sparma was more inclined to be in love with a career as a passer but legendary head coach Woody Hayes had other plans. Sparma wasn't used that much. Hayes loved the running game.

"It was kind of ridiculous," Connie said. "Unfortunately, Woody Hayes didn't understand how to run a football play. When he wanted someone to throw a pass, he'd bring in Joe. It wasn't the greatest relationship Joe had with Woody Hayes."

Sparma threw for 200 yards and tossed two touchdown passes as Ohio State beat archival Michigan in 1961. Sparma was more impressive in baseball at Ohio State, compiling a

During that 1962 season, Sparma, like most other players on the team, appeared in all nine of Ohio State's games. He didn't get to throw the ball much but he did have a teammate, who would go on to be a star receiver in the National Football League with the Cleveland Browns and Miami Dolphins.

His name was Paul Warfield.

It was a coup interview to have the privilege of talking with Warfield, who was both a rival of Sparma in high school and a teammate at Ohio State.

"I really, really enjoyed this conversation," Warfield told me after we finished our interview. Of course, I told him he was one of my favou-

Explosion

Courtesy Ohio State University
Paul Warfield played against Joe Sparma in high school and was his teammate at Ohio State.

rite players on one of my favourite teams in 1972 when the Miami Dolphins went wire to wire undefeated to win the Super Bowl.

"Joe and I played against each on an annual basis three years in high school in the mid-to-late 1950s," Warfield told me in February of 2023. "I was at Warren Harding and Joe was at Massillon Washington. Joe and I go back to scholastic football. We were rivals.

"It was a great, great high school football tradition in Ohio. There were many great highs in the state of Ohio. High school football was somewhat of a big deal in the state of Ohio. It was huge. I would say Joe Sparma was the top quarterback in the state of Ohio. His school was our top competitor."

It seemed ironic Sparma and Warfield ended up at Ohio State. They were rivals in high school, teammates in college ball.

Sparma joined the Buckeyes as a freshman but didn't play on the varsity team. In 1961, he completed 16 of 38 passes for 341 yards. His main rival at quarterback, William Mrikaski, threw 35 passes and completed 23 for 231 yards. Warfield rushed 77 times for 420 yards and caught only nine passes for 120 yards, all telling you that Hayes concentrated more on the running game.

During the 1962 season, Warfield, calling himself a "combination running back and receiver", rushed 57 times for 367 yards and caught eight of Sparma's passes for another 139 yards.

All in all, Sparma had 71 pass attempts that season, completing 30 for 288 yards, hardly the type of football he enjoyed. He wanted more of the action and the glamour associated with the game. He didn't want to be just handing off the ball to a running back. There's not much glamour in that.

"Unfortunately, Ohio State was a run-oriented football team," Warfield said. "Under the circumstances, Joe would come in to play when we'd be behind in games or we'd be trying to bounce back or if they wanted to throw a pass. He had a great arm. He was an outstanding passer, enormously talented.

"He had an amazing ability to throw the football. He was very capable of throwing it accurately. Joe's skills were not utilized. Philosophically, Ohio State was not geared to pass the football. He didn't get much of an opportunity to play. He was a great teammate. I enjoyed our relationship.

"I had a number of offers from major-league teams. I had numerous opportunities to sign a baseball contract. I decided to go to college (Ohio State). I did not play college baseball. I played summer baseball."

So what happened with Sparma? His relationship with Hayes was testy so he chose to forego his senior year at Ohio State to sign a pro baseball contract with the Detroit Tigers in 1963, a deal that came after Sparma's spring season at Ohio State, where his combined record as a pitcher in 1962-63 was 11-8 with a 3.16 ERA.

He struck out 93 batters in 1963 and threw a no-hitter against Michigan on May 18. He ended his collegiate year as Ohio State's all-time leader in strikeouts with 195.

"Joe had an outstanding reputation as a pitcher. He made the decision to change sports. He felt it was more beneficial for him in baseball," said Warfield, who remained with the Buckeyes while Sparma transferred to baseball.

"In the spring of 1963, Joe had a bonus offer put in front of his face. Detroit offered him $34,000 — at the time, it was pretty good," Connie told me. A SABR Bio Project story done by Jeff Samoray mentioned the signing bonus was $20,000 but we'll go with what Connie said.

Sparma spent the 1963 season in two places: A ball in Duluth-Superior and in Double-A with Knoxville. By 1964, he was called up to the majors by the Tigers and made his debut after another stint in Knoxville.

"When he was brought up by Detroit, he was considered a bonus baby. They had to keep him a certain amount of time," Connie said.

Sparma was 5-6 in 1964 and was outstanding in 1965 with a 13.8 record with a 3.18 ERA in 167 innings. He was a mainstay in a five-man rotation that included Denny McLain (16-6), Mickey Lolich (15-9), Hank Aquirre (14-10) and Dave Wickersham, who was 9-14.

At spring training in Lakeland, Fla, in 1966, disaster struck.

"Joe's pitching-hand finger (index) got caught in the car door and he never regained the control and confidence he had recovering from that bad injury," Connie said. "It took a while for that to heal. He didn't have the same feeling. We were there. It happened so fast."

Sparma pitched part of the 1966 with poor results. He was 2-7 in 91.2 innings. But there was good news on the horizon because he shook off his hand mishap to enjoy the best season of his career in 1967. He went 16-9 in 217.2 innings of work. He was 9-1 through the first half but didn't make the all-star team. In the rotation with him that season were Earl Wilson (22-11), Lolich (14-13) and McLain (17-16)

In 1968, he tailed off and his relationship with Smith deteriorated. He was 10-10 in 182.1 innings.

Smith often bypassed him for rotation starts and it infuriated Sparma.

"Mayo had no confidence in Joe so he would take him out of the game. It was upsetting," Connie said.

Exposion

For all the discontent between Sparma and Smith, the manager reluctantly inserted Sparma into a game late in the 1968 season, Sept. 17, and Sparma was the winning pitcher. His effort clinched the pennant for the Tigers and they went on to beat the Cardinals in the World Series.

"All I could think of was all the trouble I've been in this year and how much pain it has caused my wife and my family," Sparma told reporters after the clinching game.

Of course, all through this scenario in 1969 and in previous seasons after his accident, he had terrible control problems. He had the yips like a number of other major leaguers such as Steve Sax and Steve Blass, who had awful experiences trying to throw a ball to the plate or a base. It probably didn't help that Sparma was a chain smoker and battled his weight on occasion.

Someone joked on Facebook that Sparma exhibited control that "rivalled Greg Maddux's." Of course, while Sparma's control was out of whack, Maddux was exemplary by painting the black and hitting corners,

"I suppose it was a mental aspect, if you don't have confidence in what you are doing. It can be disturbing," Connie told me about Joe's wacky control. "He always had control problems, ever since he picked up a baseball. You couldn't catch him. He had first-inning jitters. He started to lose his confidence."

In Sparma's last season with Detroit, he was 6-8 with a 4.76 ERA and his relationship with Smith kept getting rockier.

On Dec. 3, 1969, Tigers GM Jim Campbell traded Sparma to the Expos in exchange for Jerry Robertson. The Expos knew how good Sparma could be when he was on, so they gambled to see if Sparma could change his fortunes. He was only 27 going on 28 so he was still young. He was worth the risk for sure.

"When the trade was completed, I remember the Expos brass being very high on Sparma." recalled Expos fan Pierre Miquelon. "We gave up a pretty good righty, Jerry Robertson, in exchange for Sparma."

Canadian Baseball Hall of Fame
Joe Sparma

The change in scenery didn't seem to help Sparma. He was 0-4 with a 7.06 ERA and spent some time in the minors with Winnipeg. On May 12 with Montreal, Sparma, in relief of Claude Raymond, threw only five strikes on 28 pitches. He walked four in one inning. That's how bad his control (yips?) was. Even when he was trying to intentionally walk a batter, he once threw the ball over catcher John Bateman's head. He just never knew where the ball was going to wind up.

"He was a bulldog with a great fastball," recalled 1970 teammate

Joe Sparma and Paul Warfield

Rich Nye.

"Detroit probably knew Sparma was at the end of the line when they dealt him," Miquelon said. "But then, when you consider Adolfo Phillips, Rick Coggins and Fred Breining, among others, Sparma was likely the first of several players to report to the Expos with damaged goods. But we loved Joe anyways. He was one of Nos Amours. He could do no harm."

Sparma and his lack of control were immortalized in Jim Bouton's Ball Four. Bouton remarked, "Of course, Frank Howard is out from here to there (6-foot-8) and Sparma is out of an inning in which all he threw was 10 pitches – all balls."

Later that season, the Expos dealt Sparma to Detroit's Triple-A team in Toledo, Ohio but Sparma's problems prevailed.

"The Montreal trade, it was a shocker to us. We had become so comfortable with Detroit," Connie said. "His brief time in Montreal was a hopeful time but ultimately it didn't work out. We were grateful for the opportunity.

"My memory of that time was that it snowed during the month of May. New experiences for us both. Snow in May? Where I come from (Ohio), there is no snow in the spring. The plan was to have my son born there in Montreal. Joe was traded back to Detroit (Toledo) before my due date, so Blase was born July 6, 1970 in Dearborn, Michigan."

In his "brief time" in Montreal, Sparma grew to admire Le Grand Orange ever so much.

"Joe loved Rusty Staub. He befriended him. He couldn't talk about anything but Rusty Staub," Connie said. "He loved Jim Fanning. He found him to be very likeable."

Sparma was out of baseball following the 1970 season.

"Joe didn't want to go beyond that (1970). He never asked to go anywhere else. He was a homebody. He didn't want to go anywhere. No other teams were after him so it was time to put baseball on the shelf," Connie said.

Within a short time of retiring, Sparma took a management training course and proceeded to work for many years for Buckeye Steel in Worthington, Ohio, with his last job being vice-president of sales and marketing.

Sad news came in May of 1984 when Sparma suffered a heart attack which stemmed possibly from heavy smoking. Due to complications from triple-bypass surgery, he died May 14.

"He had an irregular heart beat and was on medication for that. It was a bad situation. He never left the hospital. He was there 19 days," Connie said. "It was devastating for the children and myself. It was very unexpected. We were very close."

I could tell by talking to Connie and reading her emails that she still adores Joe 37 going on 38 years since his death.

"Again, I thank you for thinking of Joe," Connie told me. "It warms my heart to know people still remember. He was a beautiful, kind-hearted man, who loved his family dearly. Gone way too soon."

Chapter 8

Strohmayer outduelled Nolan Ryan

When Kevin Strohmayer went to the dais to speak at his father's Celebration of Life on Dec. 14, 2019, he immediately talked about the time his dad John played for the Expos, especially the game when he went toe to toe in a pitcher's duel with Mets blooming great Nolan Ryan.

It was a remarkable story. The scene was Shea Stadium in New York. The date was July 5, 1971. Strohmayer, a relatively unknown, a lithe, skinny runt at 6-feet tall, going up against the future Hall of Famer, who was pure power.

Strohmayer, unfazed by the opposing pitcher, singled to centre in the sixth inning and pitched a masterful game in going the distance, outduelling Ryan 2-1 in a real-quick game time of 2:10. Talk about one of the highlights of Strohmayer's career.

"He used to tell us that when he went up against Nolan Ryan that he couldn't see the ball in the batter's box," Kevin told his audience at Crosse Pointe Community Church in Redding, Calif. "So we used to joke with him that the only way he got that hit was if he swung with his eyes closed."

In a matinée at Shea Stadium, Strohmayer flung a five-hitter, struck out five. Here he was, a kid, born in smalltown Belle Fourche, South Dakota who grew up in smalltown Redding, Calif., doing a stellar job against Ryan. it was like David going against Goliath, the unknown average-throwing upstart facing a fireballer.

Strohmayer's sister Natalie Crowder said at his memorial service his brother's strong belief in himself aided him tremendously in many aspects of his life as an educator, athlete and career in baseball.

"He had faith in himself and he had great determination and he overcame lots of odds," Crowder said. "I think he weighed 140 pounds in high school but he excelled in three sports. Even when he went to the majors, he was still little but because of his blind faith, he was going to do many great things."

Strohmayer was taken by the Expos from the Oakland Athletics in the Rule 5 major-league draft Dec. 1, 1969 and made his big-league debut with the Expos on April 29, 1970. He came into the day game at old San Diego Stadium in a mop up role as the Padres rolled to an easy 10-0 washout. Strohmayer pitched two innings, allowing a solo home run to Al Ferrara.

His best season was 1971 when he was 7-5. He appeared in 27 games, 15 as a starter, working 114 innings. His ERA was 4.34. He was also ex-

Strohmayer outduelled Nolan Ryan

Canadian Baseball HOF *Pro Stars Publications*
John Strohmayer

emplary in 1972, strictly as a reliever. He appeared in 48 games, struck out 50 batters and recorded a 3.52 ERA in 76.2 innings.

Expos scout Eddie Lopat had worked with Strohmayer by touching up his control and pitching strategy. In 1973, Strohmayer was worked infrequently by manager Gene Mauch and was put on waivers July 10, 1973 when he was snapped up by the Mets.

In an interview with the Montreal Gazette, Strohmayer alluded to a conflict with Mauch.

"I got the feeling that it didn't matter how well I pitched, I would still be only spotted when he was stuck," Strohmayer said in the interview. "I'm just not the type of pitcher who can be called upon every eight or nine days and be effective."

It was at spring training in 1970 when Strohmayer and teammate Steve Renko began their friendship. During the regular season, they were roommates. It was a friendship that lasted until Stroh died almost

Exposion

50 years later. They clicked, just like the many Expos' friendships we have learned about: Ken Singleton and Mike Torrez, Larry Jaster and Floyd Wicker, Cliff Floyd and Rondell White, Jeff Fassero and Sean Berry, Bob McClure and Bryn Smith. And many others.

While Strohmayer was the lesser known of the two, their friendship blossomed. Renko was the ace of the Expos' staff for many years from 1969-76. Strohmayer had two relatively good seasons in 1971-72. He had never reached the echelons achieved by Renko but Renko was unfazed. Strohmayer, the person, meant more to Renko.

On off days in Montreal, Strohmayer and Renko went fishing for trout in the Laurentides. When both retired, they would rent pontoon boats and fish at Lake Shasta in California. Renko would make his way to California from Texas, Kansas or wherever he lived. Even after Strohmayer retired from his education career, him and his wife Connie would travel in their RV to visit Renko.

Rarely, if ever, did Strohmayer and Renko talk baseball.

"We didn't know any of the new players and we didn't keep in touch with any of them," Renko told Ethan Passion of the Redding Record Searchlight newspaper in Strohmayer's hometown. "All the players we knew were either retired or gone. We talked about things that I talk with my friends in town. 'How's your health?' The only thing you talk about when you're past 70 are the aches and pains. I know he had eye issues and we would just sit back and laugh about getting old."

Following the 1971 season, Strohmayer played winter ball in Caguas, located in the Central Mountain Range of Puerto Rico. Who should tag along with him? Renko. It was an experience that enthralled Strohmayer when he was interviewed by Mississippi-based writer Tom Van Hyning.

"Where else can you work in a vacation paradise, meet great people and play against great ball players?" he asked in delight. "I wouldn't trade those years for anything. They were just fantastic."

Strohmayer took great satisfaction in the Puerto Rican foods because it wasn't hot and spicy like Mexican grub. Often for road trips in the Puerto Rican winter league, he would grab local food, while most of his teammates wanted the equivalent of stateside U.S. fare.

Strohmayer, as Van Hyning pointed out, loved the delicacy asopao, a thick soup of various flavours highlighted by infusions of chicken and seafood.

But for the intentions of the Expos' brass back in Montreal, he was considered a prospect and he won player of the week a number of times with prizes including a trip to St. Thomas in the British Virgin Islands, a dinner for two at the Caguas Highway Inn, a new radio and a $100 gift certificate.

During a regular-season game in 1971, Strohmayer was facing José Pagan of the Pirates, who had become another friend of Strohmayer's in winter ball, although not near as close as Renko was. On a 1-2 pitch, Strohmayer went inside on Pagan and hit him on the left wrist. Strohmayer felt bad.

"In fact, when I hit Jose and heard that sickening thud and crack. I said, 'Oh no, geez, here's a guy, who was my friend.' I found out he had a broken wrist from a clubhouse report," Strohmayer told Van Hyning.

That same game, the great Roberto Clemente came up the plate, non too pleased with Strohmayer hitting his buddy, born also in Puerto Rico like him. Clemente hit a comebacker to the mound and as he was headed to the dugout, he shouted a few obscenities in Spanish at Strohmayer.

An even odder scenario took place the following winter in Caguas. Pagan told Strohmayer his wrist was completely healed. First time up against Strohmayer, Pagan was drilled again in the exact same spot, breaking it again. Not a word of a lie.

An arm injury forced Strohmayer to retire too young in 1975. He soon got involved in education, taking advantage of the Bachelor of Arts degree in history he obtained from the University of the Pacific in Stockton.

Over time, he spent many years as a basketball coach and as a teacher, vice-principal, principal, and head of the school board as superintendent.

Strohmayer died at 73 on U.S. Thanksgiving Day Nov. 28, 2019 of heart problems, passing away on the operating table before surgeons were going to do some surgery.

I just happened to call Strohmayer's "good, good friend" Renko on Dec. 6, 2019 to do an interview with him for a chapter in one of my books when he closed the conversation to say Strohmayer died.

"This is something you might want to know," Renko told me.

Strohmayer's death hadn't been announced. Shortly after Renko and I talked, the family placed an obituary in the local paper, the Redding Record Searchlight.

"He was a close friend. He had valves placed in his heart and they started beeping," Renko said when he told me his buddy had died. "He was put in intensive care. They were going to operate."

Thank you, John, for the time you gave to the Expos. R.I.P.

Chapter 9

Woods was a solid, part-time player

On the mean streets and the fields of Compton, Expos alumnus Ron Woods survived and thrived.

In the face of adversity and racial discrimination, he had the Patience of Job after leaving his native Hamilton, Ohio and growing up in Compton, the predominantly black community nestled in the inner-city walls of Los Angeles.

Woods used baseball as a catalyst when barriers wouldn't permit him to use certain facilities, drinking fountains and washrooms.

As a member of the Compton high school baseball team, he played against future Yankees teammate Roy White, who suited up for Centennial high school.

One of the most famous athletes to play at Compton high was Duke Snider along with current NBA great DeMar DeRozan. Others with roots in Compton include Serena Williams and former NFL commissioner Pete Rozelle.

At the age of 18, Woods got noticed by the Pittsburgh Pirates and was signed to a Class D contract. He ended up being posted to the lowly outpost of Hobbs, New Mexico, which is about five miles from the Texas border, where he played in what was called the Sophomore League. It was the last year Hobbs had a pro team because the league folded.

Oil was the name of the game in Hobbs where the Midwest Oil Company had set up shop for many years.

"Hobbs was a very small town. It was an oil town. You could smell oil all over the place," Woods's teammate Gary Waslewski said in an interview. "You got used to the oil after a while. We got paid $200-$350 per month.

"Gene Michael was on that team. He had his wife. We stayed at the Harden Hotel. It's still there. It was a dump we were in. The rate was $2 per night. There was no air conditioning. Some nights, it would be 100 degrees and you would have to put a wet towel on the pillow."

That's what low-rung minor leaguers had to put up as they tried to get to the majors. For Woods, the experience was even more daunting in an era when racism ruled its ugly head. They could not always stay at the same hotels as their white teammates.

"I don't know about Ron – him and the blacks and Hispanics may not have been able to stay at the hotel," Waslewski said.

Woods and Waslewski were two of the stars on that team. Woods batted .309 with 14 homers and 54 RBI in 63 games. Waslewski went 12-7

Woods was a solid, part-time player

in 21 starts.

"Ron was a really good guy, a good teammate, who got caught up in the racial stuff. He was a line-drive hitter, made contact. He was a good, all-round player," Waslewski said. "He could steal bases, run and he could throw.

"Our home games were unusual in that if you hit a home run, fans stuck bills through the screen once you touched home plate. You'd start collecting the bills and you'd probably end up with $200-350 per month."

Ironically, as Waslewski noted, him, Michael, the future Yankees GM and Woods, all joined the Yankees at one point in 1971 and stood around and marvelled at how they made the show and thoughts "took us back to Hobbs", Waslewski said.

That's where that racism comes in, the resilience and determination Woods needed to survive in the face of adversity.

Woods and Waslewski also were teammates on other Pirates' minor-league teams. Woods had floundered for five years in the Bucs' farm system with no chance of a run at a major-league spot and then his fortunes changed somewhat when his contract was purchased by the Detroit Tigers for $500 at the start of the 1966 season.

Woods would spend more time in the minors but finally got his break when he made his big-league debut with Detroit in 1969, eight years after he began pro ball. He appeared in 17 games. Woods received a bigger break when he was obtained by the Yankees from Detroit for Tom Tresh on June 14, 1969. It sure was a blessing for Woods.

Despite being a part-time player with the Bronx Bombers, he managed to get into 192 games from 1969-71 and was a teammate of White, his high school rival. If you look closely, Woods is White's doppelganger. It's remarkable.

White got regular-playing time, compared to Woods, in an era when the Yankees were in a rebuilding mode or transitional period. But the part-time work still meant he was in the majors and Woods wasn't complaining.

The break he got in being traded to the Yankees was sure nice, but his status was elevated even more when the Expos plucked him from the Yankees for aging Ron Swoboda on June 25, 1971. The change in scenery didn't see Woods in a Montreal uniform in 1971 but he joined the Expos in 1972.

With the Expos, he was unheralded but a steady major-league outfielder, who was used primarily as a platoon player, defensive replacement, pinch runner and pinch hitter.

On Aug. 23, 1972 during a Wednesday game at Jarry Park, Woods enjoyed the game of a lifetime against Cincinnati. He went 3-for-4 and drove in six runs with a pair of three-run homers, while Balor Moore struck out 13 in an 11-0 rout by the Expos.

"Left-hander Balor Moore stripped the gears of the Big Red Machine last night and Ron Woods pounded it down to the hubcaps with the biggest game of his major-league career," Tim Burke said in his opening paragraph of his game report in the Montreal Gazette.

Explosion

> ### Moore was close to 15 Ks
>
> Aug. 23, 1972 brings back great memories for Balor Moore.
>
> It was the best game of his career in the majors. The Expos won 11-0 at Parc Jarry in a game that went quick: 2:27.
>
> "I remember I had a shot at 15Ks which was some kind of record I think but I got the last two outs on change ups with a two-strike count on the last three hitters," Moore told me in 2023. "I'm still angry at Tim McCarver for making me throw the change up. Probably the only three changeups I threw that whole season or my career.
>
> "Funny part is I kept shaking Timmy off till he came to the mound. I said, 'I need two more Ks' and he looked at me and says, 'So rookie, how many shutouts do you have?' Duh, none. 'So, let's get this shutout and the win, let's go, beers are getting hot.'
>
> "I also remember Pete Rose standing in the dugout screaming at me every time he made an out. Looking back, it seems unrealistic I had a whole career with only two pitches. Living in the Houston area, I get asked often about the sign stealing and if I ever worried about the batters stealing my pitches. Answer – I only had two pitches. Hitters had a 50/50 chance of guessing right. Not that difficult. Does say something about the talent though.
>
> "For some reason, maybe my age, I have been reflecting back on those good times of the past."

Woods went yard the first time with a line shot to right-centre near the 400-foot mark. The second shot was another screamer to straight-away left.

"Ron Woods and cash for Rocky Swoboda. Take a bow for that, Mr. Fanning," wrote John Robertson in the Montreal Star, referring to the trade back in 1971.

"Both my homers were off pitches in almost the same place, fast and low," the wiry Woods told reporters. "I'm not trying for them (homers). When I try for them, forget it. I'm not going for homers. I'm smarter than that. All I'm trying to do is hit the ball the way I know I can, just line drives, without over-swinging."

Expos manager Gene Mauch started Woods for the second consecutive game after Woods went 3-for-4 with a two-run homer on Aug. 22 against Ross Grimsley of the Reds. All told, Woods started six consecutive games from Aug. 22-26, in my research. He was really enjoying the glow of a full-time player during this stretch, taking starting assignments away from his platoon partner in centre field, Boots Day.

The tremendous outing on Aug. 23 was appreciated much by the 13,804 fans, including the Wormington clan from Montreal.

"We're a baseball family," Bob Wormington said. "There were at least four family members at that game - my parents, my sister Nancy and myself for sure, and possibly my sister Judy as well. One of my hobbies in retirement is compiling family history. "Serendipity alert. Today (Jan. 4, 2023) in going through my father's correspondence, I found letters between him and Frank Read at Marsh & McLennan with

Woods was a solid, part-time player

Canadian Baseball Hall of Fame
Ron Woods was a solid part-time player

Frank letting my Dad know he had secured two tickets out of the company season-ticket package for the game of Aug. 23, 1972. That's the Ron Woods six-RBI game. It was also the Balor Moore 13K game.

"I also found a second letter from a gentleman by the name of James Melling at the Robert P. Fleming architectural firm who also supplied tickets for that (Woods) game. As I said, we had a fair number of family there. I have two ticket stubs from that game. Section 118 and 218."

Woods finished 1972 with decent stats for a part-timer in 87 games: 10 homers, 31 RBI, 21 runs and a .258 average.

In 1973, Mauch got Woods into 127 games and his production went like this: three homers, 31 RBI, 45 runs, 16 stolen bases and a .230 average. Again, not a bad year for a part-timer.

In one game against the Cardinals, pinch hitting for Larry Lintz, Woods fouled off seven pitches and then hit a towering pop in between the mound and home plate. Shortstop Mick Kelleher, third baseman Terry Hughes and Joe Torre all called for the ball but none took charge. It

Exposion

Canadian Baseball HOF
Ron Woods

was called a base hit by the official scorer.

"It was the nicest hit of my career. It was probably the shortest, too," Woods was telling the Montreal Gazette later.

In the off-season, Woods and Day both got unpleasant news when the Expos acquired Willie Davis from the Dodgers for pitcher Mike Marshall. This transaction met Davis would play every day in 1974, relegating Woods and Day to much less work. There would be no platooning.

Woods did get into 90 games in 1974 but his production was way down. He managed a homer, 12 RBI and a .205 average. Little did he know he would play his last game in the majors – with the Expos on Sept. 29 of that season.

Woods is another part-time player I heard a lot about. Never saw him play but I just admired what he accomplished.

Chapter 10

Ron was better than Fairly good

He loved playing for the Dodgers even though his career had derailed in Tinseltown, and when he was traded to the Expos, he was very disappointed.

At least, that's what he would say many years later, that he didn't enjoy playing for the Expos.

Ron Fairly, with his long flowing red hair, hung around the Expos for 5½ seasons and carved out a reputation as a solid hitter, establishing himself as a threat at the plate for a team not long in talent, except maybe in 1973 when they lingered around to threaten to win the NL East before fading in the end.

Not only was he solid at the plate but he sure could work pretty good leather around first base and in the outfield.

Fairly was a southern California boy, who had moved with his parents from his native Macon, Georgia when he was only three months old. From what I read in California's Santa Barbara Independent newspaper, it appears Fairly, his older brother Rusty and their parents Carl and Marjorie arrived in California on a boat that passed through the Panama Canal round about 1941.

His father Carl played minor-league ball for about 10 seasons and Rusty was a great athlete, an all-American quarterback at the University of Denver, who also played in the Canadian Football league.

How ideal and beautiful is that a California resident gets to play for his homestate team? That's what Fairly did for the equivalent of 9½ seasons, playing mostly left field for the Dodgers and putting up some better than average numbers.

In 1968, Fairly started a decline with what was deemed a subpar season with Los Angeles. He hit only .234 with four homers and 43 RBI. The home-run output was not in line with what he generally did. No. His WAR had diminished along with his OPS.

During his long tenure in the backdrop of Hollywood, Fairly's significant contribution to the Dodgers was measured by his four consecutive seasons of 70 or more RBI from 1962-65. Beginning in 1966, Fairly's offence gradually went downhill.

Taking all those factors into consideration, the Dodgers saw more decline in Fairly through the first half of the 1969 season. Mind you, Fairly only appeared in 30 games, mustering no homers and just eight RBI and batting a measly .219. Fairly had lost playing time to Wes Parker, Bill Russell and Andy Kosko and others in either the outfield or at first base.

Exposion

So on June 15, the Dodgers pulled the plug on Fairly and decided to trade him and Paul Popovich to the expansion Expos in exchange for disgruntled Maury Wills and Manny Mota. This deal turned out to be a steal for Montreal.

Fairly was only 30 years old, just weeks shy of his 31st birthday. This trade, though, was a culture shock to Fairly. He apparently had no use for the trade. He was coming from California, where he lived and where he played all his university and big-league ball in his own backyard so to speak.

You have to give credit to Fairly, though, for sticking it out with the Expos. His one-time teammate Don DeMola does not recall him being unhappy in Montreal and what was important was that his offensive numbers actually turned a new leaf during his time with Montreal.

Fairly made the Dodgers/Expos trade lopsided in favour of Montreal. He turned his career around. In the last half of the 1969 season, Fairly managed 12 homers and 39 RBI. In the first half, he had played very little for L.A.

Then from 1970-73, he returned to numbers he had produced through most of his tenure with the Dodgers. Manager Gene Mauch put him in on a regular basis and restored his confidence.

Fairly's best season with Montreal was in 1971 when he hit 13 homers and drove in 71 runs. That's the kind of production he gave the Dodgers in the early part of his career.

In 1972, his numbers were exceptional also. He hit 17 homers and had 68 RBI. He was an all-star in 1973 – he hit .298 with 17 homers and 49 RBI. 1974 saw him slip to .245 with 12 homers and 45 ribbies.

On Dec. 6, 1974, the Expos decided to trade Fairly, 36, to St. Louis at the winter meetings. The Expos didn't get much for him. Ever heard of Rudy Kinard and Ed Kupiel?

"I never saw that he hated Montreal. He may not have liked the home-field clubhouse and such," DeMola said. "I played spades with Ron on the plane flights. He used to say, 'God takes care of babies and Demola' in reference to me always getting good hands," DeMola said.

For the record, Fairly was right up and front and blunt when he talked with the Montreal Gazette some 20 years ago or so. He did not like it in Montreal. Period.

"I hated it. I didn't like any part of it," Fairly told the Gazette. "I hated the weather and I hated playing for a last-place team. In 1970, our stated goal was to win 70 in '70. In other words, we were playing not to lose 100 games and would be happy losing 90 games.

"With the Dodgers, I went into every game expecting to win, even when we were down in 1967 and 1968. That couldn't be the case in Montreal. When I showed my four-year-old son, Mike, where I would be playing (on a map) after the trade, he looked at me sadly and asked, 'Does this mean I don't have a daddy anymore?'"

Fairly said his heart sank when he heard what Mike said.

Fairly, like the true professional he was, blocked out his dislike of Montreal by thriving with the Expos, showing the Dodgers he still had a lot of gumption left in him.

Ron was better than Fairly good

Ron Fairly, right, Jim Gosger, left, and Rusty Staub at a banquet in Montreal.

Antoine Desilets photo

Explosion

City of Montreal archives
Ron Fairly with Rusty Staub

"I was a major-league player paid to perform as well as I could play. I was still getting a check and I still had the hope that some other team would come and get me," Fairly told the Gazette.

Why didn't Fairly just ask for a trade early on, if he didn't like it in Montreal? There had been no indication publicly he ever wanted a different team.

In a profile of Fairly done for the SABR Bio Project series, a writer said the St. Louis Cardinals "rescued Fairly from his Canadian purgatory" by acquiring him from the Expos Dec. 6, 1974.

"Canadian purgatory?" What the hell is that?

Remarkably, Fairly played in 1,000 games in both the outfield and infield. How about that? Fairly soon got into broadcasting and called more than 7,000 games.

Fairly published his memoirs in February of 2018 in a book co-written with Steve Springer. The book was entitled

Fairly at Bat: My 50 years in baseball: From the batter's box to the broadcast booth

Fairly died in October of 2019, in Palm Desert, California. He was 81 years old.

Ron was better than Fairly good

Inset courtesy La Pizza Royale *Pro Stars Publications*

Ron Fairly

Exposion

Missing a hat

"Ron Fairly might have broken a toe. He walked into a table leg. So he was sitting on the bench. The bench was kind of long. He was not wearing his baseball hat so he was walking up and down the dugout with his flowing, red hair. The Dodgers had runners on base and we were attempting a double play. The second baseman throws it to Tim Foli, who steps on the bag and goes to first and hits the runner on the head. The runner goes down and Foli is screaming at him, 'Get the hell out of my way.' They get into a fight and we've got all these guys who were trying to pull them apart. It was something out of Popeye. Foli takes his glasses and hat off and kicks them into the grass and he dives back into the fight. When the fight is over, Foli is running into the dugout. He doesn't have his hat. He said, 'I can't find my hat. Where's my hat? I need my hat.' Ron Fairly was about three feet from me and Gene was in front of me. So Gene looks at Fairly and said, 'Fairly hasn't worn a hat in a week. Get a hat from him.' Gene just glared at Fairly. Fairly stood there with his mouth wide open."

— Dennis Blair talking about a hilarious incident back in the mid-1970s.

Chapter 11

Gebhard tutored some good pitchers

Bob Gebhard had a short stint as a pitcher for the Expos and then played an important role for the organization in the minor leagues in the 1970s and 1980s.

In 1974, Gebhard was a pitcher under Gene Mauch. It was a short experiment.

"I was called up by the Expos and I pitched one game and I wasn't very good," Gebhard was saying in March of 2023. "It was in St. Louis."

I did some research to find some details of the Sept. 3 at Retrosheet and Baseball Almanac. Gebhard pitched two innings, coming into the game in the eighth inning. He gave up a single to Mike Tyson, no, not that Mike Tyson, and then retired the next three batters.

To start the ninth inning, Gebhard got Ted Simmons and Lonnie Smith on groundouts before running into trouble.

"I gave up a long home run to Joe Torre on a hanging slider. Joe always reminds me of that," Gebhard said, smiling.

Gebhard then allowed consecutive singles to Bake McBride, Ken Reitz and Tyson before getting out of the inning but the damage had been done. He never pitched again in the majors.

"Gene Mauch had seen enough of that. I was taken off the roster in September," Gebhard said. "I was looking for another job. The Expos offered me a job as field coordinator and minor-league pitching coach in 1976.

"I worked for Jim Fanning, who was the farm director and scouting director. He was kind of like a mentor to me. Jim was a very kind person. He always listened to what I had for thoughts and ideas. He let me do things on my own. He was a good leader for all of us. We respected what he had done in the game."

During this tenure as the roving pitching coach in the minor leagues, Gebhard sure worked with some dandy talent. To this day, Gebhard is very thankful he got to help and tutor some great arms that were the pride of the Expos' organization and the envy of opposing teams.

Gebhard sent me a wonderful photo of him posing with pitchers Bill Gullickson, Scott Sanderson, Charlie Lea, Bob James, David Palmer, Steve Ratzer and Hal Dues.

"Gully, Sanderson, Palmer, Lea – they all came through the system. They all went on to become pretty good pitchers. My favourites were probably Gullickson and Sanderson," Gebhard said. "They were very good. I respected their work effort and wanting to learn to be better. It

Exposion

Photo supplied by Bob Gebhard

Bob Gebhard, middle in back, poses with some of the pitchers he tutored back in the day. Front row, left to right, David Palmer, Steve Ratzer and Hal Dues. Back row, Bill Gullickson, Scott Sanderson, Charlie Lea and Bob James.

was nice to teach Sanderson how to throw a breaking ball. He was all smiles and worked his ass off and he was a good guy to be around."

After five years in the field and as a pitching coordinator in the minors, Fanning offered Gebhard the job of scouting director. In 1982, Gebhard spent part of the season with the major-league club as a bullpen coach under Fanning, who was manager. He threw batting practice before games and then worked with pitching coach Galen Cisco in both the dugout and in the bullpen.

"Half way through the year, John McHale asked me to be farm director. I'd put my uniform on," Gebhard said of his dual role. "It was a different way to treat the job. I tried to combine both my farm director's job and help pitchers along the way."

Gebhard continued to be farm director until the Twins came calling near the end of the 1986 season. They got permission from the Expos to talk to Gebhard and he accepted the job of vice-president of player personnel. It was a step up from what he was doing with the Expos

"I was coming back to Minnesota," Gebhard said of his new post. "I'd been with Minnesota my whole career. I had been living in Minnesota when I was with the Expos. I'd operate out of Montreal and there was a lot of travelling back and forth. I knew the Twins so I was glad to go back there."

Gebhard was born in Lamberton, Minnesota on 1940, went to Lam-

Gebhard tutored some good pitchers

Photo supplied by Bob Gebhard

Expos personnel gathered on a backfield back in the day. Front row, left to right: Rick Williams, Pat Daugherty, Gene Glynn, Frank Wren, Ralph Rowe. Back row: J.R. Miner, Leonel Carreon, Tommy Thompson, Jim Fanning, Doug Yarnus, Bob Gebhard, Felipe Alou and Mark Schuler.

Exposion

> **Daugherty was a good company man**
>
> Pat Daugherty was an integral part of the Expos organization.
>
> From 1970-743, Daugherty was the manager of the franchise's Class A team in Jamestown, N.Y.
>
> "I was a coach with a community college (Indian Hills) in Iowa and the Expos hired me," Daugherty said. "Jim Fanning hired me. I met Jim through the Major League Baseball Scouting Bureau. He was the first director of the scouting bureau and I took a part-time job with the scouting bureau."
>
> When he finished his first stint as Jamestown manager, Daugherty spent the most of his remaining time with the Expos as scouting supervisor for the state of Florida.
>
> When I asked him what player he remembers the most, he mentioned Charles Johnson, who was very high on the Expos' list of draftees.
>
> The Expos looked at him at a catching prospect along the lines of Gary Carter, who had been traded to the Mets in December of 1984. The Expos selected Johnson in the first round in 1989.
>
> "That wasn't a good time for me," Daugherty said of the Johnson saga. "I did a fair amount of work on it in the background. The kid told me he was interested in signing. Whether he got cold feet – he flipped and decided to go to the University of Miami."
>
> What goes around comes around, because in 1990, Daugherty was back as Jamestown manager and his experience in the game saw him get a new job in 1991.
>
> Daugherty was hired as the Colorado Rockies' scouting director by friend and new GM Bob Gebhard. As in the case of Johnson, I asked Daugherty who his favourite Rockies player was as a scout.
>
> "Todd Helton," he said. "He was playing at the University of Tennessee. You know what, I saw him as a pitcher. He was a great pitcher for them. He also played third base. He was not hard to like. He was a two-player player.
>
> "I don't know how far he could have gone in pitching. He could hit. I didn't know he would have the power he had. I thought he would hit 15 homers a season and hit for average but he ended up doing a lot better than that."
>
> That's right, Helton is Cooperstown-bound pretty soon – thanks to some help from Daugherty, who scouted for the Rockies until he was 80 and then retired.

berton high school and was drafted as a pitcher out of the University of Iowa by his hometown Twins in the 44th round of the 1965 June draft of amateur players.

It was the year the Twins, owned by Canadian born Calvin Griffith, lost in the seventh game of the World Series against the Dodgers and although he wasn't part of that team, Gebhard was all excited about pro ball in the Minnesota system.

Gebhard made a lot of stops in various towns and cities in America for the Twins and following a break-through 8-3 season for Portland, Oregon in Triple-A in 1970, he was called up to make his big-league debut

Gebhard tutored some good pitchers

Aug. 2, 1971 and did just fine, allowing no runs in two innings of work.

Gebhard appeared in 30 games during his Twins tenure before he was signed as a free agent by Montreal on Jan. 14, 1974.

"The first year after I signed with the Twins in 1986, we won the World Series and I stayed with them until after we won the World Series again in 1991," Gebhard said.

Then a bountiful piece of luck came across Gebhard's desk when expansion took place, beginning in 1993. He lucked out with a neat job.

"I was interviewed for several jobs. Detroit offered me the GM job but I didn't think the conditions were right. San Diego offered me a job and lucky enough, the Rockies hired me as general manager," he said. "I was thrilled to death. It was a great opportunity for me.

"I signed with the Rockies before the end of the season but I was allowed to stay with the Twins until the end of the season. The Twins won the World Series on a Sunday night and on Wednesday, I was on a plane to Denver."

Starting a team from scratch had to be a lot of fun.

On Oct. 6, 1991, Larry Bearnarth had been let go as Expos pitching coach, a job he had held since 1985. Sure enough, Gebhard grabbed his old buddy from his Expos days to join him as a special assistant to the GM and then Bear became pitching coach when the Rockies started play in 1993.

"Danny, we often worked 24/7 to try and get a major-league staff together and get things ready for 1993," Gebhard said. "I was gone all the time. Sometimes, I'd be gone 30 days at a time on scouting trips. I took an apartment in Colorado.

"Larry was very, very knowledgeable about pitching. We worked well together, we roomed together in winter ball and the Instructional league and became very good friends, I had tremendous respect for him for what he could bring to the Rockies. He was hard working. I'd made him a manager in the minor leagues for the Expos."

Gebhard hired Don Baylor as manager and following the 1994 season, he made one of the biggest moves he ever made when he signed Expos great Larry Walker as a free agent.

The move wasn't made until April 8, 1995 because the winter of 1994-95 was a mess since the players' strike dragged past the normal spring-training period of Feb. 15-April 1 or thereabouts.

Shortly after the players went back to work, Gebhard got talking to Walker's agent Pat Rooney. What had complicated things all winter was that teams had been on strike since Aug. 12 and transactions all through the winter of 1993-94 were pretty much at a standstill.

"Normally after the World Series is when free agency begins," Gebhard said. "The dates kept changing (due to the strike). All of a sudden, the strike is over and teams have to offer arbitration or the player becomes a free agent.

"Larry was not offered arbitration (by the Expos) so at midnight, a little after 12, his agent and I had discussions. It was a pretty large contract. I talked to Larry.

"Next day, he was in Tucson. He reported immediately. He was in

Exposion

Canadian Baseball Hall of Fame
Bob James was a protégé of Bob Gebhard

uniform that day. He jumped right into spring training. He was ready to play with the ability he had," Gebhard said of the signing and Walker's quick presence at spring training in Arizona.

"I might add that in 55 years in baseball, Larry is the most talented athlete I've been around. You talk about five tools – he was at the top in all five of them."

Walker was a star with Montreal but he became a superstar in Mile High City. He was prolific with Colorado and used his Rockies' tenure as a springboard to the Hall of Fame in 2019.

"I was thrilled to death he made the hall of fame – finally,"Gebhard said.

"I was with the Rockies nine years. I was a vice-president and a special assistant with the Cardinals for five years. I took a break and then I was with the Arizona Diamondbacks for 12 years as vice-president of player personnel. I returned to the Cardinals for another few years and then I decided to retire," Gebhard said.

Geb was one of baseball's finest. So glad to be able to do a chapter on you, Bob.

Chapter 12

Blair was a whiz-kid prospect

No. 1 was Bobby Goodman.
No. 2 was Ellis Valentine.
No. 3 was Gary Carter.
No. 4 was Roger DeLazzer

"And I was the No. 5 pick," Dennis Blair told me of the Expos' early selections in the 1972 June amateur draft.

Blair was born in Middletown, Ohio but he moved with his family to the Los Angeles area when he was young and then they shifted about 60 miles away to Rialto not long after that.

"My parents moved to Fontana, California in 1957. They were married in 1948 and after nine winters in Iowa, my dad had enough," Blair said. "He was tired of the cold and moved to California because at the time, Fontana had the largest steel producing facility west of the Mississippi. My dad had worked for a steel mill in Ohio."

Blair grew up a Dodgers fan, attended a few of their games at Dodger Stadium and loved Don Drysdale, the Cooperstown Hall of Famer, who eventually was a coach and broadcaster with the Expos.

"Drysdale was a fierce competitor and always threw lots of innings," Blair said. "There was no pitch count for him."

Blair would have loved to have been drafted by Los Angeles but there was no complaining really when the Expos drafted him. Blair was selected by the Expos out of Dwight Eisenhower High school. Valentine and Carter were also from California.

Blair talked about his neighbourhood and how growing up was a lot different than what he was accustomed to. He mentioned the time he was invited to Valentine's house for supper along with another Expos draft pick, Bill Bolden. This was shortly after his rookie-league season in Cocoa Beach, Florida in 1972.

"Remember Leave It To Beaver and Ozzie and Harriet? That's what it was like growing up. Rialto was not a culturally diverse town," Blair said. "I was the only white person within 10 square miles. There were a few minorities who went to my school but not many.

"I wasn't the sharpest knife in the drawer as a kid. I knew there were areas that had a black population. We got to Ellis' neighbourhood. Looking around, I'm thinking there's nobody in my skin colour around here. We got to Ellis' house.

"The whole point of this, is that for the first time in my life, I was in an area I had never experienced before. I don't want to make it a racial thing but it was definitely different. I didn't feel uncomfortable or threatened but it was a different situation or environment I had never experienced before."

As for that dinner at Ellis' house? "His mother prepared a feast for us. It was a great get-together."

So here's a kid from California sent to play rookie ball in Florida and Blair wondered if this is "the best decision I could make? For some guys, they don't have that problem. Maybe I should have gone to college. It was a tough decision."

Blair stuck it out in the minor leagues. He got rid of the malady called homesickness. He was highly touted by the Expos when other teams passed on him. How could anyone not notice a 6-foot-5 pitcher like Blair? And he was impossibly gorgeous. He boasted the package.

"I remember Colt league baseball and the summer of 1971 and I think Expos scout Bob Zuk came up to me after the game and basically, he said, 'I would like to have you work out with other pitchers this fall,' " Blair told me. "He had signed guys like Reggie Jackson, George Hendrick, Freddie Patek, Ellis, Carter and me."

Zuk zoomed in on prospects with his discreet observations of players from outside a fence or from the bushes, trying to let on to other scouts he wasn't interested in certain prodigies when in fact, he was high on them.

Zuk's moniker was The Godfather. He was tight lipped. According to a SABR Project Bio Series profile on Zuk, he also was credited with observing and signing Willie Stargell for the Pirates in August of 1958.

Blair heaped praise on California birddog John Ramey for getting the ball rolling on his selection by the Expos. Ramey passed the word on to Zuk and others higher than him in the Expos' scouting fraternity – that Blair was indeed worth looking at.

"Scouts read multiple newspapers and high school spiels and box-scores. They don't sit around," Blair said. "Bob Zuk received many newspapers in order to find prospects. Scouts see players playing Little League, Pony League ... this guy comes come up to me and said, 'There's a baseball league this fall. 'Do you want to play?' I said yes. I didn't play football.

"Bob Zuk introduced himself to me. He told me the Expos were very interested in drafting me. Other teams didn't care about me. They said, 'Good luck with your future but we're not interested.' Bob Zuk thought I had potential"

In an interview with Ian MacDonald of the Montreal Gazette for a long-long story in an Expos magazine in 1975, Zuk said he was impressed with how Blair took his stock serious when he travelled from Rialto to Los Angeles for a series of tryouts over two days one weekend.

"Dennis sacrificed himself. He drove 80 miles each way. So the total mileage was 320," Zuk told MacDonald. "We arranged for him to pitch in what we called our scouts league in Los Angeles. We play weekend games throughout the winter and we mix boys with pros. It gives us a chance to see what the young prospects have."

Without a radar gun, Blair figured he threw in the "upper 80s" prior

Blair was a whiz-kid prospect

Canadian Baseball Hall of Fame
Dennis Blair in a centrefold photo with the staples in the middle from 1975

to being drafted.

Blair apprenticed in 12 games in the weeks and months following his selection in the draft – with West Palm of the Florida State league, Jamestown Low-A ball in the New York-Penn league and Cocoa in the Florida East Coast League.

In 1973, he split time with West Palm and Québec City Double-A for a combined 7-12 record. Things got better in 1974 when he was assigned to Memphis Triple-A. He was getting closer and closer to Montreal.

In less than two years, Blair got the call every player is looking for – he was being promoted to the big show. Blair went 5-0 with a 1.83 ERA with Memphis when he was notified about some interesting news.

"I was in Tidewater, Virginia. I was going well as a starter for Memphis. Like all kids, I wanted to make the major leagues," Blair said. "I'm pretty sure it was the Mets' organization we were playing against. On May 21, I was called into the manager's office. Karl Kuehl wanted to talk with me and with him was Larry Bearnarth, the Expos 'minor-league pitching coordinator.

"They said, 'You're going to Montreal.' I almost had a heart attack. I couldn't believe it. I never thought I'd get to the big leagues. I couldn't believe I got the call for the promotion to the big leagues. It was a total mind-blower. I don't think I slept much that day. I told my parents."

Exposion

Blair flew to Montreal from Tidewater and was there for a get-away game, delayed by fog, on the 23rd won by the Expos 5-4. He didn't pitch that game. He flew with the team to Philadelphia and continued to sit on the bench and throw a bit on the side, bullpens they call them.

In the fourth game of the four-game series, Blair got the call from Mauch to pitch a day game on Sunday, May 26, and he was superlative. It was a dream debut at the age of 19 years, 355 days, making him the second youngest player to suit up in a game in the 36-season history of the Expos.

He was just short of 20 years of age. Balor Moore was the youngest player to suit up as an Expos' player at 19 years and 116 days.

Blair worked eight innings, striking out seven and walking six as the Expos won 5-3. Tom Walker came in to pitch the ninth inning as part of a double switch. Time of game was a neat 2:22.

"Yes, I had butterflies, I was stressed out and I was anxious to pitch," Blair said of how he was feeling before the game. "I said, 'When I take the mound that day, okay, nobody will notice there will be a rookie pitcher out there.' Watching the scoreboard, it said, 'Dennis Blair is making his major-league debut.' I was nervous.

"It went well. The first batter was Dave Cash. I got behind in the count 3-2 and I threw a fastball he ripped to left field but Boots Day caught it. Larry Bowa slapped a fly ball to Willie Davis in centre and Del Unser – I struck him out.

"I was in the right place at the right time. I didn't have spectacular ability. I never thought I'd get a chance to play in the major leagues.

Blair downplayed the fact he was excellent that season with a terrific 11-7 record and a 3.27 ERA. He was downright impressive. As MacDonald said in that magazine story, he was a "whiz kid" prospect.

"When I got to Montreal, it was a real urban environment. It was really quite a change from where I grew up. It was such an unique culture with so many different languages spoken in so many parts of the cities," Blair told me.

"Downtown life was incredible. I liked the Métro (subway) and really enjoyed public transportation. You wake up to bright, blue skies – I really enjoyed the city. I loved playing at Jarry Park. I thought it was a great park – it wasn't as modern as the parks in Philadelphia, Pittsburgh or Cincinnati but it was baseball and it was the major leagues. I thought it was just wonderful. I would have played for free. I was just a dumb 20-year-old kid who didn't care."

Blair said one of the highlights of that season other than his debut centred around a doubleheader the Expos played against the Cubs at Jarry Park on June 28.

"I threw a two-hit shutout but what made the game special was that it started at 11:30 at night. It was a strange time to start a game. The reason being that it was a twilight doubleheader," Blair said. "The first game started at 6 p.m. and went 18 innings. One game was two games long. We were able to start the second game under the time requirement. We had to start the game before midnight. It was over at 2 a.m. The doubleheader took 27 innings.

Blair was a whiz-kid prospect

Image courtesy Topps   *Dimanche Dernier Matin*

Dennis Blair pitched for the Expos from 1974-76

"That's what made it special. I can't remember any pitches I made. My main pitch was any that wasn't hit out of the yard," he joked. "Seriously, I relied on a two-seam fastball and went to my slider for a strikeout against righties. I didn't have an overpowering heater."

The Cubs won the opener 8-7 and oh boy, what a long game it was. Time of game was 4:55. The Expos hammered out 17 hits in the nightcap to win 15-0 as Blair went the distance with a two-hitter. Ron Hunt went 3-for-4 with five RBI and Jim Cox was 4-for-5 with three RBI.

And as Blair noted for the record, "It was my only shutout in the big leagues."

Blair's maiden campaign saw him toss four complete games, he threw only four wild pitches and allowed only seven homers in 146 innings. When you looked at the Expos' rotation that year, it wasn't that bad. The team wasn't that bad either with a 79-92 record. With a little bit of luck, the Expos should have been over .500.

Steve Rogers was 15-22, Mike Torrez came in at 15-8 and Steve Renko was 12-16. Ernie McAnally pulled up the rear at 6-13.

"I didn't have many complete games and I don't remember I approached 150 pitches per game. I was probably somewhere between 120-135. The manager or pitching coach would make a change based on how your stuff looked late in games or if the opposing team started hit-

Exposion

ting rockets," he said, chuckling.

Talking about 1974, Blair talked about the thrill he and some of his teammates got when slugger Hank Aaron broke Babe Ruth's record of 714 lifetime homers. The feat was accomplished April 8 when he connected off Al Downing of the Dodgers.

Less than a month later, Aaron and the Braves were in Montreal for a brief two-game series. Blair allowed no hits to Aaron on June 1 in a game won 7-6 by Montreal. Blair threw 7.1 innings and wasn't the pitcher of record.

Going through the Retrosheet account of the game, I noticed that Expos first-base coach Walt Hriniak was ejected by umpire Art Williams for bumping him during an argument about whether Tim Foli was out after being picked off first by Atlanta catcher Johnny Oates.

The story, though, as far as Blair is concerned, is that prior to the game, Expos' players were lined up to approach Aaron for a photo with him. Blair admitted he was shy and didn't go up to Aaron, for fear of being rejected. He has been kicking his ass ever since he neglected to go after Hammerin' Hank.

"A lot of people had their picture taken with Hank," Blair said. "I told myself, 'After that, if I'm around a superstar, I'm going to have a picture taken with them.' So in 1977 when I was with Baltimore, I told myself I was going to have a picture taken with Jim Palmer. He agreed and it's my prized possession.

"I saw Tom Seaver, Steve Carlton, J.R. Richard – but Palmer was the best pitcher I've ever seen, He made it effortless. That photo of me and him was taken at the end of 1977 and I received it at spring training in 1978. My parents checked my mail.

"I remember like it was yesterday. It's funny how the mind works. Chuck Taylor and John Montague were next to Hank and they arranged to get their photos taken. 34 years later, one of my teammates, Chuck Taylor (very ill, later to die) – I thought of getting a hold of him. His wife invited us over to his place in 2008. Chuck had a room with memorabilia from his career and one of the things on the wall was a photo of him and John Montague with Hank.

"I also was in Los Angeles in 1974 when Tommy John got hurt and walked off the field. He had Tommy John surgery. Today, that surgery is pretty routine."

Near the end of the '74 season, Blair admitted his hair was getting long and wasn't surprised when Mauch approached him.

"One day, I was walking to the clubhouse and Mauch came up to me and looked at me and said, "You need to get a haircut. We don't want any page boys around here.' Next day, I went out and got my hair cut," Blair said. "He had his expectations on what players should look and dress like."

Blair's sophomore season was of the jinx variety. He was a humbling 8-15 but you have to consider he was pitching for a bad team. Yet, still, he was almost the exact opposite of what he was in his rookie season.

Blair's ERA in 1975 was decent at 3.80 and he allowed only 14 homers in 163.1 innings of work but those 15 losses stood out. After a 79-82 season in 1974, the Expos regressed to 75-87 in 1975, prompting the Expos to fire Mauch.

That season, the entire Expos' rotation was out of whack: Rogers was 11-12, Renko slipped to 6-12 and Woodie Fryman was 9-12. That was the year Dave McNally, acquired in the off-season, quit in June and went home.

"Maybe it was the sophomore jinx. I didn't produce. I didn't have a very good year. Maybe I was trying too hard and not focusing on getting the hitters out and not going with the basics," Blair said. "1975 wasn't giving me a break. I probably should have done more to keep us in the game.

"You know, 50 years ago, it was a different lifetime. I remember more of the bad than the good. For example, in 1975, we were playing in St. Louis and I had runners at first and second and Ted Simmons, the catcher, steps up to the plate. I got the signal from the dugout to walk him intentionally," Blair recalled.

"The catcher (Gary Carter) was standing up with his glove hand to the left side. I was going to walk him intentionally but I don't know why – I threw that ball right down the middle of the plate. It was about 40 m.p.h. I let that ball go and I had this thought in my mind, in an instant, he's going to hit the ball over the Mississippi River and Gene is going to send me to the minors.

"In an instant, I was hoping I would be a coyote and try to reach for the ball but it got up to the plate and Simmons just unloads on it. He crushes it. It was smoked. The only problem is, the line drive hit a little above my left foot. I was an average fielder and I reached down and picked it and we got a double play out of it. Not a word was said when I got into the dugout."

"In 1975, wrist bands had made their way to baseball. Tennis players used them a lot. We'd blown a game and Gene came into the office off the clubhouse and he said, 'I don't want to see that pretty boy stuff tomorrow. In other words, no wrist bands. Gene just didn't care for that style at all. He didn't care for it.

"Next day, nobody was wearing wrist bands, except for Gary Carter," said Blair and he started laughing. "I don't know if Carter didn't get the message or he said, 'Fuck you I'm going to wear them.' "

By 1976, when the Expos were awful, Blair wasn't around much. He appeared in only five games and spent most of that season in Triple-A with the Denver Bears. Ditto for 1977. The magic of 1974 had vanished.

He didn't pitch for Montreal at all in 1977 and on Sept. 26, 1977, he got a bit of a shock when the Expos traded him to the Orioles as the PTB-NL in an earlier swap made on July 14, 1977 when Fred Holdsworth was sent to Montreal.

Montreal's experiment with Blair was relatively short. He enjoyed that one solid season in 1974 but he couldn't get anywhere close to that success in subsequent years.

"I thought you know, it was probably a move that was in my best interest," Blair said of the trade. "Maybe the Expos had other guys who could handle the pitching. I looked at it as a new opportunity. Moves are

Exposion

made in baseball. There were a lot of things that weren't known at the time.

"When I played in the big leagues, there were 25 guys on a team and we had Gene Mauch and four coaches. You go to a website for an MLB today and you look at the front-office staff – it's very overwhelming. You look at the Nationals and Phillies and Yankees, you look at how it has exploded. They have nutrient specialists, strength and conditioning people – you take a good look back and things have really changed. Today's pitch count is monitored closely and the bullpen is used a lot."

Blair managed to grab a few more days of service time with the Orioles in 1977, even though he never appeared in a game. Orioles manager Earl Weaver hadn't seen Blair pitch so he was going with "my guys", Blair said.

In 1980, Blair qualified for a MLB pension when he appeared in five games and got more service time in the employ of the San Diego Padres.

Blair never pitched in the majors again. He was only 26. Once a prospect, he had flamed out. Sad.

At least, Blair fared better than Goodman and DeLazzer, who were drafted higher than him by the Expos in 1972 but who never made it to the big show.

Goodman was hailed to be superior to Carter but he ran into a lot of injuries and spent most of his life as a Missouri state trooper. DeLazzer was out of baseball following the 1974 season and for many years, he has been a materials manager at ITT Flowtronek in Cypress, California.

"One thing about baseball is that it's very competitive," Blair said in explaining his early departure from the game. "It's not like being appointed to the Supreme Court and you are there forever. You get traded.

"So much of the game is mental. I should have been more mentally prepared. I didn't do much to make any highlight reels. I felt like I could have done better. I didn't produce. I'm not bitter. There are only so many throws in an arm. Maybe I lost some life on the fastball. That happens to a lot of pitchers. I was not a whiz-kid prospect. I was average at best. There wasn't anything great written about me. I didn't have that electrifying stuff.

"When I was in high school, I didn't make the all league teams. I didn't make the second all-league teams. I was honourable mention. A lot of scouts will draft players on future potential and I might have fit that category.

"There were other guys like me. Balor Moore with the Expos maybe never lived up to expectations. David Clyde with Texas, his career didn't live up to expectations like me."

That's right. Clyde was just several months over 18 years of age when he called up by the Rangers. He had to bow out after a few years later due to injuries and arm problems.

Blair made it known to me he was not overused by Mauch, who was criticized for employing pitchers like Moore and Don DeMola way too much – to the point where their arms went into oblivion. Blair also ruled out having a dead arm.

> **Blair and the Hit King**
>
> Dennis Blair went up to Pete Rose at an autograph show years ago and introduced himself as having pitched for the Expos in the mid-1970s.
>
> Rose didn't remember him, opting to save himself by saying, "You were the tall left-hander."
>
> Except that Blair is a right-hander.
>
> "You got the wrong deal not being in the hall of fame. It's a shame," Blair told Rose.
>
> "Pete was humble enough to say he made some mistakes (gambling)," Blair told me. "He's a guy who made the most of average ability. It was like Larry Bird's ability compared to other guys in the NBA."
>
> Blair said it "was not a putdown" to talk the way he did about Rose and Bird. It was just his way of saying through hard work and perseverance, they excelled to become superstars.
>
> When I checked Rose's lifetime stats at stathead.com, I noticed he faced 793 pitchers during his career. He hit 11-for-19 for a lifetime batting average of .579 against Blair and that was the second highest BA Rose enjoyed against anyone, based on at least 15 at-bats. Rose hit 10-for-17 for a .588 lifetime BA against Darold Knowles, just ahead of Blair.
>
> "I didn't know I faced him that much. He would have finished with 5,000 hits had he faced me more," Blair joked.

Blair said he "threw out most articles about me. I don't like going down that memory lane. Too many bad memories from my baseball experience but there were some unique moments."

Blair returned home after the 1979 minor-league season, not knowing what he was going to do. It was a cultural shock. All Blair had was a high school education at Eisenhower.

"Throwing a baseball, hitting a hockey puck or catching a football wasn't going to help you get a job," he said. "Like a lot of people when their playing days are over, we have to find employment and you have to adjust to the general population, not that I was so much better than anyone else.

"Geez, you pursued your dream and all of a sudden, you can no longer pursue your love. There comes a time in your life, hey, your playing days are over. We have to scramble to find employment. When most players end their careers, there aren't a lot of opportunities out there."

Not long after he packed in his baseball career, Blair put on another uniform, this time to deliver goods for United Parcel Service (UPS), one of the most famous companies in the world.

Jumping in and out of his UPS vehicle kept him in shape but it was hardly glamorous. He would have preferred a MLB uni, not UPS duds. In the end, continuing his education was tantamount for him.

"After eight and a half years, I decided that (UPS) is not for me and I went back to school," Blair said. "I always wanted to finish my degree. I wanted to have letters at the end of my name."

And he did with a master's degree from Lamar University in Beaumont, Texas after he obtained a liberal studies Bachelor of Arts degree from California State University-San Bernardino. Before long, he was on the move from California all the way across the country to Texas.

In 1997, he began teaching students with special needs in the Garland and Mesquite Independent school districts.

"I met my wife Karen in Texas in 1994. We moved there for something different. It was time for a change. Sometimes, change is very good," Blair said. "I taught school for 15 years and I was able to acquire my teachers' pension. I taught learning-disabled children.

Blair is in reasonably good health, although he has been scuffling with throat and neck cancer since 2018. He had lymph nodes removed, underwent several surgeries and numerous radiation treatments to counteract a cancerous growth at the end of his neck and tongue.

Blair is one tough dude and when I talked to him he sounded like there was nothing wrong with him. He still has a great voice despite his tonque problems.

"It hasn't been a lot of fun. At least I'm alive," he said.

Before his life gets longer, Blair would like none other than to cross paths again with Valentine. The idea of that happening shouldn't be difficult because both of them live not far from each other in Texas.

"Ellis, I mean, he had more ability than anybody I played with. When he hit, it was a shot. When he threw the ball, it was a cannon," Blair said. "They wanted to make him a pitcher. He was something else, unbelievable ability. Ellis was always my yardstick for measuring players. I couldn't believe it. He had exceptional ability.

"To this day, he's the most talented player I've ever seen. I always thought he had unbelievable talent. How good is Junior Griffey? Ellis is better. Before I depart this world, I hope we can meet up. Ellis and I were not the best of buddies but there was a lot of stuff I liked about him. He was a lovable person."

What does Blair think of Montreal's chances of getting another team?

"I can't see it. Don't get me wrong, Montreal is an awesome city. I loved playing there and in Québec City but I don't see a major-league team in Montreal," he said. "I mean, I'm not Mr. Baseball Executive but I don't see any hope. I love Montreal but Montreal is a hockey town. From what I understand, the Big O – it was a horrible place for the fans to see a game."

Blair loves going to the Indy 500 with his wife and has spent time in Arizona where he saw that he looked like the spitting image of someone playing for the Diamondbacks. Zack Greinke.

I posted a photo of Greinke on Twitter and Facebook in the summer of 2023 to see if any followers would know what former Expo resemble him. Several people pointed out Blair as a doppelganger.

"I saw pictures of him with the Diamondbacks. My God, I look like him. I wish I had the career he had," Blair said.

Dennis, many thanks for taking the time to chat. This is a wonderful story. It was a real coup to get you to talk. I appreciate you taking the time to go back and forth many times to answer follow-up questions.

Dyer came in to back up Carter

Duffy Dyer was recruited by the Expos as a back-up to Gary Carter so they signed him following the 1978 season to a three-year contract but it didn't work out that much to Dyer's satisfaction.

It's very rare nowadays that a backup catcher gets a three-year deal but back in the day, it was not that uncommon.

"I remember playing out my option in Pittsburgh," Dyer told me in an interview. "I really liked it in Pittsburgh. I actually wanted to stay and Montreal gave me a three-year deal. I was very happy with the contract. For a back-up catcher, it was pretty good -- salary plus bonuses and certain incentives.

"I was very excited. I knew I was going to back up Carter. He was a fine, young catcher."

In the next breath, Dyer said, "I didn't realize he would be a hall of fame catcher."

In 1979, Carter was just in the early stages of his career so Dyer probably was right, that it was too early to say Kid was Cooperstown material.

"We had a very good club. They had a lot of young players. It was ironic that we lost to Pitttsburgh the last weekend of the season," Dyer said. "We were in the race, if I remember right. We went right down to the end.

"A guy I really admired was Chris Speier. I became close to Chris. His wife and my wife were close in the ski resort of Ste. Adele. His wife found a place for us to stay in the summer. Chris and I came to the park every day. We became very close."

As far as playing time goes, Dyer didn't get much. He appeared in only 28 games out of a possible 162. Carter, of course, got most of the playing time. John Tamargo also appeared in 27 games behind the plate and on occasion, infielder Ken Macha caught.

"The thing about it was ironic," Dyer said. "At spring training, they said something like, 'We have that young catcher to do most of the catching. We like the way you (Dyer) handle the pitching staff and call games. We got you for your experience.' They gave me that spiel.' I said, 'Fine.' "

The Dyer experiment with the Expos ended March 15, 1980 during spring training when he was traded to the Tigers for infielder Jerry Manuel. He reported to Detroit across state in Florida and got the same song and dance..

"I get over to Lakeland and Sparky Anderson calls me into his office," Dyer said. "He tells me the same things. They have Lance Parrish. It was the almost identical speech Dick Williams gave me. I was disappointed I was not going back with Montreal."

And you are wondering how Don Robert Dyer got his nickname? It emanated from the radio show called Duffy's Tavern. When his mother went into labour to bring him into the world, she was listening to the show and asked, 'How's Duffy?' after she gave birth.

Chapter 13

Jose Morales was the Hit Man and Yip Yaw

It's one of the loneliest jobs in baseball.
Pinch hitting. Coming off the bench. You're rusty, not being in the game most of the day or night. Then in the sixth, seventh, eighth or ninth inning, you're called upon – cold – to try and help the team in a pinch.

Expos alumnus Jose Morales was fantastic at it.

Morales finished with 100 pinch hits overall as a major leaguer and future Expo John Vander Wal came around years later to finish with 129, although both were decidedly short of the all-time record of 212 collected by Lenny Harris.

Wallace Johnson is the all-time Expos' leader in pinch hits with exactly 100 but you could say Morales was the early pioneer in pinch-hitting expertise for the Expos. Morales doesn't get enough credit for his pioneering role in Montreal.

As we conversed on April 26, 2023 in a coup interview conducted after many years of on-off attempts by me to reach him in Florida, Morales quickly told me the highlight of his time with the Expos from 1974-77.

Sept. 16, 1976.

"One of the things that got me excited was the pinch-hit double with the bases loaded," Morales said of his performance at Parc Jarry. The Expos were up 1-0 against the Cubs in the seventh inning when Morales came into play.

It was a day game.

Tim Foli doubled to left to lead off the inning against a young phenom pitcher, just emerging in his first season on his way to Cooperstown. His name? Bruce Sutter, he of the nasty, split-fingered pitch. At that juncture, Sutter was anonymous, way too early in his career for anyone to expect he would be a Cooperstown-calibre pitcher.

In the Montreal Gazette's account of the game, there was no mention of Sutter imploding in that inning.

Wayne Garrett grounded out 4-3 to move Foli to third. Gary Carter reached on a fielder's choice. During this scenario, Foli was caught in a rundown but managed to make his way back to third safely and Carter scooted to second.

With first base open, September call-up phenom Andre Dawson was issued an intentional base on balls. Sutter and Cubs manager Jim Marshall decided Sutter would not pitch to Dawson. It was the first of 143 intentional walks Dawson received in his stellar career.

Jose Morales was the Hit Man and Yip Yaw

Photo courtesy Danny Plamondon

**Bat boy Danny Plamondon congratulates Jose Morales
after his record-setting hit Sept. 16, 1976.**

Just five days earlier, Hawk had made his big-league debut. Prior to this intentional pass, Hawk had gone 4-for-15 to start his career, according to my research, heading into this at-bat against Sutter.

That's when Morales was summoned to pinch hit for pitcher Steve Dunning.

Sutter went to 1-2 on Morales and then tried to jam him but Morales connected to drive home all three runners as the Expos went up 4-0 to give Canadian-born pitcher Larry Landreth his first win in the major leagues and Dale Murray got his 13th save. The final score was actually Expos 4 Cubs 3.

A tiny audience of 2,877 was on hand. Sad and bad. This was a way for Montreal fans to show their displeasure at the team's hapless performance that season – and hardly anyone came.

"Sutter came back inside and I made contact and it hit right on the line," Morales recalled with glee.

As he stood on second base, he waved to acknowledge the miniscule crowd.

"I was so excited that I waved to the bleachers as well," Morales told the Montreal Gazette. "I hoped nobody noticed. There was nobody there. That was kind of silly. But I was excited. It was emotion, I guess."

The Gazette story revealed the left-field foul line was wooden. Morales' hit bounced off the line and caromed into fair territory up against the outfield fence.

"Don't talk like that," Morales admonished a reporter, who asked if he had thought that the ball might be foul. "I saw the ball hit the wood and I said, 'No. I can't be that bad-lucky that they call that ball foul.' "

Sutter was out of the game after the double, replaced by Ramon Hernandez.

The Cubs came back to score two runs to make it close. Even though Sutter gave up three runs, he wasn't the loser. Steve Renko, who had been traded by the Expos to the Cubs in mid-season, was charged with the loss because he allowed the first Montreal run.

The dramatic pinch hit by Morales was his 25th of the season, breaking the mark of 24 set in one season by Dave Philley of the Orioles in 1961 and Vic Davalillo of the Cardinals in 1970.

According to inside70s.com, the hit by Morales was his 74th as a pinch hitter, one more than Davalillo in 1970.

"I was the first to greet him. I was one of the guys close to him," bat boy Danny Plamondon told me in 2023.

Long after the game was over, Morales was outside talking to reporters and autographing items for fans, who had hung around.

"I'm just glad that it is over," Morales told reporters about the hit that broke the record set by Philly and Davalillo.

"Once I passed the club record of 15 which I set last year, I thought about this record. Well, I couldn't help it. People kept reminding me about it. After I had 20, I think I was trying too hard. I wanted to get the record out of the way and I was pressing.

"Now, I hope that I can get back to being the type of hitter that I am. I won't think of records anymore. I just want to think about hitting."

It was interesting, though, when someone asked Morales the night of his clutch double off Sutter, if he was aiming for 50 pinch hits, considering that down the road he would reach 100.

"I got that from Roberto Clemente," Morales said about his Puerto Rican hero, although Morales was born nearby in the Virgin Islands.

"Clemente would say that if you aim for .300, you might hit .280 or .279. So, he said, 'You aim higher and then if you don't quite reach your goal, then you still have a good season.' That's why I said to myself this spring that I want to hit .350 and if they use me as a pinch hitter, I want to make 50 pinch hits. I know that it is very unlikely but I still aim for that."

With the help of that interesting trivia that saw him surpass Philly and Davalillo, Morales was voted the National League's player of the week for the period Sept. 13-19. From what I could gather in my research, Morales went 3-for-6 that week, all in a pinch-hit role, was issued an intentional walk and was hit by a pitch.

What made this weekly honour so special was that he ended up as the only Expos' player given such a monthly award through all of the team's terrible season of 1976. Wasn't that something? In all of 1976? In all the other weeks encompassing April-October, nobody else from the Expos won a player of the month award. Crazy trivia.

That's how bad the team was in general, especially under poor manager Karl Kuehl, who was dumped near the end of the season in favour of Charlie Fox, the manager when Morales enjoyed his big afternoon.

In a classy move, Topps issued a special card to commemorate Morales' 25th pinch hit of the season called the 1976 Record Breaker.

On the front of the card was Morales in an away uniform and part of the wording said

Most hits, season, pinch hitter

To some, Morales was the club's unofficial, phantom MVP for the 1976 season because of his pinch-hitting prowess which produced four homers, 37 RBI and a terrific .316 average. Larry Parrish produced more offensively with 11 homers and 61 RBI but he was a regular.

"There were four guys in the running: a guy (Foli) who didn't want to be there, Woodie Fryman, who didn't care if he was MVP or not, Steve Rogers – Steve was Steve – and the guy who set the pinch-hitting record," Plamondon told me. "Jose was a silent leader.

"Jose was hot that year. He had the nickname Hit Man. He was our best player but Woodie won. Steve Rogers was 7-17 but with that ERA of 3.21, he should have been 17-7 and he would have been lower than Woodie."

In the end, Fryman was voted by the local writers as the official MVP due to his stellar 13-13 record and a 3.33 ERA. Foli was upset he wasn't named MVP. He had six homers and 54 RBI.

"Foli was pissed. He thought he deserved to win," Plamondon said.

Due to his lack of range and mobility, Morales very rarely got to start a game behind the plate, at first base or in the outfield. He was absent from the starting lineup regularly. In fact, he had no stolen bases in 733 big-league games. He was a catcher by trade and catchers traditionally don't run very good.

When manager Gene Mauch asked if he had any plans to use Morales in the starting lineup, he replied, "Jose's position is hitter."

According to some interesting research fashioned by Expos fan Don Rice for me, Morales did appear as a starter in many games with the Expos. It's information I couldn't find but the sleuth Rice did it. Thank you, Don.

In 1973, Morales appeared in five games, all as a pinch hitter. In 1974, he started one game – as a catcher.

In 1975, his starting role improved. He started 27 games at first, three in left field and three behind the plate. In 1976, he was in the starting lineup for 12 games at first and five as a catcher. In 1977, he started a game at first, two as a catcher.

As Rice pointed out, Morales, in nine of his 11 starts for Montreal, stayed in for the complete game. He made other appearances as a position player, just not as a starter.

Whenever he did get in a game, he did his best to put the ball in play. He struck out only 182 times in 1,305 at-bats. He was also feared at times, too, because he drew 28 lifetime intentional walks.

To keep Morales busy when he had little playing time, the club utilized him as a bullpen catcher because he had experience in that field. In those days, there was no special coach to handle the role of bullpen catcher – so often, Morales would suit up in catcher's gear.

Teammates often remember how Morales had difficulty handling Dale Murray's knuckleballs or fastballs when he was warming him up in bullpen sessions. Murray could sure wing it. Murray's fastball was a really heavy ball.

Exposion

"I know that sounds kind of crazy. The ball is the same weight for everyone," pitcher Dennis Blair said. "The ball is light for most pitchers when it came to the plate but Murray's pitches were shotputs. They were heavy. He could throw the knuckleball but not like Phil Niekro. Jose was a heckuva good guy. He was really good."

1976 saw the Expos experiment of playing hotshot prospect Carter in right while Barry Foote got most of the duties behind the plate. Morales managed to be given work as a catcher on five occasions. You will see some photos or cards of him with a catcher's mitt.

"His name was Yip Yaw. He had a better chance to stop the ball with a bat than a glove," Parrish said, chuckling. "Great hitter. He used all fields. They had him and Hal Breeden on the bench when I first came up. Both could really hit and neither was real good on defence. Mauch told both to take a bat when playing first."

When I asked Parrish the story behind Yip Yaw, he replied that it was "x-rated."

"His dick was so long he used to swing it around like a rope in the shower and do a cowboy yip yaw, thus the nickname," LP said, chuckling.

"Coach Dave Bristol used to run the extra men with the balls before the games started," Morales' teammate Don DeMola recalled. "Everybody has a ball, you flip it to him, and go out for a football pass, with no glove on. Without fail, Bristol would always yell Jose right, and Jose went left all the time. It never ever sank in. Even Jose derecho (right) didn't work.

"Jose was always the first to the soup table. Between doubleheaders, that's all we were allowed to eat. Hal Breeden would always yell in his hillbilly accent, 'Jose! Soup's on!' We got our asses kicked in the first game of a doubleheader in San Diego. Gene was screaming at the team. Jose was standing by the soup, stirring it, while Gene was yelling. When he notices Jose, he saunters over to the table and flips the whole table over."

When I mentioned this about Mauch's table-flipping antics to Morales in 2023, he replied, "He did that a few times."

The lonely job of pinch hitting wasn't really that bad of an occupation. Morales was happy, waiting for his chance, with his hands on top of the knob of the bat on the bench.

"To be honest with you, I don't think negative things. I don't care how hard he's throwing it," Morales told me of any pitcher he faced. "Considering I'm the ninth batter, I'm always watching the game. I always knew when Gene Mauch was going to use me.

"I'd be at the end of the dugout and he'd say, 'Get ready.' I'd come off the bench. I remember facing Nolan Ryan one time. He was known for the fastball. He threw a curveball a little high and then the second pitch was a curveball. I was looking for a fastball and he threw a fastball and I hit a foul tip and the catcher caught it. I ran into Ryan one time the next year and told him about that. I said to him, 'What's going on?'

"On the bench, you develop your mentality. There were no computers. During BP, I'd be thinking of what to do with men on first and two out. I wanted to see what I would do in a clutch situation. I wasn't thinking of how many line drives I would get in BP. I was looking at situational hitting.

"When I went to the ballpark, I was first at the ballpark and the last one to leave," he told me. "Out in the bullpen, I'd hit balls against the wall. I don't play cards or go to the sauna. I had a connection with the manager. I was all business. I was dedicated to myself at my position.

"As a pinch hitter, you have to be aggressive. I would be facing guys like Nolan Ryan, Goose Gossage, Jerry Koosman. I'd see Ron Guidry in the off-season and I'd say, 'What's going on?' He didn't know what I was trying to find out. There was a guy in Detroit, I knew everything he threw. I can't remember his name.

"You'd be on the bench and I remember hitting a two-run double off Frank Tanana. I hit .300 off the knuckleball brothers, Phil and Joe Niekro. I hit them pretty good. When you repeat the pitch (knuckleball), you are in trouble.

"I carried a big stick, a heavy stick. I was a pinch-hit specialist that won many games coming off the bench. One game I faced Tom Seaver. He was a helluva right-hander and I was a helluva pinch hitter. I hit a line drive at goddamn Champ Summers. He caught the ball in the gap."

The date was Aug. 31, 1977 at Olympic Stadium. It was a Wednesday day game before 18,840 fans. In the eighth inning, manager Dick Williams sent Morales in to pinch hit for pitcher Santo Alcala. The Retrosheet notes said Morales "flied out to right" but he actually hit a screamer.

As you can see, Morales is a chatterbox but that's what makes a story so enjoyable.

"He loves to hear himself talk," Mike Raymond, his friend from Iowa, said chuckling. "He wasn't as talented and gifted like many players but his work ethic was impressive. He was amazing. He was very meticulous about hitting."

Morales, yes, carried a big stick. He said his bat weighed 35-36 ounces and the length of the bat was also 35-36 inches.

"Basically, he was a premiere hitter in that era," said Dr. John Cisna, another friend from Iowa. "Pinch hitting, he was really good. He had a great arm. His catching skills were just not quite as good as you would like to have."

When I asked Morales who his favourite teammate was in Montreal, he replied, "No favourite teammate." Morales was a bit of a loner not interested in getting chummy with anyone.

Plamondon. the bat boy, recalls how he used to throw BP to Morales and one day, he drilled him, not once, not twice, but three times and Morales, instead of getting mad, would just look at Plamondon.

"The first pitch was a butterfly pitch. I throw it hard and it hit him and he's not getting up," Plamondon said. "I told him sorry.

"We went in the clubhouse and he took his shirt off and there were these two humongous, dark spots on the side of the ribs. It was like the colour of the rainbow. Barry Foote came over to Jose and said, 'What happened to you?' He saw the welts on his body on his side.' Jose re-

Exposion

Cartoon courtesy Terry (Aislin) Mosher

Jose Morales told bat boy Danny Plamondon that when he was a child in the Virgin Islands, he learned to bat by hitting rocks over and over again using large tree branches. This is a hilarious rendition by Aislin.

plied, 'It was the bat boy.'

"He pointed to me at the other end of the clubhouse. I felt so small. I wanted to hide. Carter would yell that I was Wild Bird. I thought I was going to get fired and lose my job. I felt so bad. That was a horrible time. The next day, I still had a job.Who comes up to me to ask me to throw BP? Some of the other players."

Morales came over and said to Plamondon, 'It's okay." Morales would also say he "didn't do a good job of getting out of the way."

Said Plamondon, "I was one of the guys close to him. Yet, 50 years later, he doesn't remember me."

Late in spring training in 1978, March 29, to be exact, the Morales Era in Montreal ended when the Expos sold him to the Minnesota Twins.

Morales had done a yeomen's job in Montreal in a pinch and he was on the move. He had gone through most of spring training and the club decided to dispense of him.

"Bob Reece took Jose's place as a catcher. Gene Mauch also had Barry Foote and Gary Carter," Plamondon explained. "The pitchers loved Barry. He called a better game. They wanted Carter for his bat in the outfield. He was still learning. Gene Mauch would always be after John Bateman and Carter. He'd tell them, 'Watch your weight. Watch your weight.' Gary wasn't exactly a 200-pound guy."

Morales played three seasons with the Twins under old friend Mauch and thrived.

Jose Morales as Expos pinch hitter				
1973	2-for-5	0 HR	0 RBI	(.400)
1974	5-for-22	1 HR	5 RBI	(.227)
1975	15-for-51	1 HR	11 RBI	(.294)
1976	25-for-78	3 HR	24 RBI	(.321)
1977	10-for-52	0 HR	7 RBI	(.192)
Totals:	**57/208**	**5 HR**	**47 RBI**	**(.274)**
Compiled by Don Rice				

"When I was with Minnesota, Rod Carew was in a slump for two weeks and he's say, 'No matter how good you are, you always need help.' So I suggested a few things. Then somewhere, he got on a roll again. Even Tony Gwynn would ask me for help."

At the end of the 1980 season, Morales told me someone informed him that Mauch said, "I don't want Morales." So, Morales left as a free agent.

Before he hung up his playing cleats, Morales also played for the Orioles, Indians, Giants and Dodgers. On June 18, 1984, he was signed again by the Expos but never made it back to the majors. Instead, he spent the remainder of that season with the Triple-A Indianapolis Indians.

"When I saw him in 1984, he had shaved off his famous moustache," Mike Raymond said. "I asked him why? He said, 'I want to look young.' I told him, 'That doesn't work.'"

Exposion

And Raymond started laughing.

Morales soon moved into a job as hitting coach for a total of 10 years for the Orioles, Indians, Giants and Marlins.

He talked about "not wanting to kiss anyone's ass" and referring to some people as "chicken shit" for releasing him as a coach "without shaking my hand."

From reports we read, Morales was born in poverty in the U.S. Virgin Islands in Frederiksted, St. Croix, the son of a shoe salesman. He joked he had "18 half brothers and 18 half sisters", although the real figure is believed to be around 15. The joke was that his dad had so many kids because he would impregnate some women he met going door to door.

Morales grew up with few luxuries. He once told a reporter he would gain muscle strength by stuffing biscuit containers with concrete which he would then stick on the end of a bat.

Morales told Plamondon he would hit fungoes, not with a bat and ball when he was young, but what he did to simulate the situation because of his poverty, was to take a big limb from a tree and hit rocks. True story.

"Jose was so poor he had to make his own glove," Raymond told me.

Morales spent most of his youth in Puerto Rico, which is linked to its close neighbour, the Virgin Islands, and was signed by Oakland as a free agent.

"I grew up in Puerto Rico. I moved there when I was six years old. I was originally from Latimer in St. Croix. My mother was from Puerto Rico," Morales told me. "I started learning baseball in the bush. Horace Clarke is from the same town as mine. His grandfather had a big house in Barbados. He grew up with my father. My grandfather was Irish. Horace Clarke was black and white. Horace turned out to be a ball player with the Yankees.

"I'd get experience trying to hit the garbage can stuck behind home plate. Some people thought I was crazy. When I'd go to the ballpark, nobody wanted to play because it was too hot."

It was in Puerto Rico where Morales produced outstanding results in winter-league play. Imagine this: he hit .296 with 840 hits in 2,961 at-bats. He was a machine, not content to just play in the big leagues. He wanted to improve himself in the off-season and help his adopted country. He didn't take the winter off and relax.

Morales' ability to exude confidence in the face of adversity made him a crusader for positivity. He started playing pro ball in 1964 in the Giants' organization but never made it to the majors until nine years later with Oakland. Think about that. He was 28 years old, going on 29. He had the Patience of Job.

He made his big-league debut with Oakland on Aug. 13, 1973 against the Red Sox, going 1-for-4. Here he was playing with a cast of stars and superstars like Reggie Jackson, Vida Blue, Gene Tenace, Sal Bando – a gang of characters wearing white cleats and colourful uniforms.

Realizing Morales wouldn't get much playing time on a stacked team that won the World Series that year, Charlie Finley sold him – after a six-game tenure – to Montreal on Sept. 18. It was a blessing in disguise.

Think about this: it was in Montreal where he thrived, at least as a pinch hitter. All those years in the minors and keeping the dream alive paid off.

"He blossomed in Montreal," Dr. Cisna said.

Before he finally got to the majors, he had been introduced to Raymond and Cisna in Des Moines, Iowa where Morales played in 1969 in the Oakland farm system. A lot of Oakland players like Tenace, the Lachemann brothers (Rene and Marcel), Jose Tartabull, Joe Rudi, future managerial great Tony La Russa – and because I'm Canadian, I have to mention pitcher Vern Handrahan of Charlottetown, Prince Edward Island – passed through Des Moines.

To this day, Cisna and Raymond remain tight with Morales, especially Cisna, the team physician for the Iowa Oaks, one of Oakland's farm teams. Rene Lachemann also keeps in touch with Morales, who was Lachemann's hitting coach with the Marlins for a while in the 1990s.

Cisna and Raymond would remember Morales walking home after games with a bat over his shoulder, walking miles, oblivious to the distance. Morales boarded at the home of Maxine Cisna, the doctor's mother.

"He'd walk home and didn't realize it was five miles," Raymond said.

Dr. Cisna's mother would on occasion make burgers for the entire Oaks team but Morales would take the opportunity to eat all the burgers himself. It was a standing joke for years. Mrs. Cisna often baked pies for only Morales to consume.

"He was a big eater," Dr. Cisna said. "I have fond memories of him. I remember when we took a trip and we went to Puerto Rico and we never told him we were coming. He was playing that night (winter ball) and I walked into the park and he's in the batting circle.

"I yelled at him, 'Hey, you Wet Back (language used by Americans for people from the islands).' Then I shouted, 'Jose.' And he looked up and saw me. The umpire said, 'Play ball.' But Jose said, 'Wait a minute.'

"Jose had unfailing loyalty. When he has a friend, he keeps that friend forever. He always has your back, unless you step out of line. He's a talker, as you know, that's for sure. He's probably my best friend," said Dr. Cisna, who is in his late 80s. "We call each other brothers."

Morales stays in "really, really good shape" and he's currently looking after his wife Rita, who is scuffling with Alzheimer's, Dr. Cisna said.

Thank you so much, Jose, for chatting with me. Without the intervention of Mike Raymond, I would never have interviewed Morales. I'm so thankful to Raymond for setting me up with the interview.

Chapter 14

Granger played amateur and pro ball in Québec

How did a kid like 1976 Expos pitcher Wayne Granger from Springfield, Massachussets use the Canadian towns of Jonquiere and Port-Alfred, Québec in the 1960s as a springboard to a major-league career that ended with the Expos?

It has happened a lot over the years in Canada's adult leagues, or senior leagues, as we call them in Canada. I use the word adult because some Americans might not know what the word senior means. Does it mean someone in the 60s and 70s? No. In this case, it means the age range of roughly 18-45.

Former Expos Roger Freed and Bill Campbell played for the Neilburg Monarchs in the Northern Saskatchewan league in the mid-1960s.

John Boccabella played for the Saskatoon Commodores in 1961.

Chris Speier suited up at short for the Stratford Hoods in Ontario's Intercounty league in 1969. A few years later, Jesse Orosco pitched in the same league for Cambridge.

There are many others too numerous to mention.

Granger, a stringbean who looked no more than maybe 150 pounds in some photos I have seen, was lured to Québec, first by the Jonquiere Braves, a top-level team in the Saguenay Region league, in 1963, and then he went to play for the Port-Alfred Martinet down the road in 1964. Both are located near the larger metropolis of Chicoutimi, located about five hours from Montreal.

As you see on a map, Granger would have travelled by car or bus or train almost directly straight north from Springfield up through Vermont and Montreal to Jonquiere which is about 9-10 hours from Springfield, including stops for gas, washroom breaks and food. Quite a hike.

Granger was signed by Jonquiere Braves officials Rene Hebert and Harold Hicks, a scenario captured in photos in the local French paper. Below is a headline after he was signed by Jonquiere:

Les Braves aligneront un lanceur Americaine de fort calibre

I was attracted to this story about Granger after the late Stephane Harvey of Port-Alfred posted something on Facebook in June of 2023. I was aware Granger pitched for Montreal but I was not aware he had pitched in Jonquiere and Port-Alfred until Harvey made his post.

Harvey sent me clippings that showed Granger fired two no-hitters for Jonquiere. I have to pay tribute here to Harvey because he died Oct. 11, 2023 after a long battle with brain cancer. He was only 51.

Granger had played the 1962 season in his homestate Cape Cod league

Granger played amateur and pro ball in Québec

Courtesy Topps

Wayne Granger

with the Sagamore Clouters before heading to Québec. With Port-Alfred, he batted .304 based on 31-for-102 hitting.

He played the 1965 season at his hometown Springfield College. That was the year the St. Louis Cardinals signed him, although he did draw interest from the Chicago White Sox, Washington Senators and Los Angeles Dodgers.

Granger credited the great Warren Spahn for paying attention to him

Exposion

Canadian Baseball Hall of Fame
Wayne Granger

in the minor leagues.

"The luckiest break I had in my career was having Warren Spahn as my manager in Tulsa," Granger told Arthur Daley of the New York Times. "He is to pitching what Ted Williams is to hitting. It's a pure science to him.

"He taught me concentration. I can't throw within the six-inch circle he used to target, but I can hit it one out of three times and come close on the others."

The Cardinals called him up to make his first appearance June 5, 1968. He ended up with Cincinnati for four seasons and became a dominating relief ace with 27 saves in 1969 and a major-leagues leading 35 in 1970. He would lose his closer's job to Clay Carroll in 1971 but was still an integral part of the Reds' relief corps, making 70 appearances.

Granger was the first pitcher to reach 90 appearances in a season. Only four others have accomplished that feat: Mike Marshall (three times), Kent Tekulve (three times), Salomon Torres and Pedro Feliciano.

Granger joined the Expos shortly after spring training began in 1976 on Feb. 27. He spent part of the 1976 season with Montreal, throwing 32 innings in 27 games for a 3.66 ERA and two saves. His overall performance on paper appeared to be solid but he was demoted to Triple-A following his last game June 25.

During the last half of the 1976 season with the Denver Bears, Granger helped them win the American Association title while posting a 3-1 record along with a solid 2.45 ERA in 44 innings of work over 26 games. Then he was released in February of the following year.

According to Baseball Reference, after a bit of playing in the Mexican league, Granger came back to Denver in 1979. He registered one save over 24 appearances with a less than favourable 6.75 ERA. This marked the end of his professional career in baseball.

In 1982, he was inducted in to the Cincinnati Reds Hall of Fame.

With his blonde hair and lithe physique, which some called frail to coincide with his very white skin, you'd never think he would have much success but Granger proved the critics wrong.

"Whether it's the short blonde hair, the baby face free of stubble, the thin neck masked by a turtleneck, or the rail-thin upper body, Granger gives us an image of an overage batboy. He is the antitheses of Dick Radatz, The Monster. Appearances, in this case, are deceiving, but also somewhat accurate," writer Bruce Markusen reported years ago.

Chapter 15

Stanhouse was Full Pack and Stan the Man Unusual

Don Stanhouse was one of baseball's most colourful characters in the 1970s and 1980s.

As a prelude to a full-scale interview, the 1970s Expo teased me with this declaration about himself:

"Untold stories of the players that will keep the lights turned on. I have old pictures and lots of great thoughts. Have bones in my closet that just need to get out. Still got some shit in the tank."

Stanhouse is the only native of Du Quoin, Illinois to make it to the major leagues in the 20th and 21st centuries. Frank Hereford played so called MLB ball as a member of the Brooklyn Bridegrooms back in the late 1800s.

Ever heard of Du Quoin? It's five hours driving time south of Chicago. Its motto: In the Heart of Southern Illinois.

Du Quoin, that's with the space in between, has been around for several centuries. Stanhouse is as famous as the Du Quoin State Fair, the Hambletonian and the World Trotting Derby.

"Du Quoin is famous for its fair which held stock-car races," Stanhouse said. "I went back recently and they named a field after me. It was a lot of fun, standing there and watching my teammates and they all know my stories. It was a flood of emotions telling the people about what I did in high school (football, baseball and basketball).

"Bear Bryant (University of Alabama) talked to me on the phone. Dan Devine (University of Notre Dame) came to my high school. I had all of this going on. I was picked No. 9 in the nation in baseball by Oakland. I look back and they found me in a town of 4,000 (5,742 census report) people. I was one of the best baseball players in the world. I played shortstop and I pitched. I was a good hitter in high school. I hit a lot of home runs. I had a great arm."

Stanhouse sent me a sports card that showed how outstanding he was in football at Du Quoin high school. The information says he posted a three-year prep batting average of .421 and averaged 2.2 strikeouts per inning as a pitcher.

He was named all-Southwestern Egyptian League and all-Illinois all three years. He was named to the Topps all-district 4 team and prep all-American second team in 1969 as a pitcher.

On another sheet of information, Stanhouse's rushing yardage for three years was listed at 1,442, passing yardage was 3,053 and punt-return yardage was 1,136. He was a prolific offensive player. In his senior

Exposion

Courtesy Topps
Don Stanhouse

year, he scored 13 touchdowns. No wonder Bear Bryant and Dan Devine pursued him.

Baseball won Stanhouse's heart. After being selected in the first round by the Athletics in 1969 right out of Du Quoin high, he reported to spring training in Phoenix, Arizona.

"I was an 18-year-old and when they put me on a plane, I had no idea of how I got there," he said.

Stanhouse quickly observed that Campy Campaneris was playing short and Sal Bando was at third for the big-league team.

"Quick story – by the time I put my uniform on, they were hitting ground balls to me. One hit me in the chest," he recalled. "They never called me in for batting practice. Then I'm running in to hit and I trip over the foul line. They were laughing at me. Warren Hacker was a guy who threw hard. He threw me one underneath my chin and it put me on my bum. But then I hit the next five out of the ballpark. They weren't laughing anymore."

That summer and fall of 1969, he pitched for the Tri-Cities (Washington) A's of the Northwest league and Mesa in the Arizona league. He was a combined 7-2 in 20 games overall. Pretty good stuff.

Stanhouse also played third, drove in 36 runs for Tri-Cities and committed 13 errors. His first manager, Billy Herman, called him into his office and told him Charlie Finley wanted to get him to start a game – to see how he would do as a pitcher. He won and struck out 16. Then they asked me to start another game. He won 1-0 and struck out 14. His bosses saw he could throw when he wasn't pinch hitting or playing third.

"At third base, you will have to wait until Sal Bando retires, If you are pitching, I can get you to the majors in half the time," Herman told Stanhouse.

In 1970, Stanhouse was pitching Double-A in Birmingham of the Southern league where he was 7-5 with a 2.25 ERA in 84 innings. In 1971, he kept progressing – this time, he was going to Triple-A Iowa where he was 7-4 in 154 innings: 22 games, 22 starts.

"I rode the bus. I lived the minor-league life and I wouldn't have traded it for anything," Stanhouse said.

In the spring of 1972, Stanhouse was pumped up with the hope he would crack the Oakland roster. For two weeks or so, he was working with some of the Oakland pitchers and all was encouraging until he got news that would shake him up but it was all for the good.

Stanhouse was Full Pack and Stan the Man Unusual

"All of a sudden, I was called into the manager's office. He said, 'Hey, we got you a raise but with it, you're going with Jim Panther to the Texas Rangers for Denny McLain.' I said, 'What are you going to say?' I'm 21. Catfish Hunter was not happy I was traded," he said.

This was the first season for Texas in the majors. The old Washington Senators had been relocated to Texas over the winter of 1971-72.

The previous season, McLain was 10-22 with the Senators. He may have been at the end of his career but he was only 28. Oakland was hoping he still had some juice in the tank, based on some wonderful years with the Detroit Tigers, including that 31-6 mark in 1968, the last time anyone won 30 games.

Following a substandard season in 1970, McLain was traded to the Senators and he wasn't that good on a bad team managed by Ted Williams. The Senators finished 63-96.

McLain was 1-2 in 22.1 innings of work with Oakland and then was let go and went

Canadian Baseball HOF
Don Stanhouse joined the Expos in 1976

to Atlanta where he was 3-5 with a 6.50 ERA. That was his last season in the majors. Did you ever remember McLain with Oakland or Atlanta? He's linked to Detroit and nobody else.

Catfish was 21-7, Ken Holtzman was 19-11 and Blue Moon Odom was 15-6 with Oakland in 1972. Surprisingly, Vida Blue was off kilter with a 6-10 mark. That's how powerful Oakland's pitching staff was. That was in the days when pitchers logged a lot of innings, sometimes in the 300s per season.

Stanhouse left Arizona after the trade and was driving down 1-30 on the turnpike into Arlington, Texas when he found out there was a minor-league strike which preceded a major-league strike that lasted from April 1-13.

A few days following the MLB strike, Stanhouse made the Texas roster out of spring training and travelled with the Rangers as they started the season on the road against the Angels. Four games into the season, he got the call to throw in his first big-league game.

Stanhouse was excellent at old Comiskey Park against the White Sox. He worked 6.2 innings and struck out nine, allowing one run and five hits. He fanned Richie Allen twice.

Stanhouse wasn't the pitcher of record in the 2-1 loss as Stan Bahnsen went the distance for the White Sox before a puny audience of 3,199.

"The night before, I wasn't feeling very good. In the bullpen, I could barely get the ball to the catcher and if I did, it was over his head," he said. "My very first pitch to leadoff hitter Lenny Randle, I wind up and I hit the backstop," he said.

"I had the lights turned out. I battled. I didn't give in. I wasn't too

Exposion

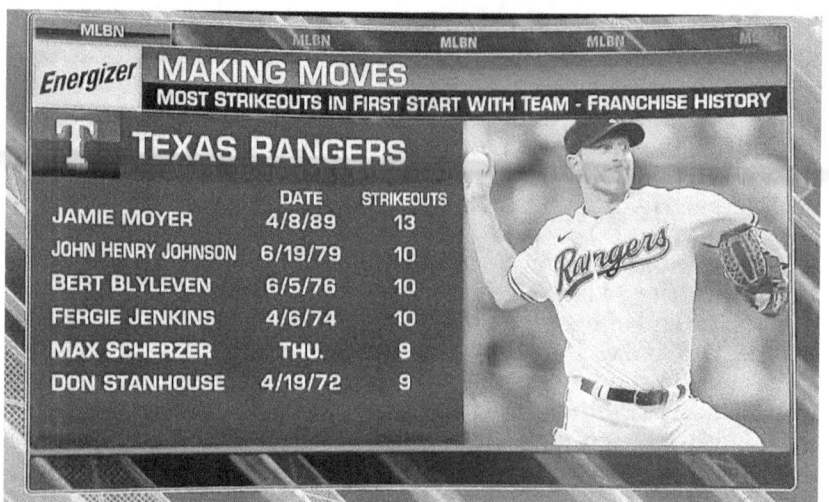

Courtesy MLB Productions
Graphic showing Don Stanhouse in inaugural debut with Rangers

bad of a starting pitcher," he said. "Over 30 years later (2023), lo and behold, they put it up on the scoreboard that I was one of five Texas pitchers with the highest number of strikeouts in their debut."

Stanhouse was tickled when he saw that graphic on his television screen. He's right up there in debut strikeouts with Jamie Moyer, John Henry Johnson, Bert Blyleven, Canadian Fergie Jenkins and Max Scherzer.

Stanhouse's 1972 season was unremarkable despite that outstanding maiden performance. His record coincided with how bad the Rangers were, still under Ted Williams. He was 2-9, the Rangers were 54-100. At least, he spent most of the season with Texas, sandwiched around a short stint with Spokane Triple-A.

In 1973 and 1974, Stanhouse was up and down from Spokane, making some appearances for Texas both years.

"Texas was a learning experience. I was a young kid," Stanhouse told me.

Then like the gift he received when he was traded to Texas and got some playing time with the Rangers rather than languish in the Oakland chain, he received another jolt when the Expos acquired him and Pete Mackanin Dec. 5, the last day of the winter meetings in New Orleans – from Texas for aging Willie Davis.

At spring training in Daytona Beach, Florida, Stanhouse started to sample the nightlife while plying his trade for the Expos. He kept the lights on at Latitude 21 when he was finished at Club Mocambo during regular bar hours. He was said to have kept Latitude 21 open until early dawn and then he'd have to go to Jackie Robinson Stadium for a round of workouts around 9 a.m.

"He was the only player who belonged to this after-hours club which opened at 2 a.m. Larry Bearnarth and I went one night and used his locker. We weren't members," his teammate Don DeMola said.

"I had my own special stall. Only problem is this bar didn't open until 2 in the morning," Stanhouse said. "We had a good time. They (management) didn't know I was doing it. We'd be getting home at 4 or 5 in the morning, then we'd go and sleep in before going to the park."

Stanhouse appeared in only four games with 13 innings of work with the Expos in his first year. With Memphis Triple-A, he was 6-5 with a 1.91 ERA.

His first initiation with manager Gene Mauch was a dose of reality. Mauch had a certain way of wanting his players to appear spic and span clean in a uniform.

"He wanted you to dress in a real baseball uniform in the 1800s. No questions asked. It was team policy. He was a micro manager," Stanhouse said. "Gene Mauch wanted me to be something I'm not. I had a no-hitter going but my arm hurts. He took me out of the game. They send me to Memphis."

In Memphis, Stanhouse ran into another military-style manager but Karl Kuehl was actually somebody he admired. Kuehl, even if he allowed no facial hair, liked Stanhouse and his results showing him as the second best pitcher in ERA.

So the next year, who's the Expos manager? Kuehl. KK was still strict with some rules and despite a subpar effort at spring training by Stanhouse, Kuehl took him north and put him in the starting rotation.

Stanhouse was outstanding on a bad team that lost 110 games. Again, he "kept the lights on" and he was appreciative of Kuehl's belief in him, although the hardline skipper was let go before the end of the season on Sept. 4.

Stanhouse was the third man in what was basically a three-man rotation of high-inning pitchers. Steve Rogers was abnormal at 7-17 and Woodie Fryman was No. 2 at 13-13.

Stanhouse made 26 consecutive starts and pitched deep often and collected eight complete games in accumulating 184 innings. As had been his habit during most of his career, he deliberated a lot between pitches.

Stanhouse was 9-12 but get this – he was 8-5 at one time, according to Retrosheet, and then lost six in a row to go 8-11 before breaking out of his slump on Sept. 24. He won his last start to finish 9-12.

He won his first two games as a reliever, working against Cincinnati both times but he soon worked his way into the starting rotation.

Remarkably, he posted an impressive ERA of 3.77.

"I thought I pitched well. I held the team together," Stanhouse observed.

One of his best memories of 1976 was some nightlife in Cincinnati, especially the overnight shift of July 14-15. Stanhouse had a few pops on the plane heading to Reds country on an off-day. Upon arrival, he had a few more pops. In the hotel lobby, he saw Bearnarth, the pitching coach, who said he was going to bed.

Stanhouse stayed out for a few hours and got back to the hotel where he saw Bearnarth in the lobby again. Bearnarth wasn't a tattle-tale but he looked at Stanhouse and said, "What are you doing up so late?"

Exposion

Down the hall in the hotel, Stanhouse and Bearnarth could hear some music playing so, they walked down to find out what was going on. They could hear Na Na Na, Na Na Na, Hey Hey Hey Kiss Him Goodbye from a piano bar.

Stanhouse and Bear checked into bed at 3 a.m. A few hours later that afternoon, the Expos were facing Joe Morgan, Pete Rose, Johnny Bench, George Foster, Tony Perez and all those guys on the Big Red Machine.

"The game started at 1. No problem. Just another day of work," Stanhouse told me.

Despite being hung over and deprived of much sleep, Stanhouse worked 8.2 solid innings, giving up a solo homer to Morgan in the bottom of the eighth, allowing the Reds to tie the game 2-2.

"Our bullpen sucks. I come out for the eighth inning. I'm gassed. I get the first out in the ninth inning. I'm bent over. Bearnarth comes out to talk to me. Gary Carter has no clue what we are doing. Larry starts singing, 'Na NaNaNaNaNa' as some form of encouragement."

Stanhouse, trying not to laugh too hard, steps back on the mound and gets another guy out. He got a no-decision with Dale Murray taking the loss, saddling him with an 0-7 record.

Talking of boozing that year, he also enjoyed Montreal's famous party circuit. On one occasion, he ran into Expos owner Charles Bronfman, the Seagram's heir.

"I was at a really nice party at a really nice hotel," Stanhouse said. "When I first came up, I drank cold beer and a lot of scotch with a little splash to dehydrate. Charles says, 'How are you? I own the team.' We started talking. He says, 'What are you drinking?' I said, 'Scotch.' He said, 'Not anymore.' He got me a Crown Royal (rye whiskey). Next day, he had a case of Crown Royal delivered to my locker in the clubhouse."

The following year, Stanhouse was working under a new manager, another one set in his own ways but not as strict as Mauch or Kuehl. Dick Williams. The way Stanhouse put it, "Williams said to get to the park on time and don't ever quit on me."

The first home game in Montreal at the new Olympic Stadium saw the Expos lose 7-2 to the Phillies April 15. As he looks back, he saw Dick Williams, Carter and Andre Dawson, prompting him to say, "all Hall of Famers."

Stanhouse lost 7-2 to the Phillies and Steve Carlton in the Expos' home opener. He lasted two innings, giving up three runs before a crowd of 57,592 on a Friday afternoon.

Stanhouse turned it around a few days later with a complete-game, 6-0 shutout of the Pirates – a five-hitter with five strikeouts. This was vintage Stanhouse, the vintage Stanhouse from 1976.

From there, it was all downhill for him pretty much as a starter. After losing on May 28, 1977 in St. Louis in front of his hometown fans so to speak from nearby Du Quoin, Stanhouse saw his record slip to 3-7. He lasted all of two innings.

Williams had enough of Stanhouse starting games. After that game, Williams sat Stanhouse down.

"Dick Williams was not happy. I had made one of my last starts. We're on a bus and he stops the bus in the middle of a street," Stanhouse said. "We get off the bus. He knocks on the doors of a restaurant and they slide open into a dining room. It was down an alley. He told me to come with him. I thought I had been traded or did something wrong.

"We go and sit down and he doesn't say a word. He ordered a drink. He finally looked at me and said, 'starting tomorrow, you are a relief pitcher.'"

From that day on, Stanhouse started to excel and by the end of the season, that 3-7 record turned into 10-10. He finished with a glittering ERA of 3.27 and recorded 10 saves on a team that finished 75-87.

"I'd pitch three innings here, three innings there and as the season goes, all of a sudden, we had a closer," Stanhouse said, meaning him.

The headline in one edition of the Montreal Gazette went this way:

Ex-starter Stanhouse a kingpin in Expos bullpen

On July 6, 1977, Stanhouse made Expos' history when he became the first pitcher in club history to hit a grand slam. It came in the second inning off Bill Bonham at Wrigley Field.

The inning began when Tony Perez doubled and scored on a Warren Cromartie single. Dawson singled, Wayne Garrett drew a walk and then Tim Blackwell hit into a fielder's choice, a scenario that saw first baseman Larry Biittner throw to catcher Steve Swisher to force Cromartie out at home.

Up stepped Stanhouse and he went "deep to left", as one online report said. Him and Scott Sanderson are the only pitchers in Expos' history to hit grand slams.

"I had a bunch of friends there. It was a little bit of a fastball on the inside of the plate. Bonham was always around the plate so I was able to hit it well enough," Stanhouse told me. "Pretty cool thing. Let me follow up on this. About 3-4 years ago, I get a letter from this guy in Chicago. He was at the game and had caught the ball and he still had it. He asked me, 'Do you mind if I send you the ball?' He wanted to know if I would take it.

"You hit a grand slam and 50 years later, this happens. He wanted nothing in return. I offered to buy it from him. I have it on my desk. I sent him some stuff in return."

Oddly enough, that grand-slam game was one Williams asked him to start. He allowed seven runs as the Cubs won 8-6.

"I was converted to the bullpen as a short reliever. I had a great ERA for Montreal. I stayed there for most of the winters," Stanhouse said. "I was single my whole career. Where the game took me, they paid me. I pitched in Venezuela and the Dominican. I really enjoyed South America. It made me appreciate everything.

"I loved the Cardinals fans, Red Schoendienst, Julian Javier. To this day, they remember where I came from, especially pitching for the Montreal Expos – the starting pitcher from Du Quoin, Illinois, 90 miles from St. Louis."

After two commendable seasons with Montreal, Stanhouse expected to be back in 1978 as the Expos kept improving their lot.

GM Charlie Fox had other plans. Stanhouse was dealt along with Joe

Mark Secheyco photo
Don Stanhouse with Expos jersey he signed for Mark Secheyco

Kerrigan and Gary Roenicke to the Orioles for Rudy May, Bryn Smith and Randy Miller in another winter-meetings transaction on Dec. 7.

"I was in Montreal and a writer calls me and I was told I had been traded? I said, 'What? Oh, great.' I never wanted to leave Montreal. I was traded to the Baltimore Orioles and that's when the story really changes," he said. "We get to spring training, we saw all the headlines. 'Who are Joe Kerrigan, Gary Roenicke and Don Stanhouse?'

"Earl Weaver, the manager, rips us in the paper. One thing led to another. We go for dinner at a country club and have a few pops. We opened up the club and Weaver bumps into my chest. He ran into me. I thought he was feeling no pain. He looked at me, I looked at him. He says to me, 'Get your ass out to the ballpark the next day. I don't care what you think of me.' And he stumbled out.

"I walk in the clubhouse and Mark Belanger says, 'You're my idol.' Lee May said I was unreal. One of the coaches, Elrod Hendricks, told me and Kerrigan and Roenicke to come with him into Earl's little, bitsy office. Earl eyeballs me. Earl says, 'This is how we play – all that garbage in the paper, we never said that.'

"Then he says, 'What the fuck's wrong with you?' I was sitting down between Elrod and Earl. I started lunging for him. Jim Palmer – he looks like a model – was a big supporter of me. He wanted me in there when the game was on the line. Earl was very business like – defence and a three-run homer."

And terrific pitching.

"I thought we had no chance in hell of making this pitching staff," Stanhouse said. "As the pitchers drop like flies, Earl calls us in. He says, "I fucking hate you guys. I don't know how this happened. You made the roster and you're going to go north. You made the roster by default."

True story. Hilarious.

So with his big, orange hair of the 1970s sticking stoutly past his ears, Stanhouse was ready to rock and roll.

"Our first game in Baltimore, Sal Bando hit a line drive five feet off the ground. He hit it so hard you could hear it. Ken Singleton handcuffed him for a line-drive out and throws in to double a guy off first. I get my first save and I walk into the clubhouse and Mike Flanagan, smoking a cigarette, says, 'You're Stan the Man Unusual.' "

A take on that man of greatness, Stan the Man Musial. Funny stuff. The Orioles started that season 0-5 but future Expo Dennis Martinez and Stanhouse shut down Milwaukee to snap the slump. Stanhouse pitched the last five outs to preserve the win for Martinez.

Stanhouse was excellent overall with 24 saves, a 6-9 record and a 2.89 ERA as Baltimore went 90-69. But on the opposite end of the spectrum, he drove Weaver crazy because of his delay tactics between pitches or because he would go deep into counts – often.

"Earl wears No. 4 and behind a pocket inside of his jersey he kept his cigarettes," Stanhouse said. "It got to a point I would go to 3-1 and 3-2 on batters. I walked guys I wanted to walk and I got guys out. Believe it or not, I knew what I was doing."

So as Stanhouse delays a lot of games, Weaver is smoking and smoking to relieve the stress of watching Stanhouse work ever so slowly. After seeing this go on and on for several games, a Baltimore writer nicknamed Stanhouse Full Pack because Weaver inevitably would smoke a full pack of cigarettes (or close to it) when Stanhouse pitched.

"We were playing the Angels one time. We were leading 10-9, I walked three guys. They got a hit, a double, and the bases loaded with two out. Brian Downing is up. I finally get him to 3-2 and I made the perfect pitch, a slider. Somehow, he fouls it off. I get up on the mound and then I step off and I step off again. Downing is built like a tank. He overswung on the slider and swings over the top of it."

After one game where Stanhouse got out of the game reasonably easy, Weaver was less stressed out.

"Were you nervous?" a reporter asked Weaver.

"I had three cigarettes. I didn't even smoke a full pack," Weaver replied, joking.

"How do I get that personality? Where does it come from? Full Pack and Stan the Man Unusual?" Stanhouse asked. "Going in the stretch, I held my head low, almost as if I went to sleep. Lo and behold, we're playing the Yankees. I put the sleeper on them in New York."

The Sleeper? That's right, another moniker for Stanhouse. He would stare straight down while in the stretch, giving the impression he was sleeping.

I looked up the date on Retrosheet and it was Aug. 4 and the Orioles edged the Yankees 2-1 but not without some delay tactics by Full Pack. Stanhouse came in and pitched the last two innings. In the eighth, there was drama. Weaver smoked his cigarettes and Stanhouse's battery mate, Rick Dempsey, was all stressed out.

"I got the ball with two out. There's a man on base with two out and up comes Reggie Jackson. There are 55,000 (actually 28,000) drunk, wet, angry fans giving me shit," Stanhouse said. "I get on the mound and they're booing me. First pitch is a ball, then it's ball two. I kind of stand there and they're looking at me. Reggie says, 'I'm going to get your ass.' I call him a few names. I do my stretch in the sleep. The ump comes out and says, 'Are you going to throw the ball – soon? Can you please throw the ball!'

"I'm standing out there and they're throwing shit on the field and Reggie yells at me. You can't hear anybody. I look at every fan. Reggie lowers his hands. I go into the sleeper and I throw him a mediocre backdoor slider. I thought he might hit it 500 feet but he hit a flair to Doug DeCinces in foul territory at third and we went home. There you have the sleeper story. I can't believe the story. I knew what was going on. It was cat and mouse in my performance. Danny, I just kept the lights on."

In 1979, Stanhouse was outstanding again like he was in 1978. He saved 21 games and his ERA was 2.85. This time, he earned all-star status and went to Seattle with teammate Ken Singleton for the mid-summer classic.

Singleton, who had been acquired from the Expos a few years earlier, had been a perennial all-star with the Orioles. In 1979, he enjoyed another banner season – he drilled 35 homers and drove in 111 runs while hitting .295. Somehow, he didn't make the starting lineup for the game.

Bob Lemon of the Yankees is the manager, even though he had been fired earlier in the season by George Steinbrenner.

"We go to the all-star festivities. We go into the clubhouse. We see Yaz, Hank Aaron. It's half the Red Sox and half the Yankees. In the eighth inning, the National League gets the bases loaded. Lemon never puts me in the game. He puts in his own Ron Guidry. He walks a guy to bring in a run. I'd gotten out of 4-5 bases-loaded, nobody-out situations that year. Ken got a token appearance as a pinch hitter in the ninth inning."

So Stanhouse and Singleton were non too pleased but they got a great deal of pleasure when the Orioles went all the way to the World Series before losing to the Pirates. Stanhouse was 1-1 in the ALCS win. He was the losing pitcher in Game 2 of the World Series and never pitched again in the remaining games.

"Pittsburgh was We Are Family. Manager Chuck Tanner, he's got Dave Parker, Willie Stargell, Phil Garner, Tim Foli, who was in Montreal," Stanhouse was saying. "We were up 3-1 and they came back and won three straight. I never pitched with a lead late in the game."

In the off-season, Stanhouse was a prized free agent. He was excellent with the Orioles in 1978 and 1979 and he was very commendable with the Expos in 1976-77. So, looking at his body of work for four consecutive seasons, the Dodgers blew him away with a five-year deal, one of the best that off-season of 1979-80 – for $2.4-million, almost worth $500,000 per season, pretty gall-darn good for a reliever in those days.

Stanhouse's tenure with Dodger Blue sadly didn't even come close to five years.

"I had an unusual relationship with the Dodgers. I wasn't in the best of shape," he said.

"In our second game, I walked a guy and the bases were loaded. Lasorda took me out of the game. I exploded. We still had the lead. We had words like you never believed," Stanhouse said.

As I looked on Retrosheet, Stanhouse had retired the two batters he faced in the seventh inning after taking over from starter Rick Sutcliffe. It was a different matter in the eighth. Harold Reynolds homered to lead off and the Astros loaded the bases with one out. That's when Lasorda went to rookie Steve Howe, making his big-league debut. Howe didn't pick up Stanhouse and the Astros took advantage. Full Pack's line saw him with one inning and four earned runs.

"I was still getting into games," Stanhouse said. "My shoulder hurt, my back hurt. They didn't believe me. I went to see Dr. (Frank) Jobe. He recommended strengthening and manipulation. I wanted to go to Southern Illinois. I thought the guy there could fix me."

Stanhouse threw only 25 innings that season but he did collect seven saves and the Dodgers came ever so close to winning the National League West title. They fell short of the Astros after the Astros won three out of four head-to-head in the last games of the regular season.

Because of injuries, Stanhouse never played during the 1981 season and didn't make the roster for the playoffs, including the NLCS against the Expos. Just when he thought he was getting back to being his usual

Exposion

self health-wise, the Dodgers decided to release him at spring training in 1982. So much for that big contract.

"We could keep you or release you and move on," Lasorda told Stanhouse.

Then what happened made Stanhouse feel good again. He was picked up by the Orioles, meeting up again with Weaver, Singleton, El Presidente, Palmer and many others from the gang in 1978-79. And he met up with Ross Grimsley, who had returned to Baltimore after spending the 1978-79 seasons with the Expos.

Stanhouse appeared in only 17 games with an ERA of 5.40. Him and Grimsley were September call-ups and when they saw Weaver, he said, 'Get the fuck out of my office.'

"I was so fortunate to make the greatest comeback in 1982," Stanhouse said. "I got a standing ovation. It's the story of the prodigal son welcomed home. One of the best things that ever happened to me."

The best fun for Stanhouse and Grimsley came in Triple-A that season.

"Ross and I were laughing and pulling pranks all the time. We had so much fun," Stanhouse said. "We were in Pawtucket, Rhode Island and we were playing for Rochester. After the game, we had arranged to meet up with Mark Fidrych (with Pawtucket). He gets really overserved," Stanhouse said. "The next day, Fidrych got a memo saying to please call Bill Brown at this number. There are four tickets for Bill Brown at the box office. Ross and I are hiding. Bird comes in, hung over, sees this message, gets undressed and he's just in his jock and shark shoes.

"Ross and I can hear when he dials the number for Bill Brown, who is dead. Bird had called a funeral home. The guy at the funeral home says, 'We have Bill Brown here. This is a funeral home.' Bird's eyes light up and he said, 'Who the fuck did that, leaving tickets for a dead guy?'

"He comes to around first base and he only has his jock on and shark shoes. He said to me and Ross, 'You got me. I can't believe it.' Bird gets a round of applause and all the concessions people come over. I started laughing so hard, we started crying. We've told this story and laughed about that for years."

Stanhouse pitched in Triple-A for the Hawaii Islanders in 1983 and that was it for his career.

"If you go back – 1979, we did not win the World Series. In 1980, we were down four games and lose the last game to the Astros on the final day of the season. In 1981, the Dodgers won the World Series. I come back in 1982 and the Orioles won the World Series in 1983."

Stanhouse wasn't around when the Dodgers won in 1981 and when the Orioles won in 1983. What he was trying to get at was this: bad luck.

Stanhouse has enjoyed great luck in the business world. For years, he has been the operator of Pro Players Power and Gas in Texas. I mentioned to him he was probably a millionaire.

His answer: "I live a blessed life. It's my first and only marriage. I've been married to this beautiful woman Kyle for 42 years. We have three beautiful kids."

Thank you, Don, for helping me out with this wonderful story.

Chapter 16

Garrett only Expo to hit grand slam vs. Seaver

Sept. 29, 1976. Expos vs. the Mets. Shea Stadium. Fan Appreciation Night. New York's last home game of the season.

The great Tom Seaver had retired the first 11 Montreal batters. Then Mike Jorgensen drew a walk. Ellis Valentine singled to centre. Larry Parrish worked a base on balls.

Bases loaded. All of a sudden, Tom Terrific was in trouble. The batter was Wayne Garrett. Not exactly known as a big threat. Seaver was no stranger to Garrett, who was Seaver's teammate with the Mets for several seasons and competed in the 1969 and 1973 World Series together with Seaver.

I've seen video of the introduction of Mets manager Yogi Berra prior to Game 1 of the '73 World Series. Garrett was seen as the first player introduced after Yogi as the leadoff hitter. That must have been some moment.

Garrett was often known as Red for his distinctive red hair, which equalled the orange hair of his one-time Mets teammate Rusty Staub, a former Expo. In this game with Seaver facing Garrett, Staub was playing right field.

Here he was, Garrett, playing in a game for Montreal, after spending 7½ seasons with the Mets. He had been a fixture at Flushing Meadows. It was a cultural shock when he was traded to the Expos on July 21, 1976 – along with Del Unser for Jim Dwyer and Pepe Mangual – because he had been so accustomed to being with the Mets for so long. He'd loved the city, the nightlife and all it had to offer.

Here he was in unfamiliar territory with the Expos. He seemed out of place.

"I am surprised, certainly, but it hasn't been a good year for me and I guess that was the reason," Garrett told reporters after the trade.

Garrett met the Expos in Atlanta to play the Braves and two days later, Garrett was facing the Mets. And when he stepped in to face Seaver on Sept. 29 after a number of games already played between the two teams, he had gone 0-for-12 against his old club and 0-for-4 against Seaver, according to my research on Retrosheet.

Anyway, so, first pitch from Seaver to Garrett was a strike. On the second pitch, guess what Garrett did? He laced a grand slam to right-centre, giving the Expos a 4-1 lead and Montreal eventually won 7-2, giving Steve Rogers his seventh win of that awful season against 17 losses.

Garrett hit what Seaver called a "hanging slider." This was an im-

Exposion

Photos from Canadian Baseball Hall of Fame collection
Wayne Garrett played for the Expos from 1976-78

probable moment for Garrett, whose beacon was unlike that of Seaver's.

Dave Kingman leaped in attempt to catch the ball hit by Garrett. He crashed into the fence, opening the bullpen cage but missed it as the ball hit the top of the fence and landed in the bullpen.

"I didn't really get all of it and I didn't need the tallest guy in the world (Kingman) out there in right field," Garrett told reporters. "First grand slam anyplace. I never hit one in high school, Little League, Babe Ruth, anyplace.

"I had a special extra feeling because it showed the management about the trade. It had nothing to do with the guys here. They're super. It's management."

Management, as in general manager Joe McDonald and board chairman Donald Grant. Garrett clenched his fists in front of reporters and said, "It made me feel like this."

Seaver was upset with home-plate umpire Rick Colosi for not giving him calls for strikes, two of them that went for balls to Parrish.

"I thought I had Parrish struck out twice before I pitched to Garrett," Seaver lamented. "It's been that kind of year. After pitching 10 years, if you make a good pitch and the umpire doesn't call it, no way you can say anything. All year has been like this."

Yet, on a terrible Mets team, Tom Terrific was still a masterful 14-11.

According to crack shot Expos fan and Saskatoon journalist Don Rice, Garrett's shot was the only grand slam Seaver gave up to a Montreal batter in 48 lifetime appearances. How's that for trivia?

"Tom didn't say anything to me after the home run," Garrett said. "But the next time up, he threw me all fastballs, all knee high."

Rice's detective work told me Seaver allowed 21 lifetime homers to the Expos. No three-run shots. He gave up 14 solo homers and six homers of the two-run variety.

Garrett finished the 1976 season with five homers.

When I texted Garrett to see if he wanted to talk about this special grand slam, he replied, "I don't do interviews for books anymore."

I went on to say I was featuring him in my book and he said, "No, you don't have to."

A few months following the 1976 season, he got some news that would cut his playing time at second base. Dave Cash signed a long-term deal as a free agent to play full time at second. Garrett was reduced to 68 games with two homers, 22 RBI and a .276 average.

In 1978, he got into 49 games with a homer and two RBI, while batting .174 through the first part of the season. The Expos decided to trade him to the Cardinals on July 21, exactly two years after his acquisition by the Expos from the Mets. He was only 30 years old.

Now, here's something interesting, a fact given me by my editor Philippe Grenier – Garrett drilled a pinch-hit, grand slam for the Cardinals on Aug. 21, 1978 against the Cincinnati Reds.

Seaver was the starting pitcher but Garrett's homer with the bases loaded came in the bottom of the ninth against reliever Doug Bair, scoring Keith Hernandez, Ken Reitz and Mike Tyson (no, not that one) in a 11-6 loss.

Twenty-six days later, on Sept 26, that was it for Red in the majors. It was his last game.

> "Gene had a dress code or expectations on how to wear the uniform. There was a way to wear the uniform and it was expected at all times. It didn't matter who the player was. He expected everyone to have the uniform over the knee and we couldn't stretch the stirrups. And we had to wear black spikes. Other teams could stretch their stirrups. I want to say this: after the 1975 season, he went to Minnesota. I'm sure when he walked into the clubhouse, he started to change his outlook somewhat. I guarantee you he did not say anything about stirrups and hair length." **Dennis Blair on Gene Mauch**

Chapter 17

Playing a prank on Cromartie

Danny Plamondon still has his diary from June 5, 1978.

The day after on June 6, the Montreal Star published a story, saying Warren Cromartie was being mentioned as a trade candidate involving a possible deal with the San Francisco Giants for pitcher Jim Barr.

The headline went this way:

Barr for Cromartie in the works?

This was in the days when the trade deadline was June 15, compared to what it is now – Aug. 1, which became a new date recently after the long-time deadline of July 31.

So in his diary, Plamondon talks of the prank some players played on Cromartie in the clubhouse at Olympic Stadium on June 5. This nugget has never been revealed until now.

"Dawson, Steve Rogers, Ellis Valentine wanted to play a joke," Plamondon wrote in his diary. "They emptied Cromartie's locker and packed his bags. Cromartie comes in and they didn't notice he came in. Cromartie pointed his finger at me to be silent."

As Cromartie saw his mates pulling their gag, he exclaimed, "Don't forget my shoes."

Dawson turned around and said, 'You're an hour early."

And everybody started laughing.

"You're known to me as homie," Cromartie told Dawson.

Russ Hansen photo
Warren Cromartie

"Cromartie always played with a chip on his shoulder," Plamondon told me in a 2023 interview. "Management always thought he was on drugs, but he wasn't, as far as I know. It was probably not true. They were always looking for players who were on drugs."

In Dunn's story, he said Cromartie was a "likely candidate" for a trade and manager Dick Williams said if such a deal did come down, it wouldn't be a multi-player transaction. Cromartie wasn't quoted in the

Playing a prank on Cromartie

Dariush Ramezani sketch

Warren Cromartie

story.

"Possibly one-for-one for sure," Williams said.

"The Giants want an outfielder from the Expos and the most logical name would be Warren Cromartie," Dunn said in the story. "Cromartie is batting .281 for the Expos and could give the Giants some of the offence they lack."

In the June 5 game against San Diego, Dunn pointed out that Cromartie picked up his eighth outfield assist, making him a stellar man in what was called the "best young outfield in baseball" – with Dawson and Valentine being the other members of the elite consortium.

Cromartie was mentioned in the trade talks because there was no way on earth the Expos would ever trade Dawson or Valentine, at least not that year, because they were so much superior to Cromartie in talent.

Cromartie and Valentine never reached the potential gained by Dawson, who made it to the hall of Fame.

"Yes, I do remember that frightening day when my locker was empty after the game," Cromartie told me 45 years later. "Yes, I was in shock, but the guys gave it away when they all started to snicker and laugh about it.

"I know my name was being tossed around at that time and I'm glad

Exposion

Russ Hansen photo
Warren Cromartie with Larry Parrish

it never happened because I was playing with such a young team and I wouldn't be able to play my career with Andre Dawson and Ellis Valentine, the best outfield in baseball."

Dunn showed his aggressive, investigative side, by tracking down Barr, who was receptive in part to coming to Montreal and possibly signing a contract extension.

In the end, Barr wasn't traded that year and Cromartie was never traded by the Expos. He stayed with the Expos through the 1983 season.

Chapter 18

Chris Smith part of Staub trade

When it came time for the Expos to trade Rusty Staub a second time, they found a partner in the Texas Rangers.

The way Chris Smith tells it, Expos general manager John McHale told his Texas counterpart Eddie Robinson, "if you want Rusty Staub, we have to have Chris Smith."

So, that is what happened. The Expos received Smith and LaRue Washington for Le Grand Orange.

The Expos loved Smith because he was coming off an excellent season in Tulsa Double-A for the Rangers, batting .331 with six homers and 54 RBI.

Staub went on to play a few more seasons in the majors while Smitty and Washington never played much.

Rusty was on the down swing of his career at 35 when this trade was made. In December of 1971, he was dealt to the Mets for Ken Singleton, Tim Foli and Mike Jorgensen. At the time of that swap, he was operating at his finest as the Expos' early franchise hero.

What is interesting about Smith is that he was a brief part of the Expos during the run to a playoff spot in 1981. And this is why I got a hold of him finally in the spring of 2023, after not getting a hold of him for my 2018 book Blue Monday about the 1981 Expos.

I knew he had lived in Japan a long time, but there was no success getting a hold of him as I tried to reach all of the living members who played in 1981, even if it was just for a short period.

In April of 2023, just out of pure luck, I ventured to call Don Nomura, an agent known for representing Japanese players such as Hideki Irabu of the Expos. Smith has lived in Japan since 1995 so I figure, hey, why not try my luck with Nomura. Within minutes of my call, Nomura had found out contact info for Smitty.

Smith was glad to be a small part of the Expos in 1981. He went 0-for-7 but enjoyed the brief experiment. He was 0-for-2 with Montreal in 1982. The Expos wanted Smith because they saw the potential he was showing with Texas. He got little playing time with the Expos because they were a stacked team.

Smith didn't get to make the playoff roster for those series against the Phillies and Dodgers. He looked on from afar with admiration.

"I was always the 25th man with the Expos," Smith told me. "It was such a good team in 1981. The Dodgers shut the Expos down. We were in the top of the ninth inning. We were so close to the World Series. Steve

Exposion

Rogers was the best pitcher Montreal had.

"Rick Monday hits the home run. I had won everything – at Bishop Montgomery high school in Los Angeles. When I was with USC, we won the NCAA Division 1 national title in 1978. We should have won in 1981."

Smith made his MLB debut on May 14, 1981 and it was a special one because he was starting his brief career in the majors in his hometown. He was a beach bum from Hermosa Beach. He had been called up from Indianapolis in May of 1981 from Triple-A Denver where he got into 38 games, batting .303 with a homer and 17 RBI. His manager was Felipe Alou.

"It was unbelievable at Dodger Stadium," he said. "That game, I had not slept in two days. I was so excited when I was called up. Felipe called me at six in the morning. He said, 'Are you ready to go? You're going to the big leagues.' I said, 'You gotta be kidding me.' I was excited to play because we were playing the Dodgers at Dodger Stadium."

In the eighth inning, manager Dick Williams summoned him and told him he would be pinch hitting.

"That first at-bat, I was so nervous. I was praying Dick Williams wouldn't call me. It so happened the pitcher was Fernando Valenzuela. It was Fernandomania. It was amazing. If I had to do it all over again – it was a different mentality, oh man."

Smith was called out on strikes in that at-bat vs. Fernando.

In subsequent games that month of May, he was strictly a pinch hitter each time. He grounded out 6-3, grounded out to first, struck out swinging and flied to centre. Then in June, he struck out and flied to right. Williams, for the first time in seven games, left Smith in the game to play second.

In 1982, in a two-game sojourn with Montreal, he struck out and flied to right. He didn't play in the majors again.

"I always pinch hit. It was terrible. I was on the bench. I was always looking over my shoulder. I was the 25th man. I never liked pinch hitting. I always wanted four at-bats," he said.

"My favourite player was Ellis Valentine. He took me under his wing. He was the greatest friend ever. I loved Ellis Valentine. I was young. Ellis was the guy that stood out."

Smith also was in love with the Rangers' organization and being tutored by the likes of Braves great and Hall of Famer Eddie Mathews.

By the way Smith sounded, he would have preferred to have remained with the Rangers.

"Eddie Mathews was a hitting instructor. I got along with Eddie Mathews," Smith said. "He was amazing. Not what he showed me or told me – but what a good hitter he was. You had to respect a guy like him. He was one of the best hitters in the game.

"One spring training game when I was with Texas, we played Boston and I hit a triple. I led the Rangers in spring training that year. Wade Boggs was there. He basically had a huge impression on me. So did Ted Williams. He was the last guy to hit .400. He told me, 'The most difficult thing is taking a round bat and hitting a round ball.' "

Smith was dealt by the Expos to the San Francisco Giants on Feb. 2,

1983 in exchange for Jim Wohlford. His manager was Frank Robinson. During spring training, he was "confused" by his lack of playing time.

"I ended up with six at-bats. I will never forget it. Frank took me aside and said, 'I'm sending you to Triple-A.' I said, 'What more do I have to do in Triple-A?' He said, 'Son, don't tell me what to do.'

"I went to Phoenix, and I won the batting title in the Pacific Coast League with a .379 average. I beat out Kevin Mitchell."

Smith also hit 21 homers and drove in 102 runs in 123 games. That output prompted Robinson to bring him to the big leagues as a September call-up.

Back in San Francisco, Smith excelled in 22 games with a .328 average with 11 RBI and his only big-league homer.

Following the 1983 season, Smith decided to sign a long-term contract to play in Japan for the Tokyo Yakult Swallows. It was a decision he regretted.

"I was offered a seven-figure contract and I jumped at it," Smith said. "It was a mistake. I was so immature to make that decision. It was the worst experience. I could easily have played in the majors for 10 years. I felt that in my heart."

The statistics show Smith's two-season stint with Yakult was a disaster. In 52 games in 1984, he batted .214. In 16 games in 1985, he hit a measly .158.

Despite this negativity, Smith has been a resident of Japan for many years and has been married for over two decades to Marrie, a model and TV broadcaster. His business niche has been buying and selling companies that are in distress and he said "we've done very well in Japan."

He was on a trip back home to California to adhere to his U.S. residency rules when I caught up with him, thanks to Nomura.

Chris, glad we connected.

Exposion

Russ Hansen photo
Expos coach Ozzie Virgil, left, and Canadian Bill Atkinson posed for a photo back in the late 1970s. Virgil was a coach under Karl Kuehl, Charlie Fox, Dick Williams and Jim Fanning. Atkinson pitched for Montreal from 1976-79.

Chapter 19

Dan Norman and A Boy and His Dog

Long before he made it to the majors with the Expos and other teams, Dan Norman was looking to work in the movies in a specific role: stuntman.

He was really intrigued by the film industry moreso than baseball while growing up in Barstow, California located about an hour from Los Angeles and Hollywood.

What got him hooked on the big screen was his time playing the role of a background extra, like I do in Canada, for a production called A Boy and His Dog.

It was shot at a military base, Fort Irwin, a national training centre for the army situated in the Mojave Desert in the Caligo Mountains.

A Boy and His Dog was characterized as a black comedy science-fiction film and was distributed by L.Q. Jones' company LQ/Jaf Productions. Looking through the cast, I saw Jason Robards as one of the actors along with Alvy Moore and Canadian beauty Susanne Benton – and the main star, Don Johnson.

"I was 19 at the time. In high school, I was very interested in being a stuntman. When I was in high school, they needed extras for this show. They came and got the football players on the team. There were 50-60 of us. I was a defensive back," Norman told me in 2023. "We were a bunch of renegades in army rag clothing.

"Don Johnson was in the movie. L.Q. Jones was the director, and he was also an actor. We were out there for a long time for a few days."

Near the end of the shoot, Jones approached Norman to see if he wanted to stick around for more work in the movie in an acting role with lines.

"He wanted me to stay longer. He said, 'If you stay longer, I will use your voice.' He wanted my voice. But I had to leave because I had a ride to go home. It may have been my big break, if I was able to stay." Norman said, chuckling.

At one point, Norman approached SAG (Screen Actors Guild) officials to see what it would cost to join up and pursue his dream of working in the movies.

"They told me it would be $1,000 to join. Oh yeah, that was a lot of money," Norman said.

Norman was also interested in pursuing a career as a lawyer but that never came to pass. So he ended up playing baseball seriously. He grew up a fan of his home state Dodgers, especially Willie Davis, who played

Exposion

Courtesy Dan Norman

Dan Norman, left, who wanted to be a movie stuntman when he was in high school, poses with movie director Ron Howard prior to a 1982 Expos game in Los Angeles

for the Expos in 1974.

"I played at Trinity Lutheran High. I was a really young shortstop. Because of my arm, I did a lot of pitching. In my senior year, I struck out 286 batters."

That's what he said: 286.

Then he was off to L.A.'s Barstow Community College and while he was playing there, he was taken by the Cincinnati Reds in the 1974 draft. He never got playing time for the Reds in the majors because their line-up was stacked with Big Red Machine veterans.

Norman did produce some good numbers in the minors, including a 134-game season in 1976 with Canada's Aigles de Trois-Rivières, a Cincinnati farm team. He batted .273 with 17 homers and 63 RBI.

The Reds did him a favour when they swapped him along with Doug Flynn and Pat Zachry to the New York Mets in exchange for this guy by the name of Tom Seaver on June 15, 1977. A 3-for-1 transaction.

"I couldn't believe I was in the trade because I had been there for three years. I was surprised," Norman told me.

The trade to New York proved beneficial for Norman because he languished in the minors with the Reds. He played in 139 games from 1977-1980 with the Mets.

And then almost five years later, he was part of another major trade. He was a throw-in again, like in the Seaver deal – the Mets were dealing him to the Expos along with Jeff Reardon for Ellis Valentine on May 29, 1981.

"We were playing in Rochester, New York and the Mets took me out of the game. The players heard the manager Jack Aker say over the phone in the locker room to get me out of the game right now before I got hurt," Norman said of the circumstances leading to the trade. "The Detroit Tigers tried to trade for me, but the Mets wouldn't let me go because I had played for Sparky Anderson in spring training.

"The Expos had Dawson and Raines and Cromartie in the outfield, and I said to myself, 'Where am I going to play here?' I was an everyday outfielder. I knew I wasn't going to play much."

In all fairness, Norman was no Valentine, but he told me, "I could run, hit for average and power." Valentine had worn out his welcome with the Expos. The club was just plain fed up with him and his antics.

Canadian Baseball Hall of Fame
Dan Norman

Funny thing, though, Norman didn't play any part of the 1981 season for Montreal. He was sent to Denver Triple-A to finish the season and he wound up with 11 homers, 38 RBI and a .272 average in 73 games. He never earned a September call-up because that fall, the Expos were full of talent as they advanced to the playoffs for the first and only time in franchise history. There was no room for Norman.

Same kind of news hit Norman at spring training in 1982. There was too much talent for him to crack the lineup, so, he started the season with Wichita, the Expos' new Triple-A affiliate in Kansas.

In the early going of that season, Norman appeared in eight games for Wichita under manager Felipe Alou with two homers, seven RBI and an impressive .348 average. Expos GM John McHale and manager Jim Fanning figured this guy deserved playing time in the majors.

So, in late April, Norman got the call everyone likes to get when they are floundering in the minors.

"I got called up. Felipe said, 'You're going to the major leagues,'" Norman said. I said, 'Are you kidding me?' I thought he was kidding me."

In my research of the Expos' schedule in 1982, I found out that Norman's first appearance in a game was May 2 against the Dodgers in Los Angeles, in his home territory, but he had been on the roster for a few

Exposion

days prior to that. He had a ninth-inning single as a late-game replacement in left field for Raines as the Expos won 13-1.

Norman played mostly part-time and through May 17, he hit a very respectable 7-for-18. All told that season, he played in 53 games with two homers, seven ribbies and a .212 average. He lost some playing time to Terry Francona and when Raines was switched to the outfield from second base, he was reduced to part-time duty and pinch hitting.

Norman never played in the majors again, but Montreal's good-will gesture to keep him with the team in 1982 allowed him the necessary service time of four years to receive a pension.

Norman was never close to any of the Expos, saying his best friends to this day are players from the Cincinnati system: Steve Henderson and Donny Lyle.

After sitting out the 1983 season, Norman played in the minor leagues for different organizations from 1984-1989 and then began coaching and managing for many years in various leagues, including a managing stint in 2002 in a familiar city: Trois-Rivières, where he played in 1976.

Over the years, Norman also managed and coached at his alma mater, Barstow College, and helped out at baseball camps in California.

In the summer of 2023, Norman, 68, was appointed manager of the new Chatham-Kent Barnstormers' entry in Ontario's Intercounty Baseball League, a team that will begin play in 2024.

"Our team will be comprised of future and former professional players, and I'm excited to bring championship-calibre baseball to the region for this new team," Norman said in a statement released by club owner Dom Dinelle and general manager Harry Muir.

"We're so excited to have Dan with the team. He is a values-based leader, on and off the field, bringing a high level of experience, an impressive work ethic, and a dedication to the fans and community," Muir said.

"The Barnstormers are bringing in a very experienced manager to lead the troops," the news release added.

In research I did, I found out Norman was only the second black manager hired in the IBL in the previous 60 years. Steve Charles managed part of the 2006 season with the Brantford Red Sox and prior to that, it was Jimmy (Seabiscuit) Wilkes with Brantford in 1963.

"It's a cool fact. I didn't know that. It's fun but it's not the reason Dan was selected. As you know, he's got good credentials," Dinelle said in an interview at the time of Norman's hiring. "It doesn't matter: black, white, gold, green. Dan was the best one. It just happens that he's black."

Norman's hiring should be a sign that more black managers should be hired in the IBL.

"Hopefully, this will encourage other people," league commissioner Ted Kalnins said at the time. "We're excited at the high calibre of Dan Norman. He has an incredible pedigree. It's great of him to uproot himself and come here."

Good luck with the Chatham gig, Dan. Appreciate the time you took to talk with me.

Chapter 20

The Pete Incaviglia saga

Gary Ward knew Pete Incaviglia as much as anyone.

Ward recalled that Incaviglia was a 10th-round draft choice of the San Francisco Giants out of Monterey high school in Monterey, California in 1982.

Former major-leaguer and one-time Giant Hank Sauer was the scout for the Giants but the Giants were not exactly awash in money. And 10th-round money wouldn't be that good. So, Incaviglia decided not to sign with the Giants.

"We knew the Giants were in financial straits. They were trying to sell the franchise," said Ward, Incaviglia's baseball coach at Oklahoma State University. "We knew Pete's brother Tony, who was a minor leaguer. All that information is what got the ball rolling, it got us on the inside."

Inside, meaning Incaviglia decided he wouldn't sign with San Fran. He decided to go to Oklahoma State in Stillwater.

"Sauer said to me Pete had major-league power," Ward told me in April of 2023. "In retrospect, he was the hardest worker that I had in 39 years of coaching. He would not leave you alone. He would wear you out. He wanted to be in the cage. He never took things for granted. He was that dedicated. He was an engaging personality.

"That's how driven he was. He had an extraordinary work ethic. He was an old school guy. He swung so much he would get blisters on his hand. He needed a lot of repetitions. He didn't have a great sense of batting awareness. He had no idea about a hitting pattern. He didn't have too much launch angle. We would train and train him to get the bat to travel in a better path.

"He was a big upper-body guy wider through the shoulders. He was drafted as a third baseman, but he didn't have the ability to play third. He didn't have the great hands. He was a big-bodied man. He worked on his speed. He did a 6.8 in 60 seconds."

Incavigliawas drafted by the Expos in 1985 on June 7, 1985. Remember the hype about Incaviglia? He was traded to Texas for pitcher Bob Sebra and infielder Jimmy Anderson on Nov. 2 of the same year after the Expos had gone through many futile months of trying to sign him.

The trade was first announced by the Oklahoma State University sports information office, which was working on the lowdown given it by Incaviglia's agent Bucky Woy.

Woy was a professional golfer and bowling executive, who was one of the early pioneers when it came to representing athletes, mostly golfers such as Lee Trevino, Julius Boros, Ben Hogan and Tom Weiskopf, but also the likes of tennis great Jimmy Connors.

Woy was known to be very tough at the negotiating table. He demanded a lot and expected a lot from the people on the other side of the negotiating table or on the phone.

"It shocked me," Ward told me when I asked him about Incaviglia going to Texas and balking at going to Montreal. "It had not been something we discussed. It was Bucky Woy's people – where the initial idea of whether Pete didn't want to play in Canada or whether Montreal would not pay enough money. I was not involved in that.

Courtesy Texas Rangers
Pete Incaviglia

"I suggested being born in California, he could travel all over the country and take a trip to Montreal. It's gorgeous. You need to go see it," Ward recalled. "Texas, in June and July, is a sweatbox. It has the worst summer environment. He just kind of bit it off (my suggestion). He never replied, he didn't answer. I said okay. It surprised me – Montreal agreed to sign and trade him."

Incaviglia's numbers at Oklahoma State were staggering. No wonder the beach bum from Pebble Beach on California's north coast was voted the NCAA player of the century award in 1999.

In his junior team year, his final year in college ball, he slammed 48 homers and drove in 143 runs in only 74 games. Imagine, what he would have done, if the college schedule was 162 games.

Geez, he was something else. He batted .464 and his OPS was a gaudy 1.140. Often, he was walked intentionally with men on second and third. Incaviglia was given the Golden Spikes Award for what he did in 1985.

"We didn't know about OPS back then. We just wanted to know about average and home runs," Expos general manager Murray Cook was telling me.

While some reports suggested Incaviglia didn't want to play in the minor leagues for the Expos, Cook batted down that talk. His recollection is that Incaviglia, despite the Rangers' poor showing in the standings during the 1985 season, wanted to play for Texas.

"Pretty sure I am right on it – he didn't want to play for anybody other than the Texas Rangers," Cook said in an interview. "He was a screwball animal with a huge ego. Sign and trade him? That wasn't the plan before we drafted him. This all transpired afterward we drafted him.

"He had that kind of year on a big team, big conference. Just like a lot

The Pete Incaviglia saga

of players, those kinds of numbers, you paid extra for it. He said he had the credentials to back up his demands. He wanted more than what the traffic would bear, as they say."

And what Inky wanted in monetary demands was conflicting. Some reports suggested he wanted $100,000 to sign. But it was more than that. Woy had shocked the baseball world when he arranged a deal for Arizona State University star Bob Horner to step in and play for the Atlanta Braves in 1978 without any minor-league experience.

In an Associated Press wire story emanating from Arlington, Texas, the Rangers' home base, Incaviglia received what was believed to be a $600,000 package, including a signing bonus in excess of $200,000.

"The negotiations with Bucky Woy were rather testy. We were not willing to pay the kind of money they wanted," Cook was telling me. "Jim Fanning and Bill Stoneman did the negotiating. There wasn't much negotiating. They were making strong demands.

"I called (GM) Tommy Grieve of the Rangers and explained it to him. We worked out a deal. Texas was willing."

The sign-and-trade deal was unprecedented. It was the first time a team signed a drafted player and immediately traded him. The AP story said Incaviglia signed with Montreal "on the condition he would be traded to the Rangers," Woy said at the time.

In most cases, players who are drafted may not want to sign with the team that drafted him and just wait until the next draft. The commissioner's office was kept abreast of the Incaviglia saga. One rule already in place was that unsigned drafted players could not be traded.

"I look at it as a chance of a lifetime," Grieve told Paul Hagen of the Fort Worth Star-Telegram following the trade. "Even if the kid never plays a game in the big leagues, it was worth the gamble."

Some 30 years later, Grieve hailed the Incaviglia deal.

"To this day, he's the greatest hitter in college baseball history," Grieve told me. "With the competition he faced and the numbers he put up, we were okay with acquiring him.

"We had some discussions with the Expos. It was one of those deals where Murray Cook knew we really wanted Pete. Murray needed to make a trade. He didn't have a lot of teams to deal with. There was not much leverage. Murray Cook would have preferred to have kept Pete, but it ended up he had no choice. I don't think Pete wanted to play in Montreal and he wanted a major-league contract.

"We might have been the only team willing to accept a major-league contract. Both teams had a high need to make that trade. Most teams had no interest in giving him a MLB contract. I don't know if he didn't want to play in Montreal and only in Texas. That may be true. We found him very desirable to acquire.

"Bucky Woy got a major-league contract for Bob Horner with the Braves. The Expos decided to explore a trade and we expressed a keen interest in trading for him. We were willing to give up Sebra and Anderson. Both of them were solid, young prospects. They were not among our top 15 prospects. We were comfortable giving them up to get a player that would be a middle-of-the-order power hitter the next year."

Exposion

There were complaints from the Incaviglia/Woy camp that Incaviglia was being "treated unfairly" financially in the second year of the contract, compared to the first year but Grieve told me a neat story.

"I agreed this is the contract. I didn't give a shit. I had a contract," Grieve said. "The reality of it was that the deal was agreed upon. We were advised of the parameters of the contract – he would be paid 80% in the second year of the $200,000 he earned in 1985. In the second year, he earned $160,000.

"Bucky Woy went to the press and said, 'Can you believe my guy, they are going to give him a pay cut?' But on the other side, Bucky agreed to that contract before Pete put a uniform on and went to spring training.

"We didn't promise he would be in the majors," Grieve said. "He still had to make the team. If you would send him to the minors, the only choice for him would be to quit. Going into spring training, it was 80% sure he was going to be on the big-league team. His contract may have been a bit high, but the contract becomes very manageable once he makes the team."

Not long after the deal was made, the commissioner's office instituted what Grieve called the Sandy Johnson Rule, named after the Rangers' scouting director, but most people remember it as the Pete Incaviglia Rule, meaning that in future, signed draft picks couldn't be traded until one year later.

"That was the rule behind it," Cook said.

Incaviglia made believers of the Rangers in 1986 with 30 homers and 88 RBI while batting .250. The only negative was his 185 strikeouts.

He spent five seasons with the Rangers and then played for a host of teams after that, finishing his career with more than 10 years of service.

"He earned the right to make the team. He earned a spot on the team," Grieve said. "He was a great teammate. He was one of our favourites. The guys on the team loved him. Just seeing him walk into a room with his chest stuck out – he was a happy-go-lucky guy. He was very personable."

Incaviglia in the majors was nowhere near what he was in his junior season at Oklahoma State. He finished with 206 homers in the big leagues with 655 RBI and a .246 average.

"We thought he had enough ability to hit 270-290 homers in the majors, not 400 or 500," Ward said. "He learned to hit the breaking ball more to right-centre."

In recent years, Incaviglia had been the manager of New York's Tri-City Wildcats of the Frontier League, but he parted ways with the club following the 2023 season because he wanted to be closer to his family in Texas.

Chapter 21

Buck Rodgers was a popular manager

Buck Rodgers was managing winter ball in Venezuela in late 1984, trying to get back to the majors as a manager when he got a call from Expos general manager Murray Cook.

"We'd just completed an 18-inning game and Murray Cook calls me at 3 in the morning Venezuela time," Rodgers told me in a 2023 interview.

"He started talking about second base and shortstop and I said, 'What do you want?' He said, 'We want you to manage the Montreal Expos! Will you take the job?' I said, 'Yes, I want to manage the Montreal Expos.'

"I got up for breakfast, thinking it was a dream or did Murray Cook really want me as manager? The Caracas paper came out and announced it and the players congratulated me in the coffee shop. That's when I realized it was the real thing.

"(President) John McHale called me. I mean, all I had was a light jacket. He said, 'Look, we'll get you a coat and suit for the press conference in Montreal. I changed planes in New York. It was colder than hell. I went from one terminal to the other in the wee hours of the morning."

Rodgers had spent the 1984 season as skipper of the Expos' Triple-A team in Indianapolis so Cook had an idea of what Rodgers could do. He had also managed the Milwaukee Brewers.

Cook had interviewed Orioles managerial great Earl Weaver, former Expo Tim McCarver and also considered Felipe Alou, but decided on Rodgers, who wasn't interviewed per se.

It was a new era for baseball in Montreal – a new general manager, a new manager and a new coaching staff for the most part, but it didn't hurt that Rodgers was voted manager of the year in the American Association with the job he did with Indianapolis.

Rodgers was just happy to be the manager of a big-league team again. He thinks he received "not much more than $100,000" per year for a salary to join the Expos.

The most surprising team Rodgers managed was the 1987 club that surprised pundits by producing marvellous results until they fell short at the end of the season. He was voted manager of the year.

"1987 – that was my biggest thrill," Rodgers said.

The 1989 club was also solid to the point the Expos surprised everyone again after they fell off in 1988.

The Expos led the NL East for much of the summer of 1989 following

Exposion

Joe Gromelski photo
Buck Rodgers, Expos managing general partner Claude Brochu
and commissioner Fay Vincent on the field back in the day.

the acquisition of Mark Langston from the Mariners for Randy Johnson, Brian Holman and Gene Harris – before folding in August and September. What a disaster.

"1989 – what happened, everything that could go wrong went wrong," Rodgers said. "That was my biggest disappointment as Expos manager. We were probably playing over our heads in the first half and playing below our ability in the last part.

"We gave up an awful lot for the last few months of Langston's contract. I liked Holman, Randy had so much ability, but he had to harness everything, and Gene Harris had one of our best arms we thought in the league as a reliever."

On June 2, 1991, Rodgers was fired and replaced by Tom Runnells. His tenure of 6½ seasons was over.

Rodgers was easily one of the most popular managers the Expos ever had, right up there with Alou. The media loved both for their charm, personality, wisdom and eloquence and funny tales.

"I liked the way I was appreciated in Montreal. I enjoyed Montreal more than any place I managed," Rodgers said. "Baseball is the No. 2 sport in Canada after hockey. You have to realize that. I always felt I had to have an answer for everything.

Buck Rodgers was a popular manager

Courtesy Debra McLean
Buck Rodgers poses with fan Debra McLean

"If I made a move, I'd talk to the press and had the reasons for making the move. That's why I spent more time with the press. It was important to explain why you did things. If you put the squeeze on, you wanted to explain why."

Rodgers turned 85 in 2023 and is reasonably good health, although he needs a cane to get around.

Glad you're doing good, Buck.

Chapter 22

McGaffigan was an unsung hero

When Andy McGaffigan joined the Expos, it was like he was coming home, at least during spring training because it was his backyard, so to speak.

He grew up near Palm Beach International Airport in the Belvedere Homes district south of Okeechobee Boulevard. As a kid, he'd go to old Municipal Stadium in West Palm Beach, now occupied by a Home Depot store, and catch foul balls hit during spring training or even the Class A games of the West Palm Beach Expos.

"In fact, I played all my Legion ball at Municipal Stadium," McGaffigan said.

In 1974, McGaffigan was drafted in the 36th round by the Cincinnati Reds out of Twin Lakes high school in West Palm Beach but didn't sign. Two years later, he was selected in the fifth round by White Sox out of Palm Beach Lakes College. Again, he didn't sign.

"They weren't offering much money. They had no money," McGaffigan said about the Reds and White Sox. "I decided to take my scholarship money and stay in school."

In 1978, McGaffigan was taken in Round 6 by the Yankees when he was at Florida Southern College in Lakeland. This time, he signed. McGaffigan didn't like the money the Reds and White Sox were offering but he took George Steinbrenner's Yankees' dough and by that time, he also had matured as a pitcher.

McGaffigan helped the Joe Arnold-coached Florida Southern team advance to the Division II Senior College World Series in Springfield, Illinois where he met up with future major-leaguer Steve Bedrosian, who was with the University of New Haven.

He was 7-1 throughout the season with four complete games and 101 strikeouts and a 3.34 ERA.

"In the minor leagues with the Yankees, they had a pretty established coaching system and Mr. Steinbrenner was pretty encouraging of our minor-league system. He put development money into coaching. My development was pretty strong in the Yankees' system," McGaffigan told me.

McGaffigan pitched in the minors in Fort Lauderdale, West Haven, Conn., Nashville and Columbus, Ohio before finally making his big-league debut with the Yankees on Sept. 22, 1981 at Yankee Stadium against Cleveland.

And it was a pretty decent start. He threw three innings, facing 14 batters, allowing one hit, three walks and no runs.

Too bad, though, that McGaffigan's tenure with the Yankees was brief.

McGaffigan was traded to San Francisco in late March of 1982, just before the regular season began along with Ted Wilburn in exchange for Doyle Alexander.

McGaffigan, except for eight innings with the Giants, spent all of 1982 in the minors. Then he got lucky in 1983 when the Giants kept him on the big-league roster. He was a regular contributor, going 3-9 with 4.29 ERA in 134.1 innings.

Then along came another spring-training trade. He was dealt to Montreal on Feb. 27, 1984 in a transaction that saw hit meister Al Oliver go to San Fran.

"I was leaving a Giants club that was not very good. They were probably going to lose 100 games. I was going to a team that could possibly be in the World Series," McGaffigan said.

The Expos had a good run of success from 1979-83 and the 1984 squad was also supposed to be a contending team but they weren't. Yet, it was a homecoming for McGaffigan because he was born in West Palm.

"1984 was not a great year for Montreal. There was a lot of turmoil. Pete Rose was there but he was at the end of his career," McGaffigan said. "Charlie Lea was great, but he was hurt. There was David Palmer, Bill Gullickson, Steve Rogers – it was a good team, but it had no symmetry. Bill Virdon was the manager and we struggled.

"It wasn't long after I was traded to Cincinnati and then Pete was back with Cincinnati after the trade with Montreal in August. Pete and I weren't fast or close friends but when he came over, it was a shot of adrenalin. Everything changed. There was a lot of hustle and bustle. Vern Rapp had been the manager, and nobody was happy and we were not playing well. The Reds were even worse (than the Expos)."

McGaffigan remained with the Reds, a team that had drafted him earlier in his career, through the 1985 season but the Expos missed him so much they re-acquired him on Dec. 19, 1985 from Cincinnati in the trade that sent Gullickson to the Reds.

That was the beginning of a renaissance for McGaffigan. His tenure with Montreal was the longest he enjoyed with any of his teams: about 5½ seasons in all.

"I was a little surprised with the trade. I wasn't really unhappy in Cincinnati. I looked at it one way and that the Reds didn't want me," he said. "It was an opportunity to go to a team that had really changed quite a bit. Buck was the new manager. We had strong, young players.

"I thought I got a really nice break there. In 1986, I did both starting and relieving and I really kind of established myself that year, a guy that could eat some innings. It was a very good era. It was good to match up with (catcher) Mike Fitzgerald. He was just awesome. I was coming into my own. I got the ball regularly.

"The highlight in 1986 was a complete game in Philadelphia. My catcher that day was Dann Bilardello. He was my roommate. It was a shutout. It was a good year."

I did research of that May 6 game on Retrosheet and McGaffigan was impressive. He scattered eight hits in going the distance. He struck out seven as the Expos won 8-0. Rarely used Bilardello went 1-for-4 with an RBI and Andre Dawson and Vance Law contributed two-run homers off aging Steve Carlton, who was at the end of his rope after a long, illustrious career. That once stifling, terrifying left arm of his wasn't useful anymore.

Then came Montreal's Cinderella season in 1987 when the surprising Expos won 91 games and fought for the NL East title right down until near the end. Tim Burke was outstanding as the leader of the club's bullpen-by-committee which was created after closer Jeff Reardon was traded by Montreal to Minnesota following the 1986 season.

Rodgers compromised with Reardon's loss by going with a number of relievers.

McGaffigan was tremendous like Burke, with 12 saves to go with a 2.39 ERA and a 5-2 record.

"1987 – truthfully, I didn't have a lot of consistency as a starter, but I had the ability to throw a few times a week," he said. "I had a pretty live arm that allowed multiple innings in multiple games. 1988, like 1987, I had great opportunities. The Expos were extremely talented those years. It was just gratifying to get as many opportunities three years in a row."

In 1988, he was strong, just like he was in 1987, with a 6-0 record and a 2.76 ERA. It was vintage McGaffigan.

Canadian Baseball Hall of Fame
Andy McGaffigan

"It was fun, just to be able to be a part of all of those winning games or close games," he said. "It was fun to pitch and more fun when the game is on the line. I was usually brought in – in the sixth inning on. We were either tied or were ahead or down by one run. My job was to eat a couple of innings. There were a few three-inning saves. I just tried to be consistent. The bullpen-by-committee – it was a collective effort, a very unique group of guys. In 1988, it was just more of the same. I was in a groove, throwing a lot of strikes. I was healthy."

McGaffigan's best pitch in his heyday tenure with the Expos? Was it the fastball, curve, slider, changeup? I asked him that question and his reply was interesting.

"My first pitch," McGaffigan answered, when I queried him in late 2022. "Strike one is the best pitch in baseball, the main pitch. It might sound funny, smart-alecky, but I threw a lot of strikes. If you get strike one, you have a better chance of getting that guy out.

"I threw a cross-seam fastball up and in on left-handers, and then I threw a two-seamer, a slider and changeup."

McGaffigan hit turbulence in 1989 when the Expos were in first place during a long summer stretch in the NL East, before they folded to finish at 81-81.

Like the club as a whole, he, too, was disappointing. His ERA had climbed to 4.68 and although he finished 24 games, he was only able to save two, and finished the season with a 3-5 record.

"1989 – I didn't have the same stuff. I didn't have the same effectiveness. I was disappointed in my outcome. I was not as good as my other years," McGaffigan said. "It was an off-year. 1989 – we fell apart.

"We lost our momentum. It was very disappointing. It's not just us, it was the other teams. There was a strong Phillies team. It was just a hard division. It was a battle and struggle all the time."

McGaffigan stuck with the Expos for 99% of spring training in 1990 before he was traded to – you guessed it, the Giants, for PTBNL Steve Hecht. It was two days prior to the season opener in St. Louis. He had to up and leave some close friends. It was a culture shock for sure.

"I was disappointed. I thought I had given the club four really good years. I would have preferred to stay in Montreal than go back to the Giants," he said. "It was frustrating. It's not hardly ever the truth – it's a business decision which I think it was. It's always been that way. It's not about personalities or friendships or loyalties. It was me and an older player with a pretty good contract ($623,000 for one year). It was unfortunate. I didn't have the best spring training.

"I went to the Giants, and I struggled, and they released me. I went to Kansas City, and I began to pitch like I used to."

That's right, McGaffigan's ERA was 3.09 in 78.2 innings. The old McGaffigan was back. By the following year, though, he was released by Kansas City and never played in the majors again.

It was another culture shock. He had been in baseball, either at the high school, university or pro level since 1975 and here now, he was out of work. He was no longer going to spring training and hanging out with teammates from Feb 15-Oct. 1.

Instead of staying home for 4½ months in the off-season, he was at home for 12 months a year. It was some adjustment. It sure required a lot of thinking on how to keep himself busy all day and stay out of his wife's hair.

"The first year was kind of a novelty. It was definitely a wake-up call. You get released and you're not quite ready to retire. When players retire, they never get to retire on their own," he explained. "The page gets turned around. Nobody plays forever. I spent about a year and a half and didn't do anything. I tried to work out what the new normal would be.

"The second year off is not as hard as the first. I still thought I could still pitch at the big-league level. The phone calls never came. It was over and done. I tried my hand at a number of things. I worked for a company dealing in golf.

"The last 22 years I've been a financial advisor. I was recruited by Northwestern Financial."

Exposion

Although his roots were in West Palm, he has lived in Lakeland for many years because that is where his alma mater, Florida Central University, is located. Him and his wife raised their kids in Lakeland, which so happened also to be the spring-training base for the Tigers, next door to the Reds' facility.

"As a teenager in Plattsburgh, N.Y., I had the opportunity to watch Andy McGaffigan pitch for the Expos," said his now-close friend Kris Doorey. "From 1985-88, he was one of the top relief arms in baseball. Since our lives have crossed paths, I've been able to learn about Andy McGaffigan the man. There is not a better human on the planet. A great person, a great father, a great husband, a great friend."

I can tell you that without Doorey's intervention, I would not have had an interview with McGaffigan. I had emailed McGaffigan at his place of work a few years ago but I got no reply. We knew each other.

All of a sudden in late 2022, I got a private message on Twitter from Doorey.

"Let me know if you would have any interest in an interview with Andy McGaffigan," Doorey wrote.

I promptly said yes. So that set the stage for an interview several months later.

McGaffigan jokingly said he would do a chat if a special request was made.

"The only thing I ask is that Plattsburgh gets mentioned," McGaffigan said, chuckling.

So, in the course of our interview, he talked about how Plattsburgh meant so much to the wives of U.S.-born Expos.

"Plattsburgh was like an oasis for the wives in Montreal. When we were on road trips, they would escape down there just to hear American English and get familiar food and supplies," he said. "All the wives – they weren't Canadians. They were Americans or South Americans.

"The French-Canadian culture was different from what we were accustomed to. It's so drastically different from the American culture. It was a unique, different culture. It was nice for the girls to break away to go back to the States to a normal, traditional grocery store and speak English.

"French is not the easiest of languages to learn. Not that they hated the French, but it gave them a respite to get into the American culture scene."

McGaffigan's teammate Bryn Smith and his wife would often say (joke?) they couldn't get Doritos in Montreal, so they had to go to Plattsburgh, which is located about one hour south of Montreal near Québec's Champlain/Lacolle crossing.

Andy, it was such a pleasure chatting with you.

Bat Masterton, Dave Schmidt and Dr. Pepper

Did you know that Bat Masterton, the famous lawman of the American Old West, was born in Henryville in Québec's Eastern Townships?

I didn't know that until I Googled Henryville on May 7, 2023.

I bring Henryville up because Expos players, their wives and children would often drive to the picturesque town to take advantage of beautiful parks, attractions and nearby Lake Champlain. It's about an hour's drive southwest of Montreal and a few miles from a U.S. border crossing at Rouses Point.

"We were having a BBQ in Henryville on an Expos off day with the Wallachs, Owens, Foleys and Dave Schmidt," recalled Roberto Greco, who worked in promotions for the Expos for 24 years, "when Dave mentioned that he missed not being able to buy Dr. Pepper in Montreal."

Greco recommended to Schmidt that he go with him to Rouses Point, which is probably the very tiny border crossing Masterton and his family crossed to head to Dodge City, Kansas, New York City and other American destinations where he became a celebrity.

"I suggested that we go shopping in Rouses Point but little did I know that we would empty out the small grocery store with two shopping carts filled with regular Dr. Pepper," Greco said. "The trunk of his car was full. He had a stash for the summer."

Chapter 23

Hesketh's debut featured a balk

Before he even threw his first pitch in his major-league debut with the Expos on Aug. 7, 1984, Joe Hesketh was called for a balk – either by home-plate umpire Jerry Crawford or first-base ump Joe West. Not sure which.

Unreal. Pretty amazing trivia or circumstance. Whatever you want to call it.

It was the first game of a doubleheader against the Phillies at Olympic Stadium. It was the top of the fifth inning. Expos starter Bryn Smith allowed a single to Juan Samuel, who promptly stole second and advanced to third on a throwing error by catcher Bobby Ramos. Next batter was Jeff Stone and he singled to score Samuel.

That series of events prompted manager Bill Virdon to lift Smitty and bring in Hesketh, who threw his complimentary eight pitches to get ready to face Von Hayes.

Here he was, Hesketh, promoted from Indianapolis Triple-A where he was spectacular with a 12-3 record and a nifty 3.05 ERA under manager Buck Rodgers, getting to throw his first pitch.

Next thing you know, Hesketh balks, apparently doing something to try and pick Stone off at first as regular catcher Gary Carter made an extremely rare start at first base in place of Pete Rose, who wasn't getting much time around first at any rate that season.

An exclamation point to start a big-league career for sure, but Hesketh settled down by getting Hayes on a fly to left. With first base open, Virdon elected to have the feared Mike Schmidt given an open pass to first with an intentional base on balls. Earlier in the game, Schmidt had drilled a three-run homer off Smitty.

Hesketh proceeded to strike out Len Matuszek and got pinch-hitter Sixto Lezcano on a 4-3 groundout to end the inning.

The oddity of him making his big-league debut and getting called for a balk got very little attention in the Montreal papers, except for a notation in the boxscore, simply because there were two games that day and usually the second game of a doubleheader gets the bigger write-up of the two games all rolled into one story. Understand?

Little did Hesketh know he would go on to enjoy a pretty decent career in the big leagues. The Expos sure were hoping for good things from the kid from the Buffalo suburb of Lackawanna.

Hesketh pretty much went unnoticed by pro scouts while excelling at Hamburg's Frontier Central, a Catholic school. He was brilliant at State

Hesketh's debut featured a balk

University of New York in Buffalo (UB) with the Bulls, securing a 1.77 ERA, including a nifty 0.91 in his junior year.

Hesketh was outstanding under the great Bulls coach Bill Monkarsh. He threw 10 complete games and pitched in two of the greatest games in school history – a 4-0 shutout against the host Miami Hurricanes in a NCAA Division I playoff game and notching the save as the Bulls beat powerful St. John's which featured future MLB star Frank Viola, a fellow lefty.

Hesketh was highly thought of in the 1980 June draft of amateur players and the Expos won out with little known Al Harper the scout leading the way. Hesketh was Montreal's second-round choice which was awarded to the Expos as compensation for the Red Sox signing of Tony Perez, who had spent the 1977-79 seasons with Montreal.

Interesting that Hesketh was the starting pitcher for the Expos in the Canadian Pearson Cup exhibition game against the Blue Jays on July 31, 1980 at the Big O and was the winning pitcher in Montreal's 3-1 victory.

The injury-plagued Hesketh underwent elbow surgery following the 1980 season and missed the entire 1981 season. Oh no.

As Expos PR specialist Rich Griffin put it, Hesketh went "684 days between appearances before beginning his first comeback on July 17, 1982 at West Palm Beach."

Not long after his big-league debut, he was returned to Indianapolis. Then, on Aug. 22, he was looking forward to seeing his parents come from Lackawanna to Indianapolis to see him pitch, but he got both good news and bad news. His parents were probably not too unhappy with the bad news, because the good news was that Hesketh was called up by the Expos to report to duty on Aug. 23.

Canadian Baseball Hall of Fame
Joe Hesketh

So, Hesketh was scratched from his scheduled start against the Oklahoma City 89ers. Instead, he flew to Montreal from Indy to make it on time for the game against the Phillies the next day.

According to a story in the Indianapolis Star, Hesketh had gone to church on the morning of his scheduled start. His roommate, the late Roy Johnson, told him Indians manager Buck Rodgers had called. Hesketh tried to get a hold of Rodgers with no luck, so he sat down with Johnson to watch the Expos/Cubs game from Chicago on television. And so, it was on that telecast he found out he had been called up.

"I was stunned," Hesketh told reporters. "After being here this long, I figured I'd probably finish the season here. I came here and did what I had to do. And it's more rewarding that way, doing well here and showing them I deserved a chance up there," added Hesketh.

"I was hoping I'd get one more start out of him," said Rodgers, who felt it was only time before the Expos promoted him.

Hesketh made his first start as a big leaguer on Aug. 26 with a no-decision to show for seven solid innings of work in a game won 4-2 by the Expos over the Cubs. He struck out the side in the third in one of Virdon's last days as a manager before he was fired.

"I don't consider myself a strikeout pitcher," Hesketh said.

Hesketh's first shutout came in his last start of 1984 when he beat the Mets with a four-hitter at Olympic Stadium.

Hesketh was superlative for the Expos in his first full season in 1985, going 10-5 with a neat 2.49 ERA. His best game all season arguably was when he outduelled storied Nolan Ryan on May 8 in a day game in Montreal. Hesketh fanned 12 Astros in 7⅔ innings of work as Montreal won 1-0 before 10,122. What a game.

Hesketh sailed through the season in beautiful fashion, being touted as a possible rookie-of-the-year candidate along with Tom Browning and others. Along the way, he beat John Tudor of the Cardinals twice in April, first on April 17 in St. Louis and then on April 27 in Montreal.

Then a major disappointment struck on Aug. 23 when he attempted to score from first on a double by Tim Raines.

Pitchers, as such, don't have a lot of experience running since they don't play another position. So, when team officials and the manager see them running, they say, "Shit, hope he doesn't get hurt." That's what the thought process is. It really is. Pitchers generally don't know how to run for the most part, they don't know how to slide or when not to slide.

Candy Maldonado fielded Raines's hit in centre, threw to right-fielder Mike Marshall, the cutoff man, who fired to Scioscia.

So, when Hesketh came close to home plate, he saw Dodgers catcher Mike Scioscia, the master of blocking the plate, had it sealed off. Hesketh decided to run into Scioscia, and he ended up falling over the catcher and somehow, he ended up suffering a non-displaced fracture of his left shin.

Oh shit, just what manager Buck Rodgers, and his teammates didn't want to see.

Hesketh should have just slid. Even then, that might have resulted in some kind of injury. Slide or stand up, team officials are worry warts when it comes to pitchers out of their element on the basepaths.

By the time Hesketh got to the plate, he was surely out of gas. He missed the remainder of the season. And you could say he was never the same following that incident, at least not with the Expos, although he did enjoy that excellent 12-4 season with the Red Sox in 1991.

"I'm sorry about what happened," Scioscia said later. "He just angled up in my leg. I feel terrible about it. I never try to hurt anybody in this game. I didn't do anything wrong and I have a clear conscience."

Rodgers, a catcher back in his playing days, acknowledged Scioscia was fine in how he set himself up at the plate to face Hesketh.

"He was having such a fine season," Rodgers said of Hesketh. "He probably would have been safe if he had slid. That was a perfectly legal play. It's not a dirty play."

Hesketh was 6-5 with a lofty 5.01 ERA in 1986 and he never pitched again for the Expos, but he went on to pitch for other teams.

Hesketh decided to retire on Aug. 7, 1994, the 10th anniversary of his major league debut. What a nice way to end it all.

Courtesy Donruss
Joe Hesketh

Chapter 24

Santovenia shuts down Coleman's 50-game streak

Nelson Santovenia recalls his date with history on July 28, 1989.

"It was the day after my birthday," Santovenia said.

On the night of the 28th with 41,000 fans on hand as the Expos were thick in the middle of a race to win the National League East championship, there was passion in the air.

It was a Friday night and Vince Coleman was in town with the Cardinals.

"I didn't know he had the streak," Santovenia was saying 35 years later when he halted Coleman's streak of 50 consecutive stolen bases by throwing him out as he tried to swipe second base in the very first inning. "I don't recall to be honest."

Santovenia downplayed his own role in ending the streak when he threw to shortstop Jeff Huson, who applied the tag. With Pascual Perez pitching, it was Santovenia's strong throw from behind the plate that eliminated the speedster Coleman.

Santovenia has always been modest, never boasting about a career that was once promising but turned out short and unfulfilling.

"That was a nice highlight for me. My birthday was on the 27th, a Thursday," he said. "It was, you know, a good thing for my career. In our scouting reports and meetings, we find out about incoming teams before each game, who was hot and who wasn't.

"A lot of strategy comes from the coaching staff and who the pitcher is. Coleman was one of the fastest runners so, as soon as he got on base, you keep him close and keep him honest."

To this day, nobody has equalled Coleman's 50-game streak. Here it is 35 years later. That same game, Coleman was also picked off first by Dennis Martinez.

To boot, Santovenia also threw out Tony Pena trying to steal second in the second inning. Not sure if Santovenia ever threw two guys out in a game. It would even be a rarity to see most catchers throw out more than one runner a game.

Oddly, the next night, Coleman was thrown out again, for the second game in a row by a Montreal catcher – this time, it was Mike Fitzgerald. It was not a good series for Coleman, at least on the base paths.

That season, Santovenia enjoyed a 35% caught-stealing percentage, compared to the 31% league average. Coleman finished the season with a league leading 65 stolen bases, while being caught only 10 times, two of which were during that three-game stint at the Big O.

Santovenia shuts down Coleman's 50-game streak

Those three games the Expos played against the Cardinals epitomized the passion and enthusiasm the fans had for the Expos because they saw the club in first place for most of the summer. This was a dream team heading for the post-season after the club acquired Mark Langston in the Randy Johnson trade.

The combined attendance for the three-game series was 118,199. The team's record was 59-41. With his win against St. Louis, the game he picked off Coleman, Martinez upped his record to 12-1.

Then the wheels fell off. The Expos were swept in Pittsburgh in a three-game set. They never really recovered and dipped into mediocrity to finish at 81-81. I don't know how many times I have talked about that year with much disappointment.

Canadian Baseball Hall of Fame
Nelson Santovenia

"We traded for Mark Langston. We just kind of didn't do very good down the stretch," Santovenia said. "Our main guys weren't hitting. We weren't scoring any runs. It was a combination of everything. It was a bad time of the year to do it."

Chapter 25

Fitzgerald's love for diving for lobsters

Mike Fitzgerald admits people rib him when he tells them he dives for lobsters.

"You know you can get them at the supermarket? Are you crazy?"the people say, as they chide him.

The popular Expos catcher from the 1980s and early 1990s has always loved the water. He has always loved "being" in the water. He loves swimming, he loves fishing, he loves surfing.

He's from Long Beach, California. He gravitates to the water. He loves searching for stuff down there in the deep, blue sea.

For close to 30 years, his passion has been diving for lobsters and putting it on the barbeque. It all started around 1995.

"Most of the time, I go to Catalina Island near Long Beach and on the California coast," he said. "It's open six months of the year and you have to use your (gloved) hands to catch them. So, when you're diving, you have to use your hands pretty quick. The lobsters have brutally sharp pangs on them. They click and kick."

"I wear a mask, a full wetsuit, special Teflon gloves, a bag on my belt and underwater light.

Joe Gromelski photo
Mike Fitzgerald

"We go out at night, diving in pairs in the dark, October-March. I would say I would be in the water most of the time about a total of two hours. We go once a month."

Fitzgerald goes with a buddy, gets dressed up in diving gear and is all pumped to see what is down deep below the surface as he discovers the state's favourite delicacies. They usually go in the Pacific Ocean sometime before "10 or 11" at night.

"There's a lot of adrenalin. When you get into the ocean, you're jumping into the food chain," he said. "There are all kinds of things in that ocean: sharks, lions – it's always an adventure when you jump

Fitzgerald's love for diving for lobsters

Courtesy Mike Fitzgerald
Mike Fitzgerald with a lobster catch

Courtesy Fitzgerald
Fitzie as a kid

into the ocean. Usually, we get a lobster that is eight pounds. The tail might be half a pound, usually for a big salad."

Fitzgerald said you must obtain a valid licence and wear a card that is issued by California Wildlife and Game. A measuring device must also be carried. It records the catches one makes and in what location.

In California, you can keep a lobster only if its length is greater than 3.25 inches measured from the rear edge of the body shell to the rear edge of the eye socket.

In order to get involved in such a strenuous un-

Exposion

dertaking, it's important you be in shape and full of stamina and Fitzgerald fits bill because he has been exercising all his life.

Thanks, Mike, for filling me in on one of your hobbies.

Dariush Ramezani sketch

Mike Fitzgerald

Chapter 26

Wainhouse only Canadian picked in first round of draft

David Wainhouse still remembers his address in Scarborough, Ontario, his house, the street name – Droxford Avenue – the house number – 6 – where he lived in suburban Toronto.

The one-time Expos pitcher remembers the house phone number was 747-7614.

"I remember I took my first grade with the kindergarten kids," he told me. "I remember I took French in the first grade. I took it every class. I went to Precious Blood Catholic School on Pharmacy Avenue

"I have three older sisters and an older brother and all of us were born at Toronto General Hospital. My sisters Patricia, Mary and Theresa and myself were given vital Bible names and Wilfred got grandpa's name. I remember we used to have a cabin at Orr Lake (Muskoka). All my family is from Madoc, Ontario. My dad came from England."

His father Paul was employed by the Lewis Refrigeration company in Toronto and his mother Aileen Tobin worked as a registered nurse after she graduated from St. Michael's College of Nursing in Toronto in 1952.

I've always been curious about why Wainhouse left Scarborough for the state of Washington at such a young age. Now, I know. His dad's work took him there.

His mother was born in Madoc east of Toronto on May 17, 1933 and grew up on a farm with her parents and six siblings. She married Paul in 1955.

In 1973, all of a sudden, Paul's company transferred him, a vice-president, to Seattle when Dave was very young – six years old. So Paul, 44, Aileen, 40, and the kids packed up and moved to the Pacific Northwest.

"We all flew out. I learned to tie my shoes right before that, so I guess I was showing a lot of the passengers my new trick for a lot of the flight," Wainhouse said, chuckling.

What was astonishing to hear was Wainhouse played only hockey in Scarborough. There were no other sports he played.

Wainhouse was born in 1967, the year the Triple-A Toronto Maple Leafs were moved out of town and 10 years before the Blue Jays started operations. Sadly, there was no professional baseball at all in Hogtown for 10 years until the Jays were awarded a franchise that began play in 1977. That's right.

"I never heard of baseball. The Jays weren't there. The only sport I ever heard of was hockey. I played street hockey with the neighbourhood kids. I'm the only Canadian who can't play ice hockey," he said, somewhat in jest, although he did skate a bit with Mark McGwire and Jim Edmonds of the Cardinals.

When the Wainhouse clan moved to Mercer Island in Washington State, it wasn't long after that when Dave was introduced to baseball, and he also saw a lot of kids playing football in the streets.

"Right away, I was into American sports. Every kid was playing baseball. I started out in T-ball. Mercer Island is a smallish community. All my friends played. I played all sports, soccer, baseball, basketball until Mercer Island high school," Wainhouse told me.

While growing up, Wainhouse grew to love the Pittsburgh Pirates, not his hometown Mariners, because they were often seen on national television, the NBC Game of the Week, whatever.

The Bucs have been around forever. Wainhouse knew they were an institution. He admired their history. They had charisma, style and brand name power. They had won the World Series in 1979. Roberto Clemente died in a plane crash when Wainhouse was seven, but he still had plenty of people to root for: Willie Stargell, Manny Sanguillén, Dave Parker, Bill Virdon, Dave Cash, but none other than somebody who worked out of the bullpen. Somebody who threw submarine style, whose fashion sense grabbed the attention of baseball in 1979.

"I really loved Kent Tekulve. I loved him and his pillbox hat," Wainhouse said. "I always wore that pillbox hat."

It's probably no wonder Wainhouse wanted to be a pitcher, just like Tekulve, although he never did throw underhand.

"I was a pitcher, but I played all positions," Wainhouse said. "Catching was actually my favourite position. I loved catching in high school. I loved throwing guys out. I wanted to do it more, but I was pitching."

"I didn't make the varsity team until my senior year. In the ninth grade, I was cut from the program. I love baseball and baseball history. Nolan Ryan was kind of not planning to play in college. I didn't plan on college baseball, when I was done playing high school. I figured I was done.

"I joined Washington State University as a walk-on, blessed with a really good arm. I didn't have a scholarship. I wasn't recruited by anyone until I saw Bobo Bryant, the head coach at Washington State. He saw me in a game, and I had a really good game.

"I pitched and swung and hit the ball well that day. He got my number. He called me and he said, 'We have tryouts. Bring your glove and spikes.' That was in August of 1985.

"In my junior year, I caught the eye of scouts. I started throwing 95 instead of 85. I had a great arm. I had great arm strength.

"I owe John Olerud. Scouts would say, 'Who is that redhead throwing 95 miles per hour?' If it wasn't for John, I would have had no exposure. I give thanks every single time because of John. I got noticed because scouts were coming in to see John hit every single ball. I played with him in my sophomore and junior years. I played at Washington State from 1986-88 and Olerud was there from 1987-89."

Line-drive hitting Olerud, a member of the Canadian Baseball Hall of Fame and a prominent Blue Jays player for many years, was phenom-

Wainhouse only Canadian picked in first round of draft

Courtesy WSU Athletics
John Olerud

Courtesy WSU Athletics
Dave Wainhouse

And who should go in the first round of the draft ahead of Snyder? Wainhouse was taken by the Expos as the first and only Canadian-born player to ever be taken in the first round and the highest-ever draft pick out of WSU.

To this day, no Canadian has been selected in the first round of the draft since Wainhouse. You're talking more than 35 years since Wainer was picked by Montreal. Many Canadians have been selected in the draft over the years, but none have gone in the first round. Quite a trivia item for Wainhouse.

The Cubs showed undue interest in Wainhouse and he took their aptitude tests. He doesn't remember the backyard Mariners showing any love for him.

"The Detroit Tigers – I talked with some of their people at the field. The Cubs had a well-known scout, Andy Peony. I got their business cards. I didn't really know anything about the Expos. I'd never spoken to an Expos' scout,"Wainhouse said.

"I'd taken those aptitude tests for other scouts, and I met with other scouts. Then 15 minutes before the draft started, I got a call from Whitey DeHart, an area scout in the Pacific Northwest for the Expos. He said, 'If we take you in the first round, will you sign?'"

"It was weird. Crazy, eh? They were one of the teams that had never talked to me. I was excited to be drafted by the Expos. By that time, I wanted to play baseball. I'm doing it. It became a real passion for me. I wanted to go and play.

"I remember the day I signed and what I was wearing when Whitey came over. I have the picture of me and him hanging on the kitchen wall. I was still fairly skinny. I was pretty tanned. After I came back from the trip with Team Canada, I wasn't that skinny. I gained all that weight on the trip."

1988 was a momentous year for Wainhouse in more ways than one. He played in the spring for Washington State, was drafted in June, Team Canada came calling to have him pitch in numerous tournaments abroad for his home country, including the Olympics, and he finished off with Instructional league tutoring in Florida to begin his Expos' apprenticeship.

"I couldn't sign to be a professional with the understanding I was going to extended spring training in October," Wainhouse explained. "I signed in my house, in our living room. I signed back then for $125,000. Andy Benes, the No. 1 overall pick, got $250,000.

"It was done pretty quick. It wasn't hard. It didn't take long. Back then, there were no million-dollar offers. It was nothing to break the bank – I just wanted to go play. They made me an offer and I doubled their offer. We were both happy. We agreed on everything. I also talked with Dan Duquette, Dave Dombrowski and Bill Stoneman from the front office.

"That was a thrill for me. I wasn't recruited by anybody," Wainhouse said about his relatively unknown status. "I could not be considered a professional for the Olympics. I had to risk a bit because if I had signed, if I gotten hurt, I was in trouble."

So, shortly after the draft, he joined Team Canada. Once he had signed with the Expos, Wainhouse worked out with the national team for close to three months in Waterloo, Ontario.

"Greg Hunter, our shortstop, was a guy they wanted to try out for the team, but they found out he wasn't Canadian (Baseball Reference does list him as born in Vancouver, B.C.)," Wainhouse said. "So, I got a number for coach Bernie Beckman and called him. He didn't know squat about me. Bernie told me, 'It's not an open tryout and we have a list of guys. Let me ask you a few questions.' He did some research and called me back. He didn't know I was Canadian."

Just like Wainhouse, Beckman grew up in Scarborough, so they had something in common.

Beckman was actually born in the Netherlands, but his family surfaced in Scarborough when he was a young kid. He played in Scarborough's Birchmount league for the most part and was encouraged by scout Bruce Prentice at age 11 to keep working hard at baseball and then Prentice's brother Bobby signed him for Detroit.

"Bob Prentice did everything he could to develop me mentally and technically. I attended tryouts in Guelph vs. Intercounty league guys. He never pressured me and with the likes of John Hiller, Mike Kilkenny, and George Korince, I felt the Tigers would be patient with a green Canadian kid and I signed with them in September of 1967 at age 16," Beckman said.

Beckman never made it to the majors but spent 1968-76 in America's minor leagues and played semi-pro in the Netherlands for several years before he took up coaching. One of his early pupils was Wainhouse.

"I was working at the National Baseball Institute in Vancouver as Baseball Canada's High-Performance Director and pitching coach," Beckman told me in June, 2023. "I was assembling our potential 1988 Olympic team, and I contacted all USA schools (2,400) to find any Canadian players or ancestorial Canadians that were playing in all USA conferences. I found 224 Canadians with citizenship or dual.

"Well, I did get a letter from Dave's mom, and I followed up on him and his successes at WSU."

This homework by Beckman came at a time when major-league teams were looking at potential players for the 1988 draft. Beckman had been on the lookout for prospects months and months before the draft to find players for the Olympics scheduled for Seoul, South Korea, beginning on Sept. 17 but also for the pre-Olympics tournaments abroad.

Remember that some cuts were made prior to the Olympics. One of them was Rod Heisler of Moose Jaw, Saskatchewan, who had pitched internationally for Canada for many years. The team photo you see in this chapter was taken prior to or during the tryout camp at the University of Waterloo. Heisler is in that photo in the back row.

"David was touted to become a No. 1 pick in the draft. I contacted him and his family and asked if he would be interested and he never hesitated to try out for Team Canada," Beckman said. "So here is a diamond in the rough and the Expos gave permission for him to play after they selected him No. 1.

"Dave was one class act, who never flaunted his draft status. His personality was just 'one of the guys' and fit in perfectly as a team player for all drills and literally never complained one bit. Teammates and coaches felt we had a class guy with willingness to do any chore or put up with any kind of accommodations presented to us throughout our world tour before the Olympics in Seoul," Beckman continued.

"I went to the training camp at the University of Waterloo in early July for about two weeks," Wainhouse said. "There were 25-40 guys at tryouts. They had to cut a lot of guys.

"I was one of the worst pitchers there. I was not in shape, I was not ready for competition, I was not good at the training camp. I had a leg up because I was a first-round pick."

Team Canada started off its summer tour of games leading to Seoul by playing in a tournament in the Netherlands metropolis of Haarlem. It was a tune-up, and the team stayed their 12 days or so. It was a homecoming for Beckman, who was born in the Netherlands, a chance for him to meet up with relatives and friends from yesteryear.

"We stayed in the resort of Zandvoort in condos on the beach. It was phenomenal. The beaches were topless. Matt and I walked up and down that beach," Wainhouse said, presumably with a smile on his face. "It was great. We hung out at the bars, and we bonded."

Then it was off to Italy for what was called the Baseball World Cup, which Wainhouse preferred to call the world championship.

"That was way more serious," Wainhouse said. "Cuba was a big-league team at every position. It was a great experience for a young man. We had meals in restaurants in little towns. We were there for 15-17 days. It was a very long trip. We ate so much. They fed us so much. I looked down and I gained 15 pounds there."

Teammate Marc Griffin said what he "remembered most about Wainhouse" was that he was a "very funny" guy and had "a great arm and, if I remember correctly, he was wild, giving up a lot of walks." Beckman viewed him as a "real competitor", who wasn't adverse to sticking up for his mates.

"That carefree personality changed. One game in Italy vs. Japan, one of our players got hit by a pitch and then the first hitter Dave faced really got hit with a fastball in the ribs," Beckman said. "In short, he was all business with a major-league fastball in the low 90s and solid breaking stuff to compliment his changeup.

"He had good composure and confidence, and you could just see his calibre as a No. 1 pick compared to the USA team which also has several No. 1 picks (nine)."

Then Japan beckoned. It was timely and essential because it allowed Team Canada to get used to the same time zone as Seoul.

In Japan, Wainhouse and the Team Canada crew always wore team clothing while out and about because of a political controversy which saw the U.S. being despised by Japan.

"The U.S. received death threats in Asia and Japan," Wainhouse said. "Whenever we went out, we wore our Canadian jersey and the big maple Leaf. The U.S. team had to go to a special part of the hotel through a stairwell with a lot of security. We had just normal rooms.

"Then I go to the Olympics for 12 days and it was the most boring part of the trip, but it was a great honour. It was super cool. I still have my Olympic pin," he said. "Me and Rhéal were the top two guys."

Team Canada lost all three games it played – 7-6 to Australia, 8-7 to the U.S. and 5-3 to South Korea. I could never get anyone from Baseball Canada, the Canadian Olympic Association or the World Baseball Federation to supply me with statistics from Seoul. All I got were scores and the participating countries. Maybe it was because it was a demonstration sport.

"I threw against South Korea. I pitched okay. I was competitive. They just beat me," Wainhouse said. "There were 15 guys in that tournament that played in the majors. That U.S. team was loaded, they were that good. Andy Benes pitched for them."

After close to three months of training and playing in various compe-

Wainhouse only Canadian picked in first round of draft

This is Team Canada that participated in various tournaments in 1988. Front row, left to right: Alan Mauthe, Matt Stairs, business manager Harve Bailie, assistant coach John Upham, head coach Bernie Beckman, assistant coach Jim Ridley, trainer Harold (Doc) Younker, Ricky Johnston and Dave Rypien. Second row: Rob Butler, Marc Griffin, Randy Curran, Greg O'Halloran, Bill Byckowski, Peter Hoy, Bullet Bob Bridges, Frank Humber, Dave Wainhouse, Warren Sawkiw and Gregory Duce. Back row: Greg Roth, Tom Nelson, Jim Kotkas, Rod Heisler, Stewart Hillman, Barry Parisotto and Rheal Cormier. Heisler and Bridges were released before the team went to the Seoul Olympics. This photo was taken during the tryout camp in Waterloo, Ontario.

Courtesy Marc Griffin & Baseball

titions, Wainhouse took a long flight home, with stopovers, from Seoul to Seattle but his baseball year wasn't complete. He relaxed a bit and "basically unpacked" before packing again for a flight to West Palm Beach for the Instructional league which lasted about a month until "about Halloween."

The Expos shared Municipal Stadium with the Atlanta Braves and inevitably, they played each other almost every day. He'd run into Ryan Klesko "all the time" while he was there.

"The Instructional league was very, very controlled. In one inning, I'd throw nine change-ups," he said, citing an example of the "controlled" environment.

This first-time apprenticeship in pro ball was an "eye opener" for Wainhouse. There were a lot of repetitions. The Expos and all other clubs would do much the same thing to introduce players to the pro ranks through Instructional league play. Just what the word Instructional says, the player is getting instructed in various categories in his first foray into pro ball.

The reps are tedious, but they made sense.

"I remember throwing a change-up and a guy hit a home run off me," Wainhouse said. "I remember Larry Walker was there. He had-had knee surgery. I remember Chris Nabholz and Greg Colbrunn were there."

In the spring of 1989, as part of his contract/signing bonus chat with DeHart, he lobbied successfully for a special consideration, something most players aren't granted. Most draft picks aren't invited to the major-league camp for several years.

"I wanted a spring-training invite. It was fairly common for a high pick to get right away," Wainhouse said. "I wanted that. It was really important to get in front of the big-league people, the higher-ups, as early as I could. It wasn't hard (to get the concession)."

Following this spring-training performance, Wainhouse started his official pro career in the Florida State League, a structured fashion in the form of regular-season play. The league and the facility at West Palm were "major league all the time."

"This was the highest A ball they had. In Rockford, Illinois and the whole Midwest league, they had pretty shitty fields. Just awful," Wainhouse said.

Wainhouse was unremarkable in 1989 with a 1-5 record.

Typically, though, those kinds of early results didn't bother the Expos. Same goes for prospects for most teams. The baptism may not be great and so, the club and the player hope for better things.

Most importantly, Wainhouse ran into one of the greatest managers he ever played for.

"Get this, my manager was Felipe Alou. I have been blessed. I've had such great managers as Felipe, Tony La Russa, Jim Leyland, Lou Piniella and Don Baylor. They were all unbelievable," Wainhouse said. "Felipe was probably the most knowledgeable of all. He was the most amazing of all. He was a special manager. He was so good. He was so incredible. His brain was so good. He taught a lot of people. I was just blessed."

In 1990, Wainhouse excelled in two markets: 6-3 with West Palm,

Wainhouse only Canadian picked in first round of draft

7-7 in Jacksonville Double A. That was the kind of production the Expos' brass wanted to see: improvement. During his time in Florida, he would occasionally go with some teammates and go deep-sea fishing with Expos scouting director Gary Hughes, who often had a cigar in his hand.

Wainhouse made this improvement in his record despite an uncomfortable injury.

"I got biceps tendinitis. I got shut down for two months. I kept playing. I had to. I slipped in the mud and put my arm in a really bad spot. It was a freak accident at our season opener in Port St. Lucie. The field was a mess," Wainhouse said.

Wainhouse started the 1991 season with Harrisburg Double-A, going 2-2 in 52 innings of work. Promoted to Indianapolis Triple-A, he was 2-0. What was dramatic about that season was that Wainhouse was sent to the bullpen. The Expos felt he was better out of the pen.

"I asked to go back to the bullpen," Wainhouse chimed in. "I was a closer at Washington State. I asked to go back to the bullpen because my back couldn't handle starting pitching. I could barely walk after I pitched (as a starter). I never did tell anyone about my back.

"It was in Harrisburg where I took off with my stuff," he said. "In my first three games at Triple-A, I went three perfect innings over nine days and then I was called up to Montreal."

With those elite performances, Wainhouse was being looked at seriously, his stock was growing and soon, the special call came.

His Indy manager was Pat Kelly, and the pitching coach was Nardi Contreras. One day, a Monday, the 2nd of August, they summoned Wainhouse into Kelly's office and Wainhouse didn't know what to expect but he did know he wanted to bring up the issue of his Triple-A contract.

"They called me in the fucking office after a game," he said. "I had played for Indianapolis on my Double-A contract, and I wanted a $150 raise, and they said no. I said, 'What about this raise?' I had asked Kent Qualls for a raise. He was the minor-league coordinator. I was promoted from Double-A to Triple-A without a pay increase. I was playing on my Double-A contract. There was no serious negotiation about a pay increase.

"They (Kelly and Contreras) said in the meeting I had a Triple-A contract to sign. They brought me in and said, 'You have to sign that contract. You have to be under contract. If you sign it, I'll give you this envelope.' They called my bluff. They had fun with it."

Wainhouse opened up the envelope and in it was the shock of his life: A first-class air ticket to Montreal for Aug. 3.

It's the dream for any prospect to play in the majors and Wainhouse was finally doing it. All the sacrifices he had made for so many years in playing baseball since he was a kid had finally paid off – his goal was being realized.

"You're going to the big leagues," Kelly told Wainhouse and they hugged each other. And Wainhouse and Contreras also hugged. Wainhouse told Kelly he was no longer worried about a pay increase. He was receiving major-league money from Montreal.

Exposion

"There was a pay phone by the locker room, and I called my parents," he said. "I stayed with (teammate) Richie Lewis that night. Him and I were close friends. I lived with him at his parents' house about an hour and 15 minutes away in Muncie. Then I had to go back to my apartment to pack up my stuff. I get back to Indy and basically, I had no sleep.

"I took my car to the ballpark and Nardi drove me to the airport about 6 in the morning. I flew to Montreal and got to the clubhouse, and they told me, 'Can you walk around the stadium outside?' They said to come back later. They were releasing a veteran to make room for me. They were letting go a very well-respected veteran, a clubhouse favourite and they didn't want me around. I felt awful. Out of respect, they didn't want me around until they had dealt with that guy and until he said his good-byes and he was gone."

That veteran was Dave Schmidt, 35, a reliever who had spent most of 1990 with the Expos but appeared in only a few games in 1991 before he was released. He was at the end of his career. So, it was a 1-for-deal: Schmidt was out, Wainhouse was in.

It's always tough for the manager and general manager to cut someone but somebody has to do it and Wainhouse was the beneficiary.

"I'd gotten to know Dave Schmidt at spring training," Wainhouse said. "Here's some sensitive information – this was the worst part – they gave me his number and they sewed his number on my jersey. That was common. That was my first introduction to the big leagues."

After a whirlwind trip, butterflies, anxiety and no sleep, Wainhouse was pressed into action late in a matinee game on the day he arrived, Aug. 3. About 3 p.m., he took over from starter Brian Barnes in the top of the eighth inning with the Phillies leading 6-1.

"The only thing I could hear in that stadium was that big plastic horn and the echo," Wainhouse said. "I was sleepless. I had no sleep. I didn't go to bed. I had so much adrenalin, serious adrenalin. You could be wired. You don't need sleep to be focused, which isn't uncommon talking to people. The first few days you are pretty tired."

As a beat writer for the Ottawa Sun, I was there for Wainhouse's debut, which made us Canadians mighty proud in the press box.

Wainhouse did fine the first inning, pitching scoreless ball. The ninth inning wasn't so great because he threw two wild pitches and the Phillies scored a run. He had been wild earlier in his career and this was another case of it.

In his next appearance, this time in Philadelphia on Aug. 6 following an off-day, he walked three guys in one inning. He couldn't find the strike zone much.

"I was nervous as hell. I was trying to throw the ball a million miles per hour," he said of his wildness in trying to impress. "I walked (pitcher) Mitch Williams on four pitches."

Wainhouse did manage to strike out Dale Murphy, the Atlanta Braves great, who looked out of place in a Phillies uniform in the dying days of his illustrious career. Wainhouse wasn't used in any games after that and then manager Tom Runnells sent him back to Indianapolis on Aug. 11. Wainhouse didn't argue with Runnells because he had little leverage.

Runnells had taken over from beloved Buck Rodgers two months earlier, but TR's presence did little to improve the team.

"I was pissed. I felt I got a bit of a shaft there, but I think I deserved it (demotion). It was a really embarrassing outing (Aug. 6). It was all my fault. The Expos were dead last, and Tom Runnells was fighting to save his job because everyone hated him. Nobody liked TR," Wainhouse said.

Little did he know but Wainhouse never pitched in the majors again for Montreal. He spent the entire 1992 season in Triple-A, and he was pleased with a "really good year except that I hyperextended my left knee and ripped all my cartilage out. I felt like shit. My knee had doubled in size."

Wainhouse required surgery in Montreal done by orthopedic surgeon Dr. Larry Coughlin. He said the operation was akin to putting a "fishing rod in your knee." Here's how Wainhouse suffered the knee injury.

"I stepped in a hole fishing that day. There was a little pond outside my apartment complex," he said. "I was looking to deep-sea fish. I tore my knee up, but I put my uniform on, and I got on the field. When I came in off the field, my knee is killing me. I went straight to the hospital and then on a plane to Montreal.

"Funny part of that story is that I was leading the league in saves (21). I was the best pitcher on our club. I was putting up great numbers. I was supposed to be called up that night by Montreal. What terrible timing. There's nothing in your contract that you can't fish. If I was riding a motorcycle, it would be different."

That fall, he went back to Instructional league to get more innings of work in and then he was traded. He was staying with one of his sisters in Seattle when he heard he was on the move. The date was Nov. 20, 1992. He got a call from Dan Duquette. The Expos' experiment with Wainhouse was over. The first-round pick was gone. His tenure with Montreal at the major-league level was short – only two games.

The first-round prospect, a Canadian born in Toronto, was no longer with the Expos.

"Are you sitting down?" Duquette asked Wainhouse.

"You just got traded to Seattle," Duquette said.

"I was so ecstatic. He knew I would be excited," Wainhouse said. "I grew up a Mariners' fan. I had tickets to the very first Mariners game. I'd catch home run balls. The Mariners' stadium was five minutes from my driveway."

Like his time with Montreal, his tenure with Seattle was short-lived. This time, it was back surgery, and he missed a year.

During his time at WSU, he incurred the back injury when he slipped while working out in a gymnasium. He didn't hurt him so much at the time. It was discovered to be more serious in 1990 but it "wasn't a big deal." Wainhouse said. It got worse in 1991 but it didn't affect him during his brief time with the Expos and when it did hurt, "I was hiding it."

Wainhouse was getting treated for his sore back and he was "still climbing the ladder" in the pro ranks.

"I know the exact moment I hurt my back. That's when I landed on

Exposion

the floor of the gym," Wainhouse explained. "You know those little pads, like mattresses, with soft rubber cushions? My heel hit on it, and I landed flying backward on my shoulder. It didn't affect me at that point. It was a non-issue.

"That happened in January of 1988. I was never as forthcoming about how much I was hurting. I refused to miss any baseball games. I've never been to a chiropractor. At spring training in 1994, my back is killing me to the point it's affecting my life," he said.

So more than six years after he hurt his back in the gym, it was time to have an operation.

"In May of 1994, I was with the Mariners at the time," Wainhouse said. "Dr. Robert Watkins of USC was the only guy I wanted, the only one allowed to do the surgery. He was the doctor of the stars. They got me a room at Cedars-Sinai Hospital. He gave me the Robert Redford Special. They were cleaning up the room when Redford was leaving so I could move in. He was in there just before me.

"They took a piece of bone out of my hip and put it in my spine. It was a big operation. I spent five days in hospital and then another five days in a hotel. I had to stay until my surgeon released me to go home," he said.

"A few months after the surgery was over and after the healing process, they were saying the hardware used in my spine surgery was not approved for spine surgery. So, the company that made the hardware flew me to Washington, D.C. so I could testify before the Food and Drug Administration. I testified that my surgery was fine. There were some people in there saying it had screwed up their backs.

"So, I missed the 1994 season. The 1995 season – I wasn't ready to play. I had signed with Toronto (Dec. 20, 1994). My back wasn't ready."

Wainhouse did get into 24.1 innings for Syracuse AAA for Toronto and was 3-2 with a 3.70 ERA. He was elated that he was "player of the month" before he was released. That summer, he also pitched in Charlotte Triple-A for the Marlins.

"I was trying to learn now to throw after 1995. I almost quit. I was almost done. Then the Pirates gave me a chance in 1996,"Wainhouse said. "An x-ray had shown how much my spine had slipped."

Just like he was with the Expos and Mariners, Wainhouse didn't fare out that good with the Pirates, but he sure loved putting on the uniform of the team he grew up loving while living on Mercer Island. He didn't get to wear the pillow hat, but he was beaming.

When he went to spring training with the Pirates in Bradenton, Florida in 1996, who should he run into but Stargell, who was there as a guest coach.

"In the dining room at lunch time, eating, I was sitting with Stargell and Dave Parker. Three days in a row. Stargell called me Wainwright. I'd been called Wainwright before by a lot by coaches my whole life. But if you're Willie Stargell, you can call me anything. Sitting next to him is something I will never, ever forget. It was a special honour."

Wainhouse also remembers with exhilaration the time he struck out Canadian Larry Walker of the Rockies.

Wainhouse only Canadian picked in first round of draft

The date was May 8, 1997. This chat about this highlight came in the second phase of two long interviews I had with Wainhouse, who admitted there were "15 more things we never talked about" in our chats. The second conversation was done to put some things into "better context"', especially the back injury.

"The highest moment of my entire career involved another Canadian,"' Wainhouse said. "I was with Pittsburgh, and we were in Colorado and Jim Leyland was the Pirates' manager. Jim Leyland was always in my corner. I also pitched for him in Colorado.

"We were up two runs, we had two out and it's the bottom of the seventh. Bases loaded. Chris Peters is the lefty on the mound. He goes 2-0 on Larry Walker. I was warming up. I was a left-handed specialist, rather than against righties. I got lefties out. You had to be ready with Leyland. He liked to have arms loose. He always had guys warming up."

To put this scenario into perspective, Dante Bichette had drawn a bases-loaded walk just before Walker came up. In a shocker, Leyland motions for Wainhouse to come from the bullpen and takes the ball from Peters.

Leyland wanted Wainhouse to come in relief to pitch to Walker on a 2-0 count! Leyland knew Wainhouse's strengths.

It's very rare that managers take out pitchers in the middle of an at-bat.

Facing one of the game's greatest stars was a challenge for Wainhouse, but he was ready for it. They were teammates briefly in Montreal in 1991 and then were mates for short periods in both 1998 and 1999 with the Rockies. Wainhouse knew how talented No. 33 was.

"Fucking Larry Walker," Wainhouse said. "Jim Leyland gave me the ball. There was a shitload of people there (48,050). I throw him three sliders and I strike him out. I threw him simply nothing but sliders. The slider was my pitch. It was the highest point of my career. I should have quit. I wish I had not gone back out. I should have walked away. I should have been done for the day.

"Larry Walker –I'd pay money to watch him play defence, let alone watch him hit. He changed the game defensively. He was special on a baseball field."

Wainhouse went back out and gave up two runs after he fanned Walker, but the Pirates hung on to beat the Rockies 10-8.

Wainhouse retired in 2000 and for many years, he has been a baseball coach in the Seattle area. He appeared in 85 MLB games, all in relief, with the Expos, Mariners, Rockies and Cardinals. He was 2-3 with a 7.37 ERA in 105 innings. He didn't record a save. He was around long enough to qualify for the MLB pension.

At the end of his career, Wainhouse realized that not only did injuries curtail his career, but he was also facing another dilemma: his mental approach to the game.

It's one thing to have good stuff and mechanics, but if your head isn't in the game to face big-league hitters, the results might not be pretty.

"With Montreal, I peaked in their possession at a certain point. I could pitch and dominate in Triple-A. I loved competing. Every ball I threw had a price tag on it," he said. "I couldn't pitch for money.

"Mentally, I could not perform at the big-league level. I wasn't strong enough mentally to perform. Physically, I could have the best stuff but mentally, I couldn't do it in a big-league game. Those guys in the majors are good.

"I could have played a lot longer throwing as hard as I could. When a decision is being made on my career, it's based on age, not skill. In my last year, I had a spring-training invite to the Cubs' camp. I turned down a better offer from Japan. The pay was double in Japan.

"I pitched in Triple-A Des Moines, Iowa and when I wasn't called up, this isn't it for me," he said. "I have no regrets."

Looking back, Wainhouse looks to Stairs as his favourite friend along the way. Starting with Waterloo and the topless beaches of Zandvoort, Wainhouse played with him during that long swing through Netherlands, Italy, Japan and Korea but also in the early going of his pro career in the minor leagues with Rockford, West Palm and Jacksonville –but not with the Expos.

"Matt and I were very close," Wainhouse said. "I was pretty close to him for years. I was also close with Chris Nabholz, Reid Nichols, Greg Colbrunn and Brian Barnes."

What is really very interesting and very nice is that Wainhouse has kept his Canadian citizenship and whenever he needs to travel outside the U.S., he goes with his Canadian passport. The kid from Scarborough sure hasn't forgotten his roots.

"I am a Canadian," he said proudly. "I want to be known as a Canadian. I have a Green Card. I haven't been outside the U.S. for 20 years. Neither one of us like to travel, but I have to renew my passport through the mail to go to Europe for a wedding (2024)."

Wainhouse was more than generous with his time with me. On top of those long chats, we did many follow-ups by text message or email. This kind of information he has never given out before to anyone, saying, "I never talk about my past."

I was so grateful that Wainhouse would open up his heart with information and comments.

Chapter 27

Perms, masks and The Cy Young Catcher

Charlie O'Brien elevated perms to a new level of fashion, caught 13 Cy Young players, was a solid defensive catcher and was a mask innovator.

He achieved a lot in his month-long tenure with the Expos in 2000. His goal was to be playing in the majors at age 40 and he wanted to play in three decades. He accomplished both with Montreal.

I got a hold of O'Brien's book The Cy Young Catcher in November of 2023 from his publisher, Texas A & M University Press. O'Brien got help in writing the book from brother-in-law Doug Wedge, an attorney and a clerk in the U.S. Bankruptcy Court in the Western District of Oklahoma, and author of other books, most notably Baseball in Alabama.

O'Brien goes into detail in the book about his time with Montreal in the final chapter called Conclusion, which aptly nailed it on the head for his career. His stint with Montreal concluded his career.

On Feb. 4, 2000, he received an invite to Montreal's major-league camp and he stayed with the team all through February and March but was sidetracked on March 19 when he strained an arch while jogging the bases after he hit a home run.

Canadian Baseball Hall of Fame
Charlie O'Brien

"I tore my plantar fascia ligament again," O'Brien said in his book, explaining the arch problem. "That set me back. If I hadn't have gotten hurt, I think I would've have made it through the season. But the injury held me back. Kept me in Jupiter, Florida for extended spring training.

"Going in to spring training, I figured that would be my last year in the big leagues. I figured right."

On April 2, just as the MLB regular season was about to begin, he was assigned to minor-league camp on the day fellow catcher Lenny Webster signed a major-league contract for his third go-round with Montreal.

O'Brien took the move in stride and reported to Double-A Harrisburg and was rewarded with a promotion to the majors on May 25 when

Exposion

catcher Chris Widger went down with a left-hand contusion.

"To be honest, Montreal was a nightmare. There was such a language barrier where most folks speak French," O'Brien wrote for the book. "They were in the process of selling the team. There was all sorts of talk about moving the team because attendance was so bad.

"We played in Olympic Stadium. Huge place. Sometimes, it felt like there were 100 people in the stadium. It was just miserable. Hard place to stay motivated."

On June 22, less than a month after he was called up, O'Brien was summoned to manager Felipe Alou's office at the Big O.

"Hey, Charlie, we're bringing up a pitcher. We're going to let you go. Do you want to be the bullpen coach?" Alou asked O'Brien. "We'd love to have you stay in coaching."

That's one revelation I found in O'Brien's book: he was offered the opportunity to stay around and be the bullpen coach. He would continue to be part of the team and make a contribution in helping out the pitching staff. He decided not to take Alou up on his offer but his book gave some insight in how he was feeling on being released.

He mentioned getting his 1995 World Series ring from the Braves with a drop-off at his house from a UPS delivery man. He thought that was odd and cold. Same with leaving the Expos and baseball.

What happened on June 7 against the Yankees in Montreal didn't help O'Brien's cause. Five New York runners stole bases on him.

"Somebody telling you that you're not good enough anymore. You kind of want to slink out of the clubhouse and not have anybody notice you leave," he said of being cut.

O'Brien had brought his two sons, Chris and Cameron, into the lockerroom that day. They were playing video games with Vladimir Guerrero when Papa stepped out of Alou's office.

"Boys, we gotta get out of here," O'Brien told his sons.

"Why aren't we staying here?" they asked, not understanding the situation.

"They're letting me go. They just told me they didn't want me anymore."

The O'Briens packed up and headed home to the family's Catch-22 ranch that encompasses about 1,000 acres outside Tulsa. Always a country boy – that's O'Brien.

Like he did as a catcher for three decades when he played the dirtiest position on the field, he loves wearing denim clothes, high rubber boots, cowboy hat and hunting and being a cattleman, pitching hay and straw and stepping into poo and whatever it takes.

Despite his bad game on June 7, what I found remarkable about O'Brien is that he threw out 37% of runners trying to steal throughout his career, beating the average of 31%. In 1990 in a combo season with the Brewers and Mets, the percentage was a mighty 45.7, a statistic he proudly points out in his bio at the back of his book.

His fielding percentage lifetime was a solid .990, he committed only 47 errors in 4,884 chances and he allowed only 21 passed balls in 782 games. His defensive work outdid his somewhat mediocre offence.

Perms, masks and The Cy Young Catcher

O'Brien, Ron Hassey, Gary Carter and Brian Schneider are four Expos catchers, that I know of through my research, who recorded a hit in their last time at the plate for the Expos. Crazy trivia. They went out with a bang on a positive note.

The day before he was released, O'Brien singled to right in his last at-bat, Ron Hassey hit a pinch-hit single in his last AB Sept. 3, 1991, Carter famously doubled Sept. 27, 1992 and Brian Schneider did the trick Oct. 1, 2004.

As for those Cy Young claims, The Baker's Dozen were Pete Vukovich, David Cone, Frank Viola, Dwight Gooden, Bret Saberhagen, John Smoltz, Greg Maddux, Tom Glavine, Chris Carpenter, Jack McDowell, Steve Bedrosian, Pat Hentgen and Roger Clemens.

In the case of Vukovich, O'Brien caught him in spring training. That was enough for O'Brien to be able to say he caught a Cy Young winner in Vuke.

O'Brien talks like a brilliant scientist throughout the book, laying out a path of explanation for how he dealt with all 13 pitchers and their quirks. He had to be a mediator to deal with various personalities and figure out what pitches should be thrown.

O'Brien took it in stride when Gooden teased him during a conversation in the Mets' clubhouse about his unusual hair.

"We'd flip each other shit. He made fun of me, saying I was the only white catcher in the league with curly hair, that I had a Jheri-curl," O'Brien said of Gooden in his oft-hilarious book.

As far as I know, O'Brien and Carter (short period) were the only Montreal catchers who were enamoured with short perms. O'Brien has been a perm guy since the 1990s.

The Irishman from Oklahoma was also a pioneer, an innovator, a groundbreaker when it came to improving the lot of catchers with better head-gear protection. The model or a facsimile of the facemask used by most catchers today originated with O'Brien's work in getting something approved while he was with the Blue Jays. He began wearing a mask approved by MLB on Sept. 13, 1996 when he was with Toronto.

O'Brien said he first told Toronto radio reporter Bruce Barker of his idea and Barker put him in touch with Eric Niskanen of Van Velden's Masks out of the Canadian city of Hamilton, Ontario located south of Toronto by about an hour.

Owner Jerry Van Velden had begun tinkering with goaltender masks when he was 16 years old so he knew what he was doing.

"We worked with Charlie. We helped him get started on a concept. It was fun. Glad we were able to do something," said Van Velden, who currently operates a waterproofing company called Rubber Shield Ltd.

O'Brien and Niskanen first met in the Jays' clubhouse and then they brought along their wives for another meeting to lay the groundwork for a special mask, one that was easy to keep on, if a catcher was running off for a foul/fair ball, one that provided protection around the jaw line where catchers normally didn't have much protection.

And there had to be shielding behind the mask and the chin cup was padded to make it more than adequate. The ears had to be protected.

Exposion

"Bruce Barker was a friend of mine and he knew I was involved with a goalie-mask manufacturing company," Niskanen explained. "He said Charlie was looking for a hockey mask. I thought it might be something for a kid, not thinking it was for baseball. The next day, the Toronto Sun had a little note about it. I asked Bruce who the Sun was referring to and he said, 'They're talking about you.'

"Funny part of the story is that all the goalie-mask manufacturers read the article. They were all trying to put something together for baseball. When I sat down with Charlie, he said, 'I don't care about money. I want to get involved with a better item for catchers.' He loved the fact we were from a very small company."

Niskanen went back to his employer and got someone to make up a prototype mask with some adjustments. Then there was the issue of getting approval from MLB's rules committee and marketing department.

Van Velden Masks presented several different prototypes to O'Brien. Getting the OK from MLB wasn't easy. There were several rejections.

O'Brien and Niskanen then decided to approach the Canadian Standards Association (CSA) for testing of his proposed mask. During that meeting, the duo met Henry Tran, who is currently the organization's senior engineering technologist and certification specialist.

Tran told me CSA offered certification and testing for bicycle helmets, hockey helmets, motorcycle helmets, actually all kinds of helmets but did not have a certification program per se for what he called "back catcher masks for baseball."

What a CSA laboratory technician did at CSA's testing facility in Rexdale, Ontario which is Niskanen's hometown, was to drop a mask connected to a computer, instead of a ball hitting the mask on the stationary baseball test fixture. Physics was involved in this scenario.

"During the testing, the impact point is right at the front of the mask which is at eye level," the official said. "The proposed baseball back catcher mask was raised to a certain height at a level of about 15-20 feet, quote, unquote in a vertical position.

"At that height level, the proposed baseball catcher mask is released and allowed to free fall, according to gravity. The ball is stationary and the mask is in motion. A speedy sensor was used to obtain the impact speed at the point of the contact between the mask and the baseball to yield a speed of 90 and 100 m.p.h."

During this testing procedure, O'Brien was in attendance along with Niskanen and Bill Murray from the MLB commissioner's office.

"It was a huge, huge change in baseball," Niskanen told me of O'Brien's endeavour. "Making the mask – that was Charlie. He was definitely an instigator. From a technology dynamic, the ball deflects off the mask, it doesn't take the full force. Charlie was tired of taking balls off his mask and seeing stars.

"He wanted a partner. We worked with All Star Sporting Goods in Massachussets with Stan Jurga. They had a licensing agreement with MLB."

Niskanen said he worked out a confidential agreement with O'Brien,

Van Velden Masks and All Star. What that entailed I don't know.

O'Brien said in his book he stood in front of a pitching machine and bravely took balls on the mask to see how the new mask worked.

"Charlie, in his very calm demeanour, said, 'oh, by the way, I can wear it tonight (Sept. 13),' " Niskanen recalled. "MLB was very, very hard to please. They had no choice (but to accept it)."

As you can see in the majors now, a hockey-style mask is what is being used for the most part. That old facemask going back decades and decades with a hard covering for the chin and no protection for the back of the head is laughable, very archaic and past its 'best before due date.'

"EvoShield is our partner in this space but one particular brand is not mandated throughout the league, so catchers can choose whichever brand that they want so long as it abides by certain standards," MLB publicist Michael Teevan told me.

"The bottom line: the hockey-style mask gave the catcher better viability and better protection," O'Brien said in his book. "That's why I liked it. Why I wouldn't drop it when Major League Baseball kept throwing up these roadblocks and kept dragging its feet before finally saying I could use the mask in a game.

"I think they thought I'd just go away. I didn't drop it, though. Took near an entire season to get them to approve the mask. I don't know how many concussions I had with the old-style mask. I'd see stars. Ears ringing. Wanting to vomit."

So give O'Brien a round of applause. He helped better the game for catchers.

That was 28 years ago. It's all a feather in his cap. He introduced sexiness to head gear to the staid MLB system.

Exposion

Reed managed a career of 17 seasons

Jeff Reed was never a star but he was a solid player.

He worked that trade into 1,234 games as a part-time catcher in the majors, including 118 games with the Expos in 1987-88.

Reed showed that through hard work and perseverance he could thrive.

Reed, fellow Expos alumnus Bill Gullickson and Blue Jays great Jesse Barfield were likely the best baseball players to come out of Joliet, Illinois.

Reed received excellent tutoring from his late dad, Don Reed, who was an institution as a coach, not only in Joliet, but later in the Cape Cod league and in Florida.

Jeff was signed out of Joliet Township West High School by the Minnesota Twins in 1980.

"Jeff Reed was phenomenal," said Jack Schimanski, a rival coach with Joliet Catholic Academy where Gullickson pitched. "Him and Mark Grant, who has been an announcer for the Detroit Tigers for about 30 years, were contemporaries in playing in high school against each other.

"Jeff was the best player we ever faced. He was unbelievable, a great left-handed hitting catcher. He legged out a nice career."

For Joliet reporters such as Dave Parker, covering Reed, Gully and Barfield was a joy.

"When Bill was pitching here, he was a man among boys," Parker told me. "He had five or six no-hitters. He had a great curveball, an off-speed pitch.

"Jeff Reed, in a regional tournament or a regular-season game, hits a rope off Gullickson down the first-base line and turned it into a triple. He really turned eyes. People were saying, 'Who is this guy?' The scouts thought he was a terrific hitter, much better than anyone else at the time.

"He was hitting off a hitting machine at a very, very young age in his father's backyard. I'm not surprised he made it to the majors but him doing 17 years was a bit of a surprise."

Following a few years with the Twins, Reed was traded to the Expos in the deal that sent Jeff Reardon to the Land of 10,000 Lakes. Tom Nieto also went to Minnesota and going to Montreal with Reed were Neal Heaton and Yorkis Perez. That transaction went down just prior to spring training in 1987 on Feb. 3.

Reed spent a season and a half in a platoon role with Mike Fitzgerald and sometimes Nelson Santovenia.

On July 13, 1988, the day after the all-star game, Reed was traded along with Randy St. Claire and Herm Winningham to the Reds for Pat Pacillo and Tracy Jones. Not long after that, Reed went 5-for-5 in a game for Cincinnati but it was rare that he played full-time.

Part-time duty, though, still got him tenure and stature: 17 seasons of it.

Chapter 28

Gardner threw no-hitter through nine innings

Mark Gardner pitched in 200 games for the Expos, but the one game people remember him for took place July 26, 1991 in Los Angeles.

That's the first thing you think of when you think of Mark Gardner. That game. It seems like nothing else matters when you talk about Gardner. He pitched a no-hitter through nine innings but lost the game.

It was a Friday night in the middle of an awful season for Montreal under new skipper Tom Runnells.

Hitters were off kilter, except let's say for Ivan Calderon, who was hitting .313 and Dave Martinez at .271. Montreal batters were in a general slump. Delino DeShields was hitting .258, Tim Wallach was at .241, Larry Walker came in at .247, Andres Galarraga was at .244. Tom Foley was at .239.

That night at Chavez Ravine, The Hook, as he was known for his splendid, awfully slow curveball or change-up, was working on overdrive. His 1991 season had it ups and downs but on this night, in front of his hometown fans – he was born in Los Angeles – he was on top of the world.

Gardner's feat was a chance for Expos media guru Rich Griffin to capture in print in the 1992 media guide.

"Gardner's up-and-down season can be best capsulized by his 41 hours and 45 minutes in the spotlight at Los Angeles in late July," the devilish Griffin wrote. "On July 26, 1991, a total of 11,064 days after the opening of Dodger Stadium on April 10, 1962, Mark became the first pitcher in stadium history to throw a nine-inning no-hitter vs. the hometown club.

"Through nine innings, he walked two and struck out four, retiring Brett Butler on a ground ball to second for the final out in the ninth on his 108th pitch."

Equalizing Gardner, though, through this wonderful game were Los Angeles pitchers Orel Hershiser and Kevin Gross, who held the Expos scoreless through nine innings.

At the end of nine innings, the Chavez Ravine crowd of 38,957 gave Gardner a standing ovation for his no-hitter. But the game wasn't over. Gardner was seen with a towel over his head, waiting to go back out for the 10th inning. He knew then he was getting fatigued.

"They all congratulated me, but it wasn't over. I was coming out of the game after the 10th. I just didn't have it anymore," Gardner told Bill Plaschke of the Los Angeles Times.

Exposion

The Expos went scoreless in the top of the 10th. In the bottom of the 10th, Lenny Harris broke up the no-hitter when he reached on a cheap bouncer past the mound. Spike Owen ran in from short to try and make a play, but it was an infield single.

"I thought I might have a play on the ball. And Spike made a terrific try for it. He did his best, like he always does," Gardner told reporters later.

Eddie Murray singled to right as Harris scampered to third. Then Runnells elected to bring in reliever Jeff Fassero to pitch to Darryl Strawberry. Gardner tipped his hat as he approached the Expos' dugout.

Strawberry singled off reliever Jeff Fassero to give the Dodgers a walk-off win and Gardner was the loser, dropping his record to 5-7. He became the seventh pitcher to lose a no-no in the 10th inning.

Canadian Baseball Hall of Fame
Mark Gardner

"I was taking out Mark all the way," Runnells told the media. "But when I got there (to the mound), Eli (Tim Wallach) suggested we put a play on to pick off the runner. That threw me for a minute, but I decided I wanted the lefty to pitch to Strawberry."

Gardner lamented his inability to get the bunt down. He was on first base after a fielder's choice when he tried unsuccessfully to bunt Owen to second. Dodgers first baseman Eddie Murray picked up Gardner's bunt and fired to second to force Owen. Marquis Grissom moved Gardner to second on a single, but Ivan Calderon couldn't get him home.

"Had I got the bunt down, I might have won the game," Gardner said, shaking his head. "But I still take satisfaction out of this. You have to. My family's here and we'll probably just go back to the hotel and talk about this. Maybe I'll cry. No, not really. Deep down, I know I pitched nine innings of no-hit ball. I just wish we'd won."

Gardner almost became the first pitcher to throw a no-hitter against the Dodgers since Johnny Vander Meer did it on June 15, 1938 against Dem Bums in Brooklyn at Ebbets Field.

"Just two days later, same two teams, same locale, Dennis Martinez tossed his perfect game, erasing Gardner's feat from the public imagination after just 41 hours and 55 minutes," Griffin wrote, with tongue in cheek. "Mark's cap and an autographed game ball are, however, at the hall of fame in Cooperstown."

One reason Gardner might have been tired was because of his shoulder surgery the previous year. He went under the knife with famous Dr. Frank Jobe of the Dodgers staff and Expos orthopedic surgeon Dr. Larry

Coughlin doing the honours on Nov. 16, 1990.

In September of 1990, Gardner had flown home with what was called a "tired arm". Jobe examined him and prescribed a program of exercise and rehabilitation. As Griffin noted in the 1992 media guide, surgery was required to repair a small posterior labrum tear.

Likewise, Hershiser was a Jobe patient, and he also had surgery in 1990.

"I'm going to be mad at Dr. Jobe if he doesn't put an outing like that in my shoulder," Hershiser jokingly told Plaschke, referring to Gardner.

The last no-hitter prior to Gardner's effort was the five-inning gem posted by Pascual Perez in a rain-shortened game in Philadelphia on Sept. 24, 1988. The last complete game no-hitter by an Expo prior to that weekend was recorded by Charlie Lea on May 10, 1981 at the Big O against the Giants.

David Palmer also threw a five-inning perfect game April 21, 1984.

Little did anyone know what Dennis Martinez would do two days after Gardner's game.

Gardner was a highly prized prospect, who moved with his family to Fresno from L.A. when he was four. He was a star at Fresno high school and Fresno State.

Just a few weeks after Bob Fontaine Sr. and Tom Hinkle drove to idyllic Grass Valley in northern California to sign the great phenom Randy Johnson following the June draft in 1985, Hinkle and Loyd Christopher, got the honour to ink Gardner to a deal a few hours away on July 4.

Both Hinkle and Christopher, both deceased now, were able to see Gardner develop and pitch at the major-league level.

Chapter 29

Duquette had his eyes on McGriff in 1993

In the heat of a pennant race that saw the Expos front and centre in 1993, general manager Dan Duquette was looking for ways to improve the club.

Somebody playing for the San Diego Padres caught his eye: Fred McGriff. He was a seasoned veteran obtained by the Padres from the Blue Jays in the famous Joe Carter trade in December of 1990.

Like he had done for most of his career, McGriff was a power hitter with San Diego, but the Padres were open to offers on a trade. Even with McGriff earning $4.3-million that season, as I saw on Baseball Almanac, Duquette kicked the tires on him.

Padres general manager Randy Smith was told/ordered by ownership to trade McGriff as part of a firesale. Managing general partner Tom Werner and his investors wanted to cut salary and they had been doing that, going back to 1992.

Looking back at the 1993 Expos roster and statistics, I saw that guys like Greg Colbrunn, Oreste Marrero, Derrick White, Archi Cianfrocco and Cliff Floyd were used at first. So, you can see why Duquette sought out McGriff. The Expos needed somebody full time at first with power.

"I always liked McGriff and he would have fit into our club while we were waiting for our farm system to mature," Duquette told me in 2023. "And he would have been an excellent veteran bat in the middle of the order which is the reason for our interest."

There have been rumours since 1993 that McGriff told the Expos he wouldn't report if the Padres made a trade. The word "veto" was actually used.

"I don't remember us getting that close to a transaction whereby he could veto a trade to Montreal," Duquette said.

Not sure how McGriff could veto a trade unless he had it in his contract because he wasn't a 10-and-5 guy, meaning at least 10 years in the majors, the last five with the same team. But I got an explanation.

"Fred had a no-trade clause to Montreal," Smith confirmed to me in August of 2023. "We ended up with a very, very limited market for Fred due to his no-trade rights and that we could not take money back. I cannot remember the number of teams on his list – 6-10. I just cannot recall exactly.

"We did have some early conversations (with Montreal) and probably could have been a match, but we never got very far due to the no-trade clause and that San Diego could not take back any money."

Duquette had his eyes on McGriff in 1993

What Smith was referring to when he talked about the Padres not being able to "take back any money" is that Werner and his investors told Smith they would not send any money to the other team to help pay for McGriff's salary.

Prior to the trade even coming down, the Braves were the team most likely to take McGriff. Smith told the Montreal Gazette in 1993 that McGriff's salary was also a factor in where the Padres would trade him.

"When you get guys making his kind of dollars, less than a handful of teams can afford him," Smith told the paper.

In the end, the Braves stuck up their hand and said they would take McGriff. The Padres traded McGriff to Atlanta July 18 for Melvin Nieves, Donnie Elliott and Vince Moore, a swap that disappointed many Padres, especially Tony Gwynn, because the return in players was poor.

Crime Dog sure would have looked good in an Expos uniform. At least Duq gave it a try. He could have offered Colbrunn, Marrero, White and Cianfrocco (not Floyd) in exchange for McGriff and the Padres would likely have said yes.

"Without getting specific, we discussed all prominent young players – not Cliff, but some good, young players, with less than three years of service," Smith told me. "I certainly believe we could have made a deal that would have benefitted both clubs, had Fred wanted to go to the Expos."

Courtesy Topps
Fred McGriff

The Expos and Padres had warmed up for these talks with a smaller trade, a 1-for-1 trade in June when Cianfrocco headed west in exchange for Tim Scott.

McGriff had played in Canada for the Blue Jays, so he probably had no interest in playing again in our great country, what, maybe because of the extra taxes paid in Canada? We don't know.

McGriff went on to hit 493 homers and drove in 1,550 runs and finally was elected into Cooperstown through a veterans-committee vote in January, 2023.

A month later after McGriff went to Atlanta, Duquette faced another veto-trade scenario when his own pitcher Dennis Martinez nixed a trade to the Braves on Aug. 26 during a month when waivers must be obtained before a trade could be made.

"Dennis had a right to decide if he would accept an assignment of his

Exposion

Canadian Baseball HOF
Dennis Martinez

contract to another club," Duquette told me for this book. "In this case, since we needed a waiver from other clubs to assign the contract which we didn't receive from Atlanta, we didn't have the right to assign his contract.

"We were not intent on trading Dennis. However, the practice of putting all the player contracts through the system after the Aug. 1 trade deadline to obtain a waiver from clubs to trade the contract was standard operating procedure," Duquette explained.

"It's difficult for a club to trade a pitcher of Martinez's calibre with the club in a pennant race. Dennis was a free agent at the end of the year, and we knew that we couldn't afford the money to re-sign him at the market price and pay our young stars in 1994 so we were exploring our options to obtain compensation.

"El Presidente made 35 starts for the '93 club which won 94 games!!! We had a good ball club and were in the hunt for the entire season. In today's structure, we would have made the playoffs but unfortunately, we played in the same division as the Braves."

Chapter 30

Various roles got Boucher into Canadian hall

April 12, 1991. The SkyDome. A Friday day game.

It was an electric moment for Canadian Denis Boucher of Montreal. It was his major-league debut, as a starting pitcher for the Blue Jays. The butterflies, the adrenalin, the moment of truth had arrived.

"One of the greatest days of my life," the quite, unassuming, modest Boucher was saying Feb. 1, 2023 on a Zoom call after he was elected into the Canadian Baseball Hall of Fame. "I walked to the mound after pitching in the bullpen. I'm on the mound. A lot of friends were there, my parents were there, my grandparents.

"I faced Paul Molitor, Robin Yount and Gary Sheffield. That's who I faced in the first inning."

Boucher shook off any worries he had. Molitor popped to third, Yount grounded out 6-3 and Sheffield flied to left. In the Milwaukee second, Franklin Stubbs lined to first, Greg Vaughn was called out on strikes and Dante Bichette popped to first.

After retiring the first six Brewers, Boucher went on to record a no-decision, finishing with 5.1 innings of commendable work, allowing three earned runs in a game won by Toronto in the 10th inning.

More than two years later, Boucher was in a similar situation at Olympic Stadium in Montreal on Sept. 6, 1993 when he pitched for the Expos with Joe Siddall of Windsor, Ont. behind the plate and B.C.'s Larry Walker in right field.

It was the first time in modern baseball history that three Canadians were in the starting lineup for the same team. With the start, Boucher also made history as the first Canuck to have suited up for both the Jays and Expos.

Like the game in 1991, the atmosphere was electrifying with 40,006 in attendance with the Rockies in town as the Expos chased a playoff spot. Again, Boucher got a no-decision, but the Expos won, just like the Jays did, with the help of solo homers by Walker and Sean Berry. Boucher pitched six, solid innings, giving up only one run, a solo homer by one-time Expo Andres Galarraga.

"I've never seen anything like it," Boucher told the reporters on the Zoom call about the atmosphere in that special game in 1993. "There were 3-4 ovations after the game. It was incredible. Andre Dawson was my hero growing up so pitching at Olympic Stadium was a special feeling."

In the days prior to the game, Michael Farber of the Montreal Gazette recalls the build up to Boucher's Expos debut.

"Boucher was throwing on the side in Denver prior to his Sept. 1 call-up," Farber recalled. "I was watching with Duquette. I think the Expos had already announced that Boucher would be starting on Sept. 6. Duquette turned to me and offhandedly said, 'Tell people not to get there late.'

"I do recall the press box was crowded with people who normally would never be there, including (retired NHL player) Mario Tremblay, who was working for some network or something. I teased Mario that he showed up because he heard the Expos were a rondelle, a puck in the outfield."

Farber was also referring to the fact the Expos had called up Rondell White around the same time as Boucher.

Along with Dawson, Boucher felt a strong allegiance with Québec hero and long-ago Expo Claude Raymond, who in 1993 was an Expos' broadcaster. As for comparing the atmosphere and the scenario in 1991 and 1993, Boucher found it difficult to choose any game over the other as a favourite.

"It's hard to pick one of the two. One was my major-league debut and then you get to home and pitch for your hometown team," Boucher said. "Both were incredible days. They both brought great feelings."

Prior to and after his short, modest, big-league career was over, Boucher was involved with Canada's national team as a pitcher or coach. He pitched for Team Canada at the 1986 world junior championships and for the senior team at the 1987 Pan-Am Games.

Since 2003, Boucher has been a coach for Team Canada. He began his coaching stint with Team Canada at the 2003 Olympic Qualifier and then within a short time, the 2004 Olympic Games in Athens and the 2005 CONCEBE Baseball Regional Olympic Qualifier.

All in all, Boucher has spent 20 years off and on for Team Canada at various tournaments around North America and the world. He's been a superb Canadian very loyal to his country.

Boucher never made into the Canadian hall because of what he did with the Expos or Jays or Indians. He had no tenure or stature with either team. He pitched 146 innings in his short MLB career of 35 appearances.

When he appeared at his selection news conference via Zoom, he was wearing a Team Canada uniform with a Team Canada banner in the background. I'm guessing that Baseball Canada asked him to appear that way.

The photo of him appearing with the other elected members for an online hall announcement also showed him in a Team Canada uniform. Then several months later as it got closer to induction day, his photo on the poster was that of him in an Expos' uniform – and his plaque on June 17, 2023 had him in an Expos' uniform.

So a little bit of this and a little bit of that and Boucher was in the hall. A little bit with the Jays, Indians and Expos, a lot of time with Team Canada and a lot of time as a Nationals/Yankees scout. He has scouted for the Yankees for close to 20 years.

Various roles got Boucher into Canadian hall

Canadian Baseball Hall of Fame *Courtesy Baseball Canada*
Denis Boucher

When Boucher reached the majors with Toronto, it was somewhat of a pioneering moment in Canadian baseball history because at the time, very few Canadians were playing in the majors. That was a proud moment for Boucher and for Canada.

What should be emphasized also is Boucher's long-time role as president of the Lachine Baseball Association in suburban Montreal. His name is on Stade Denis Boucher in Lachine.

Keep up the good work, Denis.

Chapter 31

Financial concerns about the team in 1993

Expos fans don't have a grip on how difficult it was to run a franchise when there was less than adequate fan support, especially from 1991-1994 and then from 1995-2004.

There were serious financial problems in the operation of the club back in 1993 – that is true when I wrote a story for Toronto's Globe and Mail.

Can you believe that? Not many people remember that.

I wrote a story recounting how Montrealers, including then mayor Jean Doré, were trying to find ways to help attract more fans to Expos games. The headline went this way:

Saving Expos a task for business, mayor says

In that story, I wrote that late city councillor Nick Auf der Maur, Doré and "everyone else" knows what was needed to "save the Expos from leaving the city after this season." That's right, after the 1993 season! In that story, I quoted acting commissioner Bud Selig.

Auf der Maur said the Expos' future in the city beyond that season was "very iffy," even with the city as a part-time owner. Auf der Maur was genuinely concerned. He blamed the situation on a fierce war for the entertainment dollar.

"Ultimately, it's the people who vote and they vote with their ticket stubs," Auf der Maur told me at the time. "And people don't seem to be voting much. The Expos are up against a high volume of competition that most baseball teams don't have. During the summer, there's an endless parade of festivals and endless crowds of 200,000 and more for an event. The events end up against baseball half the time."

Doré told me his top priority in making the Expos viable included a vast improvement in season-ticket sales and better contracts with the national television networks. Doré even admonished the city's business community for not supporting the Expos.

"The first problem with the Expos is that they do not have enough tickets sold through the corporate citizens of the city," the mayor said. "The top priority this year and next fall is to substantially increase the number of season tickets. The basic problem is that the business community has taken the franchise for granted.

"The club has to be supported more by the smaller, medium-sized businesses. I would be pro-active with the Board of Trade and the Expos to make people aware that a franchise is a terrific asset for any city. With a metropolitan population here of about 3.1-million people, we should

Financial concerns about the team in 1993

have 15,000-17,000 season tickets, double the norm."

Earlier that year in February, Expos vice-president Bill Stoneman had told me how serious the situation was.

"We have to be very careful about how we allocate our resources," Stoneman said. "Money doesn't fall out of the sky."

Stoneman was commenting in light of Dennis Martinez's request for an extension beyond the 1993 season. El Presidente was signed through 1993 and he was told the club wouldn't give him a contract prior to or during the '93 season.

"The fans want us to be here for a while," Stoneman said, referring to Montreal's precarious financial situation.

This whole scenario in 1993 and 1994, and even in 1991 – and the dying years of the franchise put the Expos' future in doubt– when no individual owner stepped up to purchase the franchise from Major League Baseball.

No blaming Brochu. Blame the fans for not showing enough support to keep the team in town.

Two times in 1993, I quoted George Steinbrenner in two Globe and Mail stories, saying he expressed concern for the Montreal franchise.

At the start of the 1994 season, I wrote a story for the Globe and Mail, quoting Brochu who as much as said the team was hanging by the threads financially and that it was close to bankruptcy.

"I feel the financial precarity of the team was just a part of the ensemble," said my editor, Philippe Grenier, who knew a lot about the Expos' situation. "The political instability of the Province of Québec sure didn't help, but the constant backstabbing, jealousy and power struggle within Québec Inc (Expos minority shareholders) weathered away the man that wanted the most for the team to succeed. Brochu wasn't perfect, and sometimes was a bit clumsy in his approach, but people that worked for him back then are still loyal to him today. I'd say that's worth a lot in my book."

Chapter 32

Forkball made Rojas a star

Melquiades Rojas showed up at a free-agent tryout in the Dominican Republic way back in 1986 with uncle and Expos scout Jay Alou on hand to check him out.

"There were five teams interested," Rojas told me in January, 2023. "Jay (Jesus) showed up. He said I was a top player. I signed for $2,500. In those days, it was a lot of money."

And Rojas started chuckling.

"I wanted to play in the United States. It wasn't the money," he said.

The son of Francisco Rojas and Maria Socorro Rojas then made the trek to North America to play professional ball. He didn't speak any English but "I got a lot of help. I learned English real quick with a lot of guys helping out."

He polished up his English and got to hone his pitching skills in Burlington, Iowa, Rockford, Illinois, West Palm Beach, Jacksonville and Indianapolis.

Rojas did some starting and some relieving in his minor-league days but when he got to the majors, it was a different story. On or about Aug. 1, 1990, he was told he was being promoted to the Show. In Triple-A, he was 10-7 with a 2.49 ERA with 17 of 34 appearances in relief.

"I got the call. It was my first time in the big leagues," he laughed. "I said 'Wow'. In my first game, I pitched two-thirds of an inning."

Rojas entered the game with men on first and second with two out in the top of the 12th after Bill Sampen had a rough outing that led to the Mets scoring the go-ahead runs to win 6-4 at Olympic Stadium.

Rojas induced Dave Magadan to hit a pop up in foul territory to Tim Wallach and then he struck out Tom O'Malley looking.

Rojas finished his inaugural season with 40 innings under his belt and his work was commendable. He was 3-1 with a 3.60 ERA.

What happened in all of his time in Montreal was a new era: he was strictly a reliever. In some games in the minors, he was a starter.

Rojas spent some time again in 1991 with Indianapolis but he managed to get back to Montreal for 48 innings of work. He was 3-3 with a 3.75 ERA and six saves in a really awful season for the Expos.

In 1992, he had earned his keeps and was excellent with a 7-1 record and a glittering 1.43 ERA in just over 100 innings. In his early years with the Expos, he was not a set-up guy but in 1992, his role had improved to the point where he became the set-up guy for closer John Wetteland, who had been acquired in the off season from Cincinnati.

As the team got better under new manager Felipe Alou, Rojas' uncle, so did Rojas and the bullpen. His won-loss record in 1993 wasn't a good look at 5-8 but his ERA was very commendable at 2.95 and, he found himself being installed in end-of-game scenarios as a closer. He collected 10 saves that season.

In the strike-shortened 1994 season, a bad/sad scenario for the Expos and fans in Montreal, Rojas again was outstanding as the team cruised most of the season before being shut down by a players' strike which was followed by the cancellation of the season on Sept. 14.

"Ugh, that was real bad in 1994," Rojas said. "We had a lot of fun. We won a lot."

Rojas shone in 1994 in 84 innings of work. Wetteland closed most of the games, but Rojas saved 16 on his own. He was 3-2 with a neat 3.32 ERA.

The trick at the end of a game when the Expos were leading by several runs went like this: Tim Scott in the seventh, Rojas in the eighth, Wetteland in the ninth. Game over.

The highlight of Rojas' 1994 season took place May 11 when he pitched an immaculate inning, striking out David Segui, Todd Hundley and pinch-hitter Jeff McKnight, all on three pitches each, retiring the side on the minimum nine pitches. How about that for trivia? In those days, Rojas was humming the ball at 98 m.p.h.

Rojas became the 28th player to accomplish the feat but it was/is something that doesn't seem to cause him to rank it as a highlight.

"I laugh when people bring that up. How did I do that?" Rojas said. "I say, 'No way.' I get them out no matter what."

Rojas said the highlight of his career with the Expos was not in 1993-4 but in 1995 after the fire sale when he inherited the closer's job from Wetteland, who had been traded to the Yankees. It was an unusual circumstance that made this outing so much more memorable because he had been sicker than a dog prior to taking the mound.

It was a Saturday night at old Jack Murphy Stadium in San Diego. June 3. Only 9,707 were on hand. Too many people stayed at home and missed Pedro Martinez's perfect game through nine innings.

"Pedro was pitching a no-hitter. I had a fever all day and all night," Rojas recalled. "Felipe came up to me and said, 'Can you pitch?' Everyone was surprised I was in the bullpen. I felt strong. I was not weak."

So Pedro, facing his 28th batter after retiring the first 27 and fanning nine, gave up a double to lead off the bottom of the 10th to Bip Roberts, who laced a ball past Tony Tarasco to the wall in right.

Alou immediately took Martinez out of the game after 96 pitches to bring in Rojas to protect the 1-0 lead the Expos had created when Jeff Treadway singled to right to bring home Shane Andrews in the top of the 10th.

Rojas immediately got himself in trouble when he wild-pitched Roberts to third. Still, nobody out. With the infield in, Steve Finley came up and bounced out to Andrews, playing a rare game at first, keeping Roberts at third.

Up came the feared Tony Gwynn. He grounded to second and Tread-

Exposion

Joe Gromelski photo
Mel Rojas and his son Mel Jr. have fun at a Family Day function in the 1990s.

way fired home to catcher Darrin Fletcher, who tagged Roberts out. Two down.

Then Rojas got Ken Caminiti on a pop in foul territory to third baseman Mark Grudzielanek.

"We got Roberts at home. That was so great," Rojas told me of getting out of that quagmire after feeling so rotten for a day.

Rojas finished the 1995 season with 42 saves and was excellent again in 1996 when the Expos challenged for a playoff berth. He recorded 36 saves in 40 chances with a 3.22 ERA, all due to a heavy sinker and devastating forkball.

The forkball is similar to the split-fingered pitch, the difference being that the forkball is jammed deeper between the first two digits on the hand and fired hard, snapping the wrist.

Rojas' Expos teammate Ken Hill was also known for this special pitch which produces a tumbling kind of action and drops sharply off the plate before it reaches the batter.

One of the first to use this pitch was 1969 Expo ElRoy Face, who had popularized it while he was with the Pittsburgh Pirates for many years prior to coming to Montreal.

In the end, the Expos couldn't afford to keep Rojas. He was another example of the type of expensive player the Expos could no longer keep around.He signed with the Cubbies on his 30th birthday – Dec. 10, 1996. Cool. It was the biggest birthday present he had ever received.

"I got three years for $13.75 million. It was very good," Rojas said.

Two days later, his cousin Moises Alou left the Expos as a free agent and signed with the Marlins. Two key Expos lost within such a short period of time, one a great stopper, the other a tremendous offensive player.

Rojas would later resurface with the Expos in 1999 but by then, his stature had diminished, He was hampered by right-shoulder problems and surgery. He tried his hand that season with the Dodgers, Tigers and then Montreal.

He hatched on with the Expos on May 17 but was released July 3 and never played in the majors again. He was 33. He threw 2.2 innings for Montreal, allowing five runs in five games.

"I was excited when they brought me back. I was surprised," he said.

Rojas later tried his hand in independent leagues and spent one season in Korea where his son Mel Jr. is currently excelling as an outfielder.

Exposion

Marrero's debut was memorable

Oreste Marrero bypassed Triple-A to make his big-league debut with the Expos Aug. 12, 1993.

Pretty neat. That doesn't happen too often.

The Expos decided to call up Marrero from Harrisburg Double-A on the same day he debuted.

Harrisburg is in Pennsylvania, which is about a two-hour drive northwest of Philadelphia, where he met the Expos for a day game.

"One of my girlfriends gave me a ride," Marrero told me of his jaunt to Philadelphia.

The Puerto Rican native was the starting first baseman in his debut and he excelled with 10 putouts, an assist and he went 2-for-5 with an RBI. A dream beginning to a short career in the majors.

When he posted a video of his first hit on his Facebook page on the 30th anniversary of the game Aug. 12, 2023, I saw that he almost hit a home run. This-close. It ended up as a double off the left-centre field wall in the third inning. He drove home Moises Alou and almost immediately, the ball was taken out of the game.

The video clip sees third-base coach Jerry Manuel throwing the souvenir ball to Larry Walker in the dugout. Walker was seeing rubbing the ball a little before he placed it in a secure area for Marrero.

Although he didn't get to play much in the majors thereafter, Marrero will remember that game. What was nice, too, is that the Expos kept him for the remainder of that season which saw the club fall short of the NL East title with a 94-68 record.

Marrero appeared in 32 games for the Expos in the last two months, batting .210 with a homer and four ribbies.

He qualified for his MLB pension that season because he was on the roster 52 days, surpassing the required 43 by a bunch. He also played briefly for the Dodgers in 1996.

Marrero played in 1,088 minor-league games with 4,056 plate appearances.

Chapter 33

Moises was the best Alou of all

On May 22, 2023, just out of the blue, out of curiosity, I looked up Moises Alou's stats on Baseball Reference.

What I saw was breath-taking. I knew he was a tremendous player because I saw him play for the Expos as a beat writer when he was just coming into his prime, but I didn't realize he finished with 1,287 RBI.

Holy shoot, if he hadn't missed the 1991 and 1999 seasons due to injuries, he very likely would have finished his career with close to 1,500 RBI and more consideration for Cooperstown. And he played only 93 games in 1995.

He collected those 1,287 ribbies quietly. He wasn't really a guy walking around looking around for attention from the media. Nope. He avoided the spotlight, but he was often in the spotlight because he was such a player of unending talent and prestige and because he was bred from baseball royalty. He thrived on a high-tempo Latino passion for the game with full-head-of-steam intensity.

Alou hit lifetime what is really the goal of many in the game – over .300, .303 to be exact. He played in 1,942 games, hit 332 home runs with a lifetime .885 OPS and an on-base percentage of .369. Just prolific. Holy shit. All the while without using batting gloves, just rubbing urine on his hand, or peeing on his bat, as he disclosed one time.

He was the best of all the Alous who played in the majors, outduelling his dad Felipe and his uncles Matty and Jesus. Interestingly enough, Moises collected 2,134 hits, Felipe 2,101.

On his Griff's The Pitch Podcast on April 10, 2023 which featured an interview with Moises, the widely respected Rich Griffin, a long-time Expos media-relations guru, centered out Alou as "one of the most respected players in Expos history."

Alou doesn't get enough pats on the back for his role with the Expos from 1992-1996.

"No doubt, absolutely," his outfield partner Marquis Grissom told me in an interview in May of 2023. "He was such a prolific hitter. He's a Hall of Famer. He doesn't get a lot of credit because there were a lot of guys around him (who were stars in their own way)."

In Montreal, Grissom and Larry Walker probably got more of the ink and Grissom also played with Alou in San Francisco in 2005.

"When Moises was in Houston, they had Craig Biggio and Jeff Bagwell. He gets overlooked, just like guys like Freddie Freeman and Paul Goldschmidt. They are unbelievable," Grissom was saying. "Moises be-

Exposion

came a better player when he left the Expos.

"I remember when we (Braves) went to Houston when Moises was with Houston and Moises said to me, 'Come over to the batting cage and listen to the sounds off the bat when I hit the ball.' It was loud, really loud. He's a true professional."

Alou arrived in the Expos organization on Aug. 8, 1990 in a trade with the Pirates and he's forever grateful to Montreal general manager Dave Dombrowski for getting him to Montreal where he began his ascent to stardom.

When he was recalled from the minors that year by the Pirates, the move created some interesting trivia as noted by Griffin in the media guide.

"His cousin, pitcher Mel Rojas, was called up by the Expos within 24 hours, creating what is surely a record for time elapsed, cousins, recall to majors, first time," Griffin said in his great sense of humour.

Alou missed all of 1991 at both the minor-league and major-league level due to a right-shoulder injury. He underwent surgery April 10 of that year in Los Angeles with the fabled Dr. Frank Jobe providing the heroics.

According to the 1992 Expos media guide assembled by Griffin and cohort Monique Giroux, what exactly happened is that the surgery "repaired a large superior labrum tear and a slight rotator cuff tear of the right shoulder."

Alou hurt his wing on Nov. 28, 1990 while playing for Escogido in the Dominican Winter League – diving back into first on a pick-off attempt. When he got to spring training in 1991, his shoulder wasn't getting any better, so he soon had surgery. He spent all of that season rehabbing and travelling with the team on the road in the press box with a speed gun.

In 1992, under an air of uncertainty, Alou reported to spring training, competing for the fourth right-handed hitting outfield spot with veteran Phil Bradley and Darren Reed. Alou made the Opening Day roster out of West Palm Beach.

Oddly, Alou didn't make his first start until Game 10 on April 16 when he went 3-for-3 with a double and an RBI. That exclamation mark led to an excellent season on his part, even though he got nowhere close to 500 at-bats as a full-time player. On several occasions, he would venture into the manager's office to try and get more playing time that season, either under his dad or his predecessor Tom Runnells.

He hit .282 with nine homers and 56 RBI in 341 AB in what Griffin described as a "wildly successful debut season capped by a second-place finish behind Dodgers' Eric Karros in National League rookie-of-the-year voting."

Based on that kind of season, Alou and agent Bob LaMonte wanted some kind of extra compensation salary wise for the 1993 season. That wish wasn't forthcoming. The Expos and contract negotiator Bill Stoneman adhered to a strict financial policy for players who fell short of three years of salary arbitration. At the time, Alou had two years and 37 days of service which included the 1991 season when he didn't play.

Because Alou missed 1991, Stoneman decided Alou wouldn't be paid the usual $315,000 which he normally gave players between 2-3 years of service time, players such as John Wetteland.

When all was said and done, Stoneman told Alou and LaMonte early in 1993 that Alou's salary would be $185,000. I found this out about Feb. 20, 1993 by calling LaMonte.

No discussion allowed, no negotiation. I was on the beat in those days and when I got LaMonte's phone number from Expos special assistant Marcia Schnaar, I called him in California. First and only time I ever talked with him until recently.

In one of the very few times LaMonte has ever expressed umbrage in the media about a contract negotiation involving anyone, except maybe for Dave Stieb's dealings with the Blue Jays, he ripped into the Expos for low-balling Alou in a story I wrote for Toronto's Globe and Mail.

"Moises is very frustrated," LaMonte told me for the story. "This contract just isn't going to get done. It's not right. The offer is not fair.

"Moises said he may not show up at camp on time. He said he just can't live with that salary number."

It was a business decision. Stoneman was only following major-league protocol that younger players were at the team's mercy and never mind that Felipe was Moises' father. Moises and LaMonte were looking for $250,000 and LaMonte said he was hoping the Expos would at least bump it to $200,000.

An integral part of the Expos planning for this negotiation was an historical case that involved Larry Walker's winter-ball knee injury that kept him out of action the entire 1988 season. Stoneman used that case to match up with Alou, who missed the entire 1991 season. Walker's salary after his second season (.241, 19, 51) was $185,000.

"The Expos brought up Walker's contract to compare but Moises had better statistics," LaMonte told me in 1993. "And he was second in the voting among the NL rookies and made the league's all-rookie team.

"I don't like to negotiate in the media but there are times when you have to do it. Walker's deal was two years ago. This is 1993. Moises' figure should be higher because of inflation."

The Globe story stirred up controversy and was moved on the Associated Press wire service out of New York and prompted follow-ups by the Montreal media, especially when Moises showed up at spring training – late. Without my story, there very likely would have been no publicity about his salary and his unhappiness. But the media knew about the story and the Expos were ready for the controversy that followed.

I've always been a keen observer/admirer of those players not eligible for arbitration. They are called pre-arb players. They get short-changed with small raises over the previous season so I kind of sympathize with them and I have often done stories about them, especially the prominent players.

When I knew Alou was one of these guys in 1993, I got on the phone to LaMonte.

On Feb. 27, a visibly upset Alou appeared at spring training two hours late, prompting a New York Times headline Alou Does Show Up, as I found out reading online June 7, 2023. Alou told reporters he had sat

Exposion

Joe Gromelski photo
Moises Alou was one, heckuva ball player

down for breakfast with Stoneman that morning and said some deal was being worked out.

Alou said he didn't want to stir up any trouble by sitting out any workouts, so he joined his teammates on the practice field at Municipal Stadium. No boycott, no holdout. When the dust had cleared and the animosity had subsided, Stoneman gave Alou a salary of $210,000, a $25,000 raise from the original $185,000.

"He can be stubborn but he's a lot like me," Felipe Alou told reporters after his son arrived in camp. Felipe brought up a similar type story involving himself when he was with the San Francisco Giants. He said he was hitting .281 when the club decided to send him to the minor leagues and put up a nameplate for a guy by the name of Willie McCovey. Alou said, "No. No way."

And so, Felipe went back home to the Dominican. He was encouraged to come back but not to the minor leagues. To San Francisco.

Felipe also brought up instances where Moises was involved. When Moises was 2, he was caught playing with matches and caused a fire. Another time, the kid was found by his dad facedown in water at a beach. There was the story that came up where Moises' life was saved by a gardener when a German Shepherd dog attacked Moises.

When Felipe's dad Jose died, Moises was 9 and he sat close to his grandfather's coffin without shedding a tear. Felipe thought his son had a really tough exterior when he never cried.

"Moises Alou is a tough SOB." his dad told reporters that day in February in 1993 after citing all those examples. "He's a tough out at the plate and he's a tough base runner. Last year, he was supposed to go to Triple-A (after missing 1991 because of injury) and he refused to go down by playing his way onto the team."

As far as that contract went, LaMonte, 30 years later, said, "What I'm saying is that it was very difficult. Montreal was difficult to deal with. We had conversations with Montreal but realizing it was Moises, you knew he was going to change agents. He was going to arbitration (after the 1993 season) and it came to pass he found another agent (Fernando Cuza)."

LaMonte, a teacher at the time, had met Alou at Canada College in San Jose and through the late Don Oderman, a stockbroker. LaMonte continued to represent him through his time in the Pirates organization' and in the first few years of his tenure with the Expos.

"It was really – how can I say it, it was really delicate. He had a famous father. I never had a situation like that, helping him as an agent," LaMonte said.

"Moises then was really lanky, about 150 pounds. He didn't speak a lot of English. I spoke some Spanish. Oderman asked me if I would help Moises out. Moises and I became friends. We worked together. It was a very friendly relationship – it was a difficult situation only because of the fact in that period it was just hard.

"It's not that we didn't get along. Eventually, it just reached a point where it wasn't going to work. We were moving away from each other. No hard feelings. It wasn't like a breakup. No animosity.

"Just the fact I lived in California, and he lived in the Dominican, the whole nine yards. He lived in Montreal, I was in California. It would have been different if he lived in San Jose. How can I say it – there was no connectivity. It was hard. I haven't seen or talked to Moises in 25-30 years.

"There wasn't a lot of players we had (to represent). It was coaches. My genre is football. It was certainly unusual. That was it pretty much.

"I had Dave Stieb, a partner of mine in high school where I coached. We both lived in San Jose. Now, we live in Reno, Nevada. We talk constantly. I've known him for decades. I did many multi-year contracts for Dave Stieb."

When I went to spring training several weeks after the Globe and Mail appeared and after the controversy died down, I walked up to Alou in the tiny clubhouse and we shook hands.But before I could say anything, he just up and left and went to another part of the clubhouse. He most certainly knew what I was going to ask him.

Alou shook off the slight of a poor contract and went on to produce an outstanding season in 1993, although a terrible injury sustained on the turf in St. Louis Sept. 16 dropped him out of the lineup for the remain-

Exposion

der of the season. It was the eve of a weekend series in Montreal vs. the Phillies.

Alou rounded first hard, all out, just in case he was going to second and trying to draw a throw from Bernard Gilkey – and then he backtracked to first in a sudden stop and while doing so, caught his left ankle on the Astroturf. Oh shoot. His leg folded. A very cringe moment.

In video from the game, Cardinals second baseman Luis Alcea and second-base ump Bill Hohn could be seen putting their hands to their faces in horror at what they were witnessing. That was an awful sight to behold. He snapped his ankle real bad.

Felipe came running out and stood beside him and told his son to be calm, despite the agonizing, throbbing pain.

"My foot was hanging," he told Griffin on the podcast in 2023. "I can't look at mine (tape). I still can't look at it – still. I was more disappointed in the pennant race. We were only a few games back of the Phillies and I was down and out for the year. I felt like I let the team down because I got hurt."

Teammate John Vander Wal, responding to a Facebook post involving me and John Hagmaier in June of 2023, said he was overcome with emotion when he had to deal with the Alou accident.

"I was there. Horrible with Mo on a stretcher. Felipe sent me out with Moises to the street outside of the stadium while was game was still being played and we waited for the ambulance," Vander Wal said.

"I was still in shock from what had just happened. Mo calmly asked me a question. 'Hey, Vandy, I need a dip (tobacco).' We both threw in a dip and went over what had just happened. The ambulance finally arrived. I walked back to the clubhouse with tears in my eyes, the worst thing I have ever witnessed on a baseball field."

Alou spent the night at Jewish Hospital in St. Louis and then flew to Montreal the next day. The official declaration was that he had dislocated his left ankle and suffered a fractured fibula. With Expos orthopedic surgeon Dr. Larry Coughlin helped out by Dr. Mitchell Rubinovich doing the honours, Alou was fixed up at Queen Elizabeth Hospital. Two fixation screws were placed in the ankle to stabilize the joint and the leg was placed in a below-the-knee cast.

Pirates manager Jim Leyland came to visit him, football great Joe Theismann, who suffered a similar revolting injury on the field in 1985, called him. Magic Johnson called the clubhouse. Alou came on the field on crutches several days later and received a standing ovation.

He went home to the Dominican Republic prior to the end of the regular season and then came back to Montreal in early November to have his cast removed. He also spent three weeks of vigorous therapy of the leg under the guidance of assistant trainer Mike Kozak. At one point, he attended a number of Montreal Canadiens' hockey games and he would get ovations and he would hug scalpers he knew from Olympic Stadium.

Alou had enjoyed an outstanding season until this wretched accident occurred. He had belted 18 homers, drove in 85 runs and batted .286. His RBI total was the second highest total for one season by an Alou. Felipe drove in an amazing 98 runs for that tremendous 1962 team, the San

Francisco Giants.

In his last 27 games prior to The Injury, as Griffin said in his media-guide notes, Alou hit .337 (33-for-98). Alou could get out of bed and hit more than .300. He was that cognizant of what pitchers were throwing.

Miraculously, Alou, that determined, passionate player that everybody knew – defied all logic and predictions and prognosticators and returned to play for the start of the 1994 season. It was the Comeback of All Comebacks. That was something to behold. Alou's bravery and courage and desire to come back was a testament to his will and desire.

He took up where he left off, as the expression goes, in 1994 in a season that will go down in emotions of good and sad and bad – the strike-shortened season and Bud Selig's announcement of the cancellation of the season. Selig always likes to say he never cancelled the season but that he announced it.

Until the players under executive director Donald Fehr decided to go on strike to protest a salary cap promoted by the owners, Alou was hitting an illustrious .339 and with 139 hits, was on pace to collect 200 hits in 1994. He had scored 81 runs and would have gotten close to 140, if the season had stood up. His OPS was .989, his OBP .397. Remarkable. He hit 22 homers and drove in 78 runs.

Regarding Alou "what-if" stats, there were partial-parallel cards issued by Topps in '95 that were called CyberStats, said my editor Philippe Grenier, who boasts 29,000 Expos cards in his collection.

"These cards extrapolated the stats using computer-simulated data for a few keys players of the 1994 season, and Alou was one of those," Grenier said. "So, according to Topps, Alou would have had 186 Hits, with 45 doubles and 28 homers, 98 runs, while driving in 102 runs, and finished the season with a .311 batting average. It would have been a fantastic season for him!"

Despite the season ending on a bad note, the two leagues decided to go ahead with award announcements and Alou finished third in MVP voting in the National loop.

The Expos boasted a lot of swagger with their offence, defence, starting pitching and bullpen. After starting off slowly, they had a record of 74-40 at the time of the strike and were headed for a 106-win season. Larry Walker had 44 doubles and was on pace for about 66.

"People bring that up," Alou said on the podcast with Griffin about the swagger. "I think it was from my dad. We were a family, man. My dad was a big part of that. They (players) felt he was their dad. He created that culture in the clubhouse.

"Often, you'd see 3-4 players in the manager's office with my dad. We became the team we were working on. We had the confidence. I remember on the road we'd be stretching, guys would be running – and the other teams would be afraid of playing us."

Reality set in on Sept. 14 when Selig made his announcement.

What was very forthcoming in Alou's chat with Griffin on his podcast were revelations that the papa and son had a few spats.

"I was very upset with my dad. We had a few disagreements. There

Exposion

are some things I regret," Alou said in the interview. "I was thrown out at third base with two out and I had my hands between my legs," he said in the interview, alluding to the embarrassment of being the third out on a play where he shouldn't have tried to go to third.

"In St. Louis, after a game, I had two beers in my hand in a brown paper bag and I wanted to take them back to the Adams Mark Hotel where we stayed and my dad told me I shouldn't be taking beer out of the clubhouse," Alou said.

All these years later, Moises loves his father so much he has a photo of them together on his @moisesalou18 Twitter (X) page and they share a strong belief in Jehovah God. Each day on his Twitter page, Moises quotes from the Bible.

Alou played two more seasons for his dad and the Expos and then he walked away as a free agent and signed with the Marlins Dec. 26, 1996. Dombrowski was the GM of the Marlins like he was with the Expos when he acquired Alou from the Pirates.

"I have a lot of respect for Dave," Alou told Griffin. "It was mutual love. I lived in Miami, so the Marlins were close to home. I was waiting for them to call. Finally, they called. I was hoping they'd sign me before they ran out of money."

Alou helped the Marlins to the World Series championship the following season and then was traded in a fire sale after one season. He proceeded to play for Houston, the Chicago Cubs, San Francisco, once again under Felipe in 2005-2006, and finally the New York Mets before packing in his career following the 2008 season.

"He was a great kid. You couldn't say a bad word about him," LaMonte said. "He was phenomenal. He hit line drives. Every ball he hit was a bullet. I've never seen a guy hit so many line drives, not just in the gaps. He had one of the strongest outfield arms, one of the best I've seen. He was special."

When his career was all over, Alou had produced a quiet, silent career of major production. He doesn't receive enough credit for his outstanding defence, fielding and offence.

Just a remarkable player.

LaMonte agent extraordinaire for NFL coaches

On his Professional Sports Representation website, the list of people Bob LaMonte represents in the NFL is eye-catching.

I can't help but mention how prolific LaMonte has been as an agent. He specializes in contracts for NFL coaches and associated employees, including the highly successful Andy Reid of the Kansas City Chiefs and Sean McVay of the Los Angeles Rams.

Reid reportedly earns $15-million per season with the Chiefs, McKay $14-million with the Rams.

LaMonte has close to 50 NFL coaches/assistants and front-office executives under his tow. Wow. Can you imagine the cut he gets off each contract!

LaMonte said his "break in football" came when he represented Rick Campbell in the early 1980s before "I had Dave Stieb" of the Blue Jays.

"Then it just blossomed. We're a husband and wife (Lynn) agency. We've been pioneering in football. My epiphany was I had an epiphany. I'm just an old guy, not afraid to buy green bananas."

And that epiphany was to improve the salaries of NFL coaches

"When I came in, NFL coaches were making about $297,000 a year and now it's gone up to about $7.5-million a year," LaMonte said. "We've got assistant coaches, general managers, front-office executives. It used to be the GMs who made all the money. Now it's the coaches."

LaMonte and Stieb are good friends, talk often and meet each often because they both live in Nevada.

LaMonte made the point of saying salaries for sports figures vary. I know that NBA coaches make obscene money and NHL coaches have really come on board for decades after they were penny-pinched for a long time.

"In baseball," LaMonte said, "it's the GM who is making all the money. Unless you are a Tony La Russa, you don't make money. It's getting worse and worse for baseball managers."

Chapter 34

Grissom sure had a lot of talent

Marquis Grissom had longed for a career as a pitcher after being drafted out of Florida A & M but the Expos had other plans.

"I was drafted as a pitcher. I always wanted to pitch in the big leagues. I thought I was going to be a major-league pitcher," Grissom told me in May of 2023.

Then Jerry Manuel, who would eventually be the Expos third-base coach for a good part of the time Grissom was in Montreal, went up to him at spring training in his first year.

Manuel looked out to the outfield on occasion in the early days of rookie-league ball in 1988 and would see Grissom throwing bullets and running like the dickens. Almost immediately, Manuel, a minor-league field coordinator, told Grissom his new job would be in the outfield.

"I pitched in an intrasquad game. I never pitched in a minor-league game," Grissom recalled.

Grissom said he was initially unhappy about his new role, but he accepted it.

"It was the quickest way to the majors. I wanted to play every day," he said.

By the 1989 season, Grissom was in the majors. Can you imagine? On Aug. 22, 1989, Grissom made his MLB debut, going 1-for-3 with an RBI single as the Expos wanted to add some punch to the lineup in the midst of a bad, bad slump that saw the club fade into oblivion after leading the NL East for much of that summer.

The Expos saw the potential for Grissom to be a star early and they put him into the fire very early to try to revitalize a fading team.

Grissom would continue his way to stardom with the Expos in 1990 and by the 1993 season, he was in full swing with 19 homers and 95 RBI. He was something else. The Expos fell short of the NL East title and Grissom did his best to get them in the playoffs.

1994 was a season like no other for Grissom and so was the off-season stuff that preceded the season of glad tidings and then gloom. A salary-arbitration case reared its ugly head for Grissom. When you're called into a board room and hear bad things said about you, it's not good.

It was during spring training in 1994 when Grissom and agent Eric Goldschmidt squared off against a collage of Expos' people and lawyers trying to win their case.

"I was a small company working for a big company," Grissom told me, as he started to laugh in reference to the arbitration case. "I learned a lot more about the game when I went to arbitration. The two biggest things that happened to me in 1994 were going through arbitration and going through a strike. That was tough.

"I remember my agent and I went into the hearing. We didn't know what to expect. Until you go through it, you don't know. It was really different. In fairness, we're trying to prove I am a good player and the other side felt bad about saying I was a bad player. They talked about my play and my performance.

"I was a little pissed off. Then I saw the business side. Then you know exactly how the game goes. Going to arbitration, that was tough."

Grissom ended up getting a salary of $3.575-million for 1994 in the middle of spring training. Then it came down to brass tax and being a member of one of the greatest teams in Expos history.

The year before, Grissom was involved in his first arbitration case. He was so upset with what happened he cancelled an appearance in Montreal.

Grissom shrugged off the hurt and the pain and the suffering associated with the inner workings of an arbitration hearing and put together a tremendous season in 1994, bearing in mind he knew, like his teammates, that there was gloom on the horizon in the form of a strike.

Grissom, up until the strike, had batted .300 with 11 homers, 45 RBI with 96 runs and 36 stolen bags.

"My teammates, the players, the coaches, Felipe, coming up through the organization – we had so many players with so much talent. We had a wonderful team, unbelievable," Grissom was saying. "We probably had the best coaching staff in all of baseball. We had a stellar pitching staff. We were scrappy, grinding, clawing. We had so much love and chemistry for each other. We had fire.

"The biggest thing that happened was the little brawl against the Cincinnati Reds. Pedro had a perfect game going. To think that Reggie Sanders was saying Pedro was trying to hit him was crazy. With that, Pedro prepared us to be that kind of team, to go inside, do the hit and run, steal bases. We had the dynamics.

"We could hit for average and hit for power. We had five-tool players. We had guys who were getting to the majors and fighting to get on that team and get established. We were on a roll all year."

The Expos were 34 games over .500 at 74-40 after they lost to the Pirates in Pittsburgh Aug. 11. They were so good they would have made the playoffs for the first time since 1981. You couldn't just say they would have won the World Series because there were other good teams out there. Remember the 2001 Mariners, who won 116 games and never made it out of the American League.

The strike officially started on Aug. 12.

"We started to feel real gloom at the first of August," Grissom said. "We had player reps (John Wetteland and Darrin Fletcher). A lot of guys didn't understand what was going on. It was a no-brainer that we were going to go on strike."

Little did Grissom know that game in Pittsburgh would be his last one

Explosion

in a Montreal uniform. He went back home to Atlanta Aug. 12 and then two days later, him and good friend Lenny Webster flew to Montreal, cleaned out their apartments and drove back to Atlanta in separate vehicles.

I asked Grip if he stopped in at a bar to have a drink before he left for Atlanta. He said no. Then he quipped, "But Danny, I was in a lot of bars and hotels during my playing time and had a lot of drinks."

And then we laughed and laughed, geezus, for about two minutes. Belly laughs.

"We packed up and went home," Grissom said. "I drove my truck. I had a GMC Yukon. It had just come out, it was not fancy, just an SUV. It took me 20 hours to get home. I don't know how many times I stopped to find a room. In the small town in the mountains of Carolina, one lady at a hotel looked at me. She said she had no rooms. I was pissed off. I pulled over on the side of the road."

Was it racially motivated that she wouldn't give him a room?

"Most definitely," Grissom said. "But I was looking crazy, half sleepy. So tired, so beaten."

In April of 1995 when the strike ended and Judge Sonia Sotomayer issued an injunction, Grissom reported to spring training and was soon traded along with Ken Hill and Wetteland while Larry Walker wasn't offered a contract.

"The strike happened, and they had to break the team. If we had stayed together, it would have been great. I'm not going to say the Expos were the best team," Grissom said. "1994 was a helluva team. The Atlanta Braves were a helluva team. I go to Atlanta, and they have four hall of fame players (Glavine, Smoltz, Maddux and Chipper). Cleveland, with Manny Ramirez, that was a great team."

Grissom went to the rival Braves in 1995 and they won it all that year.

Many years later, Grissom experienced the joy and sadness of everything when Hank Aaron died in 2021.

He was asked by the Braves and Aaron's wife, Billye, if he would deliver a eulogy at the slugger's Celebration of Life at Truist Park. No way he was turning that assignment down.

"They asked me to speak at his memorial. I was elated. I was happy. I was more than honoured. I was nervous, all those things. I was so appreciative. I just felt that of all the people I met over the years, what he meant to people around the world," he said.

This connection between Aaron and Grissom began years earlier when Grissom attended Florida A & M. His coach was Rob Lucas, the son of Bill Lucas, considered to be the first black general manager in all of baseball in 1976. To boot, Grissom's outfield coach was Larry Aaron, Henry's son.

"We were playing North Carolina one game in 1987 in the middle of the season and Rob Lucas and Larry decided to bring the team to Hank Aaron's house, the whole team, for a motivational speech from Hank," Grissom said. "It was probably 4-5 hours from our college in Tallahassee.

"It's kind of like a fairytale story – 26 players and the coaching staff.

Grissom sure had a lot of talent

Joe Gromelski photo
Marquis Grissom gets high-fives from Tim Raines and Tim Burke

It was my second year in college. You're talking about all the accolades of probably the greatest player of all time.

"His speech was about creating an opportunity and possibly getting drafted. He said to take advantage of that opportunity and don't let it go away. There's a short window. He said, 'If I can do it, you can do it.' That lit me up. Those chords struck me. That was part of my speech at the memorial.

"Hank Aaron, Willie Stargell, Rickey Henderson, Tony Gwynn, Barry Bonds, so many guys – they really inspired me."

Grissom said it was "very emotional" to make the speech because he also had gotten to know Aaron in the last eight years of his life since Grissom lives near Atlanta.

"I spoke from the heart, and I was hoping I didn't screw up anything. I had stuff written down but was ad-libbing once I got to the podium. I spoke from my heart and talked about the effect Hank had on my life."

Nicely done, Grip.

Chapter 35

Webster played his heart out

As a kid growing up on the south side of the tracks in Chicago after moving from his native New Orleans at age 3, Lenny Webster was "just trying to hang on" and survive in the midst of challenging times for him and his dad Washington Jr., his mother Barbara and brothers Jermaine, Elston, Terrell and Jason.

"So many things were happening," Webster told me in the summer of 2023.

"I remember my mom giving me a $10 bill and asking me to go to McDonald's on Stoney Island Ave.in the Jackson Park area to get her a chocolate milk, fries and a filet of fish. I was about 12 years old.

"I go to McDonald's. I walked two blocks. After I get the food, I get the change and walk out of the store.I get to the corner and there are six kids waiting for me, including a kid from the park. They jumped me and robbed me. They took the food and the money. I was mad. I was a stubborn kid. I was angry.

"I said, 'How am I going to tell my mom they took the food and money?' I told her I was going back. I was going to grab a knife. It never happened."

Several years after getting robbed, Webster and his family moved out of Chicago to Mississippi because "violence started to pick up", gangs were running rampant and before any of the boys "got caught up" in what was going on. It was the mid-1970s.

Leonard Irell Webster grew up tough and thrived in the face of adversity to become a solid major-leaguer, including three different stints with the Expos, one of those stints with the fabled 1994 squad.

"I was really happy to move back south. Most of my family is in Louisiana and my parents are from there," he explained of the move to Mississippi, located about 2½ hours north of Louisiana.

Webster went to Gautier Middle School on Mississippi's Gulf Coast along the Mississippi Sound at the northern extreme of the Gulf of Mexico. He went there, despite efforts by his parents to make him attend high school in Louisiana. He stayed with an aunt and uncle. He excelled in football at Gautier and played baseball in the summer league.

"I was the MVP, I won the home run crown, I had the highest batting average. It was a pretty good summer," Webster was saying.

Then he moved to Lutcher High School in Louisiana, and he excelled there, too.

"I go there and the ninth-grade baseball season had started. I missed

Webster played his heart out

Grambling University   *Canadian Baseball HOF*
Lenny Webster had three different stints with the Expos

the baseball season. I couldn't try out for the baseball team," Webster said. "Next year, I played sophomore football in my sophomore year. I played off the ball, as a linebacker, nose guard on the defensive side of the ball.

"After my sophomore year, I made the varsity team, which is something. It was a prestigious program. I was 15. I was able to start as a sophomore. I made the all-district team."

Going into his sophomore year, Webster became aware that his coaches didn't think he could play baseball. They tried to get him not to play baseball, that he should beef up and concentrate on the gridiron. The coaches didn't realize how competent Webster was at baseball.

In his mind, he was saying, "I'm playing baseball. I grew up in baseball."

In the spring of 1980, Webster ignored the 'don't play baseball' oogling and made the Lutcher team, pitching and catching as a freshman. He had a senior, Terry Rousseau, playing in front of him behind the plate so he spent that season excelling as the designated hitter. He had a "decent year", and he was voted all-state DH.

Webster continued to play for Lutcher in 1981-82 and by that time, he was attracting the attention of scouts. In June of 1982, Webster was selected by the Minnesota Twins in the 16th round out of Lutcher but he didn't sign.

"I was 17. I thought that was too young. I was not ready to go on my own," Webster said.

Explosion

So that's when the recruiting started among many colleges interested in taking Webster on a scholarship. Near the end of his high school career, he was invited to participate in a high school all-star game in Louisiana and that's where he ran into Grambling baseball coach Wilbert Ellis.

Before he met Ellis, Webster already knew where he was going because he had made the decision when he was 12 years old. Imagine.

He said he was watching television, still living in Chicago, when he took much delight in the airing of the Bayou Classic, an annual college classic rivalry game played in New Orleans between two Louisiana schools: Grambling and Baton Rouge's Southern University.

Webster loved the pomp and the drums and the crowds and decided then and there Grambling was the place for him. No recruiting from Ellis was required.

I didn't know until July 11, 2023 that Grambling is one of the Black Niners: big-name colleges or universities that are all-black. Pretty cool to see Webster in a Grambling team photo with all the players black.

"Let me explain it. I could have gone anywhere on a full-ride scholarship but I went to Grambling on a half-ride scholarship. That is where I wanted to go. They gave you a bargain," Webster said. "I went there for football. Little did I know I'd be playing baseball."

In June of 1986, the Twins came calling again, drafting Webster in the 21st round out of Grambling. This time, he signed. He was ready to play, emotionally and physically and he had matured. He received a total bonus of $25,000, including the rest of his schooling. That brings into account his explanation of a half-ride scholarship at Grambling where he majored in criminal justice.

"Lenny is one of my all-time favorite players so it's a pleasure to talk about him," said Kevin Malone, a Twins scout, who really liked what he saw in Webster. "I got to know him when I did the advanced scouting for the Twins-Braves series in 1991. In Double-A, I noticed his approach, about how he played the game. He was a glue guy when things were going good and not going good.

"He had a calming effect on players. He was not a superstar. He didn't put up big numbers, but he was one of those guys, who could come up with a big hit for a big play."

Webster spent a few years in the minors for the Twins and when he was playing Double-A in Orlando, where he currently lives, he was surprised when his manager Ron Gardenhire, a future MLB skipper for Minnesota, called him into his office on Aug. 30, 1989.

Gardenhire took the occasion to raise his voice and was facetiously giving Webster shit.

Not often are players called up from Double-A to the majors so Webster was taken aback. He wondered what the heck was going on.

"Gardy was my manager in A ball and Double-A ball. We had a really good relationship. This time, he got mad. Through and through, I thought I had done something wrong," Webster said. "He wanted me in the office – now. He told me to sit down. I was wondering why he was talking to me like that. I said, 'Gardy, what's going on?'

"Gardy said, 'You're going to the big leagues.' I said, 'What?!' It was one of disbelief. Once I got up there (September call-up), I said, 'Wow, this is baseball.'"

Webster was up and down with the parent team and another surprise came during spring training in 1994. It was the Expos who came calling for his services. It was the dog days of spring and it was getting down toward the end before the season started and clubs were trying to figure out who should make the team, be assigned to the minors or traded, released, whatever.

"Let me explain it. Ah man, I remember it like it was yesterday," Webster said. "Jerry Manuel had managed against us a long time. When he was in Double-A, he managed against us. By the time I got to the Expos, he was coaching third.

"The Twins weren't playing me a lot. I was wondering why. They weren't letting me play a lot. All of a sudden, about a week and a half later – I hadn't played, and I was sitting at my locker next to Dave Winfield and I said, 'I wonder why I'm not playing.' Winfield said, 'Hey, TK (Tom Kelly) loves you.'"

So, what happens? The Twins are at home in Fort Myers and the Expos come to town in a rare visit across state from West Palm Beach. In this game, Webster is in the lineup. He isn't aware that he's being showcased to the Expos, who were zeroing in on his talent.

"I went 2-for-3 and I went to shake hands with the Expos and they were all looking at me – Manuel, Felipe, Luis Pujols, Tommy Harper. They were just staring at me. Then a clubhouse guy told me the manager (Kelly) and general manager Andy MacPhail wanted to see me in the clubhouse," he said.

"Once I saw Andy MacPhail, I knew something was going on. Kevin Malone was the Expos general manager and he knew me from my years with the Twins. They told me I was traded to the Expos, one of the best teams. I was upset with the Twins' organization.

"I was behind Brian Harper and they gave my job away to two young kids. You know, here's the thing – it's a fresh start. I was excited. Maybe I'll get a chance to play. The Expos wanted me."

The trade was made March 24 and Webster was a little shell shocked. What player isn't taken for a loop after a trade? He headed to his truck he had been driving, while in Fort Myers, and packed it up to join the Expos – when he runs into somebody familiar in the parking lot.

"First guy I saw was Marquis Grissom," Webster said, "Grissom said, 'Lenny what are you doing?' I said, 'I just got traded. Just like that, we've been friends ever since."

Off to West Palm Webster drove in his truck. The regular season had yet to start but this trade was a clear indication Webster was staying with the Expos and there would be no sending him to Triple-A. He would be a back-up – along with third-string receiver Tim Spehr – to Darrin Fletcher, who was slated to catch a majority of the games.

"I was hungry to be with a new team. They didn't trade for me to send me to the minors. They made a trade for me to platoon with Fletcher," he said.

Exposion

Webster was an unsung hero among a team of mostly studded stars that was getting better and better following a fantastic 1993 season, and he quickly realized the impact he had on the team. He became Jeff Fassero's personal catcher and he would come in occasion and get some other starts and catch for other pitchers.

Webster was a warrior, a tank, 5 foot 9 and built like a brick-shit house. Your typical catcher, who had little speed but who worked his ass off.

"He was a quality receiver who knew how to handle a pitching staff, not just on the field but off the field," Malone told me. "The pitchers felt he could get the most out of them. He could frame pitchers, block balls, throw runners out. He felt comfortable behind the plate. He was not a tall guy. Pitchers just felt comfortable looking at him.

"He might have been a part-time player on the field but he was full time in the clubhouse, off the field and in the community. He was the consummate team player. He knew what he could do and what he couldn't do. He just had a feel for the game. He knew the little things needed to win a game."

As I would see online, Webster would sometimes catch fledging superstar Pedro Martinez, who had been acquired in the off-season from the Dodgers. In one such video I saw from Aug. 5 on the Twitter account @exposblog, Pedro went outside with a fastball and Webster decided to run out to the mound to talk with Martinez, to give him some advice.

As they stood on the top of the mound, Webster put his arm around Martinez's right waist while giving him a pep talk. Martinez listens with his back to Webster and all of a sudden, he turns around and actually looks at Webster, listening to what his catcher had to say and then suddenly, he thrusts his gloved hand onto Webster's chest in a show of appreciation.

"Pedro was young and I spent a lot time with Pedro," Webster said. "I think Pedro – he was a helluva competitor. Pedro competed to prove that he belonged. He was 5-foot-10 and weighed 150 pounds. He had something to prove. He had a chip on his shoulder.

"The highlight for me that year was that it was just a tremendous group of guys we had, a hungry, young group. I've never been around a group like this. We used to beat up teams with speeds, pitching or hitting. It was so exciting, Danny – we felt like we could win it all. We were definitely not cocky but we were confident. If we'd stayed healthy, we definitely had a chance to win the World Series."

Then the strike and the cancellation of the season.

Webster and Grissom flew back to Atlanta from Pittsburgh, site of the team's last game, and within days, both flew to Montreal to clean out their apartments and drive back to Georgia.

"We were hoping to get it (strike) worked out, to get it ironed out. It was a kick in the gut," Webster said of the work stoppage.

In a part-time role that season, Webster had batted a neat .273 with five homers and 23 RBI and an impressive .817 OPS.

When the players went back to work in April of 1995, Webster didn't return with the Expos. Almost immediately, he signed a major-league deal with the Phillies, who offered him more money.

"In 1996, I came back with Montreal. I enjoyed playing for the old man (Alou)," he said. "I had good rapport with the old man. One of the most solid managers I ever played for. I mean, he treated me like a professional. He was a straight shooter."

Webster helped the Expos to a surprising 83-79 mark that almost won them a NL East title. He batted .230 with six homers and 40 RBI.

In 1997, he made his way to the Orioles where Malone was the GM and Pat Gillick was running the show. Malone knew what he could do from their days with the Twins and that 1994 season in Montreal.

Not to be denied, Webster came back for a third stint with the Expos in 2000 for another go-go with Alou. He was 35 and wasn't quite the same as he was in 1996 and 1994. He never made it back to the majors with any other team.

How did Webster fit in with the pitchers, whether it was Fassero or whoever?

"I think for me, not just the Expos, but any staff, I think what I tried to do was tell the pitchers that 'I care about ERA. Your ERA is my ERA.' It wasn't so much about my batting average," he said. "It was basically always about the ERA. That's why I was able to get through to those guys. I cared. They took that to heart. I wanted to do the best I could."

As his agent Ron Shapiro told me, "Lenny played hard. He was special. He earned a lot of respect from everybody."

Webster finished his career with nine years and 61 days of service, falling just over 100 days shy of the magical 10 years of a full pension.

"The earliest you can take the pension is at age 45. I waited until 52," he said. "I think Major League Baseball has the best pension plan in professional sports. I'm blessed in the situation I'm in. I don't take it lightly. I earned my pension. I worked for it.

"I valued my moments in baseball. Here's my take – I wasn't allowed to become a superstar. You couldn't take away the way I played the game or the way I would think. That's what was so special to me."

Great talking with you, Lenny. It was a blast.

Chapter 36

Remembering Tom Brady again

Tom Brady's decision to finally retire in 2023 from football brought back more memories of his brief audition with the Expos June 11, 1995.

It was a Sunday morning.

Brady woke up early at his parents' home in San Mateo, California, hopped in the family car with his mom and dad and sisters, got on Route 101, drove north past San Francisco International Airport by way of the San Francisco Peninsula and found his way to Candlestick Park on Jamestown Avenue on San Francisco Bay.

Brady went to Candlestick for a morning batting practice session with the Expos before an afternoon game with the Giants. It was cool, as it usually was at Candlestick.

Candlestick was familiar territory for Brady. He would often go to see the 49ers play NFL games there in his youth because he admired 49ers quarterback Joe Montana.

Brady brought along a pair of cleats and took hacks in the batting cage as some players, manager Felipe Alou and coaches looked on. Players milled around Brady in the clubhouse, some suggesting to him he was better off going to the University of Michigan. His father Tom Sr. had already told the Expos he was headed to Michigan.

"Just fun. We just enjoyed watching him swing and interact with other ball players," Tom Brady Sr. told the author in late February of 2023 of that June day. "We remember it well. Fun day for Tommy. Things were going pretty rapidly at that time."

There was little publicity about Brady's visit to Candlestick. Although he gained some notoriety at Serra high school, Brady was just another draft pick, a needle in a haystack so to speak.

Just like the rest of us, who would have had any idea Brady would be a star in the NFL for 23 seasons and an automatic inductee in the Pro football Hall of Fame in Canton, Ohio in 2028?

At that time, who knew Tom Brady would become a cultural phenomena, a celebrity and household name ranking up there with the likes of Tom Cruise and Tiger Woods?

The Expos had drafted Brady in the 18th round, 507th overall. The Expos loved his catching instincts and his bat and were prepared to offer him $500,000 to sign but he had already made plans to go to Ann Arbor.

"The Expos had 18th-round draft pick Tom Brady take BP yesterday. There's some work to be done getting Brady signed, however. He's signed a letter of intent for a football quarterback at Michigan as a quarterback," The Montreal Gazette wrote in a short spiel the next day about Brady's visit.

The Expos were told by Brady's father his son was indeed going to Michigan.

"As I have always said, I could have ruined the history of the NFL if I had signed Tom Brady," quipped Expos area scout John Hughes said.

Currently a pitching cross-checker for the Oakland A's, Hughes was the main man who had followed Brady in high school and met with him, his father and mother and his sisters at the family home and at Candlestick – for the kid's BP session.

It's a tradition where MLB teams bring in many of their draft picks for a taste of the big-league life. So that is what happened with Brady on that day. Hughes said the Expos wanted to recognize his status as a baseball player and show their appreciation to him so, they brought him in for BP.

"It was arranged that day in the Brady house that he would come to Candlestick that day," Hughes said. "I met him and his family at Candlestick. I introduced him to some people. He met Felipe. I introduced him to Rondell White. It didn't take long for the players to gravitate to him. He was a most impressive high school kid, the way he carried himself and he was a good looking guy.

"It wasn't a work out. It was a normal, pre-game batting session where he was put into one of the

Courtesy John Hughes
John Hughes scouted Tom Brady many times

hitting groups about 90 minutes before the game. My recollection is that it was a miserable, cold day. He was doing his best to hit one out of the park. I think maybe he hit one home run."

I took a guess that Expos bullpen coordinator Pierre Arsenault was the BP pitcher throwing to Brady and I emailed him with my guess. I was right.

"Your instincts are right. I was the guy who threw BP to Tom Brady," Arsenault said. "Back then, I was the one getting abused – since I was the youngest – throwing BP, especially early to the extra guys. They did that almost every year, bringing in a drafted player so they could experience a day with the big-league club.

"Guys were impressed with Brady because he was going to Michigan to be their quarterback. I remember the Expos had brought Tom in after the draft, to entice him to quit football and sign with us. Looking back, I think he made the right choice.

"He was a classic high school kid with lots of tools that were still raw. You could see the potential for power in the bat but it was hard to tell in one session of BP, especially on a windy day in a big MLB ballpark. At first glance, his frame and size were impressive.

"He had lots of strength-gain potential, especially for a catcher and also being a left-handed bat. You could see he wasn't rattled by the events. He already had a certain maturity and our players were impressed by him. Usually those draftees would be reserved, sitting in a corner and a little star-struck but not Tom Brady – he was in his element."

Hughes had looked at Brady "I would probably say four times." Hughes went to one workout where they were actually looking at another team, another player, Greg Bols. "Tom had a lot presence. He had power in his bat. He was 6-foot-3," Hughes said. "When we drafted him, I had to go to the house to do some paper work – this is what you did. We had to get him to sign a Consent to Release form. We had the right to meet him and his family. That was just more getting to know the family a little bit. That was prior to the Expos coming to town (San Fran).

"Me and his dad would have conversations about Tom's future. Tom is an awesome guy. It became very evident he didn't want to sign. We were ready to make him an offer of second-round money. We obviously viewed him as a true prospect. I remember his dad saying Tom was not the best athlete in the house. He said the best athletes were his sisters."

Also coming in to observe Brady was Expos cross-checker Jim Fleming and he brought along another cross-checker, Dave Littlefield.

"Serra high school was a very good school," Fleming was saying. "They had great football players there, not just great baseball players. Tom had really good tools, he could really throw. He was still learning to catch because he was a big guy. We would have drafted him higher, if it wasn't for football."

When I asked Hughes if he could send me the scouting report he wrote up for Brady, he was hesitant. After all, Brady was a generational talent, a celebrity. He wasn't just going to give that document to anyone, including me.

"I'm just going to wait," Hughes told me. "The hall of fame in Cooperstown wants the report. I'm going to wait and see if Tom wants it before I disperse it to the public."

Brady would be an ideal minority partner in the Expos, if some group makes a bid for an expansion franchise. He loves the fact he was drafted by the Expos. In an April Fool's Day joke he posted on Twitter in 2022, he said he was looking forward to being the president, general manager and manager of the Expos in 2024 – with Olympic Stadium in the background.

And on Sept. 30, 2023, he wore an Expos' top at Topps card functions at the MLB flagship store at 51st and Avenue of the Americas and at a venue in Linwood, New Jersey – where he interacted with card and memorabilia collectors.

At the time, it was never revealed who convinced Brady to show up but I found out it was billionaire Michael Rubin, the CEO of Fanatics, which owns Topps and is a licensed producer of sports merchandise.

"Mr. Brady happens to be a friend of Mr. Rubin and he invited Mr. Brady as a guest," said Ken Turner, the chief marketing officer for Fanatics. "Mr. Rubin posted on one of his social outlets that Mr. Brady was going to attend."

Considering Rubin's wealth, he also would be an ideal partner in unison with Brady in any Expos group wanting a new team. At one point, Rubin was a part-owner of the NBA's Philadelphia 76ers and the NHL's New Jersey Devils. His value is estimated at $10-billion.

Turner seemed to think it would be a logical suggestion that Brady be used on Topps cards in an Expos uniform or a top.

"Mr. Brady is an icon obviously, a brand himself," Turner said. "At some point, we could get him in partnership with one of our products. It's something that could be in the works."

Sure enough, on the 12th day of the 12th month in December of 2023 – Brady's football number in the NFL was 12 – Fanatics, Topps and Bowman celebrated Brady's connection to the Expos with a parody social-media video that lasted 79 seconds and the introduction of Brady cards with him in an Expos' hat and uniform top.

Courtesy Major League Baseball
Tom Brady in Expos attire at card event in New York

I was told the excellent video was shot at a bar in mid-November in New York City. The bar is the fictional Montreal establishment Brady's Brasserie and featured Expos greats Vladimir Guerrero, Larry Walker and Pedro Martinez, who were watching a TV screen and praising their 'former teammate' Brady.

The video spoofed Brady's fictitious career with the Expos. All shots of him in the video in Expos garb were photoshopped. He wasn't present at the shoot.

There are 81 autographed Tom Brady cards in the 2023 Bowman Draft set — and a number of non-autographed cards. Hobby boxes (local card shops) and blaster boxes (available at regular retail, like Target and Wal-Mart). To underline: his card is inserted randomly into packs. Not every pack — or box full of packs — will have a Brady card in it.

Exposion

What I found really nice is that Topps did an interview with Hughes and posted it online to give him credit for his time in watching and scouting Brady – in conjunction with the release of the video. Really cool. Scouts are underestimated, undervalued and underappreciated. They are almost nameless.

"I have done numerous radio shows and newspaper interviews. Everytime Tom went to the Super Bowl I did interviews and did a couple when he announced his retirement," Hughes told me.

There are many out there who hate/dislike Brady, what, because he was successful and won seven Super Bowl titles? I love this thin connection he has to the Expos. All of this publicity helps keep the dormant franchise's legacy alive.

And now you wanted to know about Rondell White and what he did the day he was introduced to Brady?

This is what White did with a sore hamstring: he went 6-for-7 and obtained the very rare fortune of hitting for the cycle, including a 13th-inning triple as the Expos beat the Giants 10-8.

Brady set White on fire.

Chapter 37

The good and bad of Grudzielanek

Grudzielanek on the back of a uniform from the left arm pit to the right armpit wasn't exactly an easy job for Expos tailor Yvon Gendron.

Very likely the name had to be shrunk down in font size from normal names like Walker, Grissom, Rogers, Guerrero, Raines, Carter and Dawson.

Mark Grudzielanek made that name stand out a long time. He had impossibly good looks and he sure could play ball.

He appeared in more than 1,800 games. How about that? Very impressive, and he did it with aplomb from a fielding standpoint and from an offensive perspective. He played with drive, determination and passion. Maybe it was that Polish desire of his that drove him.

After he retired in early 2011, he told reporter Jon Morosi how tickled he was to make it to the major leagues, especially when he recorded his 2,000th career hit for the Kansas City Royals on July 12, 2008.

"I remember thinking, 'No way would a kid from Milwaukee, Wisc., play this long and have a career like this," Grudzielanek said in an interview with Morosi.

When he got hit No. 2000, it was a "very emotional" time for him. His family was there. They stopped the game.

"It was pretty cool," he told Morosi.

Grudzielanek, thanks to some watching by Expos scouts who believed in him, was selected by Montreal in the June draft in 1991 out of Trinidad State College, not in the Caribbean country, but in Trinidad, Colorado.

He made his debut with Montreal April 28, 1995, striking out swinging as a pinch hitter in the eighth inning at Wrigley Field against Bryan Hickerson of the Cubs.

Grudzielanek played in 78 games in his inaugural season, batting .245 with a homer and 20 RBI, while finding defensive time at second, short and third.

In 1996 and 1997, he was outstanding, playing on a full-time basis at short. The doors for Grudzielanek opened wide at short when the Expos traded incumbent shortstop Wil Cordero and Bryan Eversgerd to Boston on Jan. 10, 1996 for Rhéal Cormier, Shane Bennett and Ryan McGuire. The trade meant Grudzielanek was handed the job out of the 6 hole.

Grudzielanek went on a tear in 1996. He almost reached the 700 plateau for plate appearances with 696 as the leadoff hitter. He collected 201 hits, missed the century mark in runs with 99. He batted .306. He was never a power hitter and during this particular season, he hit six homers and drove in 49 runs. He stole 33 bases. All in all, it was a tremendous season.

As he showed for all of his career, he went up there swinging. He was not your definitive lead-off hitter. Nope. He was not up there, trying to get on base anyway he could. He was never one for taking pitches. He walked only 26 times.

Grudzielanek was honoured with his exceptional season by being named an all-star. Somewhat fittingly, his appearance at the all-star game came in the same year the great shortstop Ozzie Smith was making the last of his 15 ASG show times.

"I just remember being there pregame, chatting with Ozzie. He was one of my heroes - a joy to watch. For me to have that experience with him, in his last go-around as an All-Star, I'll never forget that," Grudzielanek told Morosi.

Grudzielanek was the personification of what the Expos accomplished that season, a season of unexpected success. It was a miracle actually. He spearheaded a drive by the Expos for a playoff spot, two years removed from the year the Expos' chances of reaching the playoffs were erased by a players' strike and cancellation of the season.

Who would have ever thought the Expos would do what they did when their roster was decimated at spring training in 1995 with the departures of stars Larry Walker, John Wetteland, Ken Hill and Marquis Grissom. This 1996 team boasted a small payroll, but the talent was impressive, driven and gritty.

The Expos were 17-9 in April and collected six grand slams before May 1. They slipped to 14-14 in May but improved to 16-10 in June before dropping to 11-15 in July and 14-14 – again – in August. They finished strong at 16-12 in September to finish 88-74, two games behind the Dodgers in the wild-card standings. Who expected them to be this good so late in the season?

Grudzielanek was one of two shortstops in the 20th century to hit .300, collect 200 hits and steal 30 bases in a season. The other shortstop was pretty good company: Honus Wagner.

In 1997, Grudzielanek pretty much duplicated his heroics from 1996. This time, he had 688 PA, drilled 54 doubles, batted .273 and drove in 51 runs. He had four homers. He drew only 23 bases on balls. He broke the Expos' club record for two-baggers, topping the old mark of 46 set by Warren Cromartie in 1983.

Larry Walker, with 44 doubles at the time, would likely have broken Cro's record in 1994, had it not been for that silly strike.

One thing we can't forget is Grudzielanek's longevity and pretty decent career. Then the rails came off Grudzielanek's short, amazing tenure with the Expos. As quick as you say Jack Robinson, he was gone, traded to the Cubs.

"It's the little things that win ballgames," he told Morosi, "and that's how I kept my job all those years."

We should mention that during his time in the minors with three different teams, he was a good friend of the late Canadian Derek Aucoin.

The good and bad of Grudzielanek

They would hang out a lot when they were together. A special moment for both was when Aucoin made his big-league debut for the Expos in San Francisco on May 21, 1996. Grudzielanek was playing third.

Later in life, not long after he retired, he was embroiled in a controversy when he left his spouse Danielle Martin to shack up with his 1995-97 teammate, David Segui.

On March 26, 2021, Grudzielanek was investigated for alleged child abuse in Scottsdale, Arizona.

The Scottsdale police department was notified Grudzielanek allegedly abused a child inside his home. For some reason, no media outlet got wind of it until TMZ exposed Grudzielanek eight days later on April 3, 2021.

There were no details given as to what Grudzielanek allegedly did. Then the story essentially disappeared.

You may recall he was under investigation for child abuse, stemming from a late-night incident on March 26, 2021 in Scottsdale, Arizona. It apparently was a physical altercation.

Whatever happened there very likely ended his chances of managing in the major leagues. He had reached Triple-A as a manager with the White Sox from 2017-19.

His son Bryce Martin-Grudzielanek was a recruit from the University of Southern California. He has another son, who may have been the victim of the assault.

Curious, I decided to look into this. I found out Grudzielanek was never charged or fingerprinted or taken to a police station for an interrogation. He was only interviewed on the phone.

Secured, exclusive documents I obtained from Scottsdale police revealed new details to coincide with the two-year anniversary of the incident.

Grudzielanek sprayed a liquid of some sort – a chemical or vinegar solution – into the eyes of a 12-year-old boy, who had been taunting him and his mother all day – and for a few months.

That boy was identified as Brock Segui, son of David Segui, Grudzielanek's Expos' teammate. Grudzielanek is the fiancé of Donna Moniz, Segui's former wife, who had gained full custody of her three kids at the time from Segui.

The police report said Brock's taunting and mischievous activity included throwing dog toys at Grudzielanek, spitting at windows and throwing a football at security cameras – which he had just erected – and by spraying the contents of a plastic container at Grudzielanek.

The police report says Grudzielanek was sitting at a table having a discussion with Moniz when Brock sprayed the contents of a bottle at Grudzielanek, who responded by taking the same container and spraying the kid in the face with the solution.

While this was going on, Brock's brother, Shai, who also was cited in the report as acting up along with his brother, filmed part of the altercation. He sent the video to a family friend, who, in turn, called police.

Shai told police Grudzielanek sprayed his brother "4-5 times" while "grabbing" his brother's left shoulder.

Explosion

When police officer Ryan Willkomm showed up at Grudzielanek's house, he asked Moniz if she could talk to him about what happened with her boyfriend. She corrected the officer quickly by saying, "Fiancé."

Moniz gave her side of the story and then shortly after midnight, Willkomm called Grudzielanek, who had left the house after the incident to take a breather after Shai had shouted at him.

"He (Grudzielanek) continued to state they (Brock and Shai) had been acting this way for the last three months since their mother had gained full custody of the children," Willkomm wrote in his report. "He then stated they (Grudzielanek and Moniz) were sitting at the table, and he was having an adult conversation with their mother and her friend when Brock grabbed a bottle of unknown liquid and sprayed it in his face.

"He stated since the children had not been respecting him or their mother all day, he took the bottle and sprayed it into Brock's face and said, 'How does it feel to be disrespected? How could you be so disrespectful?' I asked him if he knew what was in the bottle and he stated he thought it was half water and half vinegar but was not completely sure.

"I then asked him if he sprayed Brock out of anger, to discipline him, or make him learn respect and he replied it was to "try and get them to understand." He said it was "not that he was mad or going to hit him."

As an aside to the policeman, Grudzielanek said, "He's a baseball player I might add." Online reports say Brock, a switch-hitter like his dad, is eligible for the MLB draft in 2027.

Grudzielanek told the officer he didn't grab Brock by the shoulder and only sprayed him once.

After due diligence, the case was turned over to the Maricopa County's Attorney General's office for review. After reviewing the matter, the attorney general's office decided not to lay charges against Grudzielanek.

If TMZ had not been advised of this incident, Grudzielanek would have gotten away without any unwanted publicity because he was let off by the Attorney General's office.

"We declined to prosecute the case – no reasonable likelihood of conviction," said Jeanine L'Ecuyer, deputy chief of staff for the Maricopa County AO's office.

L'Ecuyer said in an email exchange with this writer that "in general, no likelihood of conviction means a case was reviewed by several attorneys in the office who determined the available evidence didn't support a likely conviction."

Grudzielanek is the second member of the Expos' fraternity in the last few years to escape a brush with the law regarding alleged child abuse. In September of 2022, John Wetteland was acquitted when a hung jury couldn't reach a verdict on charges he sexually molested a relative many years ago when the relative was a child. The judge declared the case a mistrial and prosecutors so far haven't pushed for a new trial.

Segui told me in an interview March 23, 2023 he's very upset that Grudzielanek was let off. Segui has read the police report.

The good and bad of Grudzielanek

"It's the definition of assault. He said he was angry, held my son and sprayed him in the eyes," Segui said. "In the video I saw, my son put up the phone and recorded it, but my ex-wife erased the video but not after my son had sent it to someone else. My son still has blurry eyes. She won't take him to a doctor. She takes him to Costco.

"Mark is a low life. It's so disappointing when you think you know somebody and then you find out they are a completely different person. I never thought he would abuse kids or women. He abused a child. Mark is a coward. You can print that. If he wants to put his hands on my kids, he's a low life. He knows where I live. If he doesn't like me saying this, he can come knock on my door. I live a mile and a half from him."

Segui's kids were initially ordered by an Arizona court to attend the controversial Family Bridges reunification camp in California as part of his custody battle with Moniz, according to Celeb Magazine.

"She's been going through a custody battle with her ex for the last five years," Grudzielanek told Willkomm of Moniz. "It's been a very gruesome and ugly situation. This has been really tough to deal with throughout this time. They (kids) disrupted the house many times, without me doing or saying anything to be understanding to the situation. It's very hard for me to swallow my tongue when they are treating her (mother) like absolute terrible."

The police report indicated the Segui kids don't like to be around Grudzielanek, preferring instead to be with Segui, their biological father.

Grudzielanek and Moniz couldn't be reached for comment. Grudzielanek was sent both email and text messages.

I've been told by Grudzielanek's former spouse Danielle Martin that he and Moniz have been together for about six years. Segui confirmed this.

"Mark likes married women. That's his thing. He sleeps around," Segui said. "She took off and Danielle told me. I didn't know they were together. My ex-wife left me. She left the family. She just took up and left.

"Mark and I got along great when we played together. He was more of a softer person, not aggressive. I never saw that aggressive side in him. He had a soft and passive personality. My father (former major leaguer Diego Segui) is a real man, old school, who taught us to protect women and children. That's in my blood."

Segui, a first baseman, threw grounders to Grudzielanek between innings hundreds of times and took 6-3 putouts from him during games many times during their time together.

Now, they are estranged.

"David Segui has been put through a real living hell," Martin said. "It's despicable. David's case is on a whole other level of shocking. He lost years with the kids. He's one of the best dads I've ever seen. He's a really warm, kind soul. He's amazing. He's a great influence in my sons' lives."

At some point in 2023, Segui finally gained 50% custody of his kids. He told me he had not seen his kids in two years. For the summer of 2023, he said Donna gave him the kids for that period of time.

Exposion

"It's disgusting what they (courts) are doing. They are protecting the abusers. It's actually unreal," Segui told me. "They are taking the kids from the good parents and giving them back to the bad parents. That Family Bridges camp is a scam. This has been my life for the last seven years, fighting this crap. They know I am going to sue them. They've violated my constitutional rights."

Grudzielanek was also embroiled in a court battle in San Diego over child-support payments with Martin, a sports-performance coach, professional surfer and former women's softball player at UCLA.

In 2023, a court ordered Grudzielanek to pay each of his sons $500 per month in child support. The previous amount had been $100 per kid but because he was $40,000 in arrears, the court ordered him to pay up even more.

Until the $40,000 is paid in full, Grudzielanek doesn't get use of his passport.

Martin doesn't have anything good to say about her ex. They have two sons, Bryce and Brody.

"It all started when he chose to have an affair with David Segui's wife," Martin said in a phone interview. "I bet David would like to tear his head off. This could be a movie with what's taken place. David didn't know for a year his wife was fooling around with Mark. I exposed them to David.

"Mark has crushed our family and aside from the emotional damage, he also left us with nothing. He sold our house out from underneath us and went above and beyond to harm us."

Martin said Bryce doesn't want to have anything to do with his dad. She said her son often calls Segui for batting tips. Grudzielanek and Martin met in 2000 and separated in 2010.

"Mark and I didn't get married because I just felt he had a problem with cheating," Martin said. "I didn't want to get married to him. He was not a very committal type of person.

"My sons both resemble Mark a lot, but Mark wouldn't know that since he's been out of their lives going on seven years now," Martin said. "He bowed out of being a Dad long ago and sadly was never really interested in fulfilling that title anyway. He was always a convenient Dad, being there only when he chose and not when the boys needed him."

Martin said Bryce received a text from his dad recently, telling him he was dropping him from the MLB insurance plan two weeks following a labrum surgery Bryce underwent. The insurance plan costs Grudzielanek nothing, but he deleted his son from the plan anyway. Hrrmph.

"Mom, look at this," Bryce said, in showing the text to her.

"That's the lowest of the low," Martin said of Grudzielanek's decision about the insurance benefits. "It's a shocking and sad situation but reality for us all. There has been no contact from him. It's tremendously sad. When I say no contact, nothing. No texts, no calls, no gifts, nothing," Martin said.

"These boys have been raised to take the high road and also that their Dad's behaviour and choices do not reflect them. It's not easy what their Dad did to them but they have reached a space of indifference toward it."

There have been occasions when Bryce has played at tournaments and Mark shows up but walks right by his son, as if he doesn't even know him.

Said Segui, "Mark is just one of those people who has never seen the values and blessings of having children. Put it this way – people are very surprised I have maintained my composure. In God, I trust."

Vitiello's stint par for the course: platooning

Joe Vitiello had so much potential the Kansas City Royals liked him so much they selected him in the first round of the 1991 June draft of amateur players.

He never got much of a chance to prove himself with Kansas City, the Expos or the Padres. He never reached his potential but many people thought he was a really good player.

Joe's dad Joe. Sr. found it hard to believe the Royals wouldn't treat his son better.

"He dominated every level he ever played in," Joe Sr. told me. "He was drafted seventh in the country by the Royals. When I sat down at my table to sign him, I thought they would give him more than Bo Jackson and take care of him but that's not the way it works.

"He was a starter his whole career. The Royals platooned him in his rookie year. It went from there. In Kansas City, I ran into the owner, David Glass's son, in the elevator and he said, 'I can't believe everytime I see your son, he hits a home run.'"

"It's a shame. I really would have liked to have seen what he could have done right from the get-go. Give him 500 at-bats, not 100 at-bats, in 162 games. That was his spiral. You're labelled because you've become a platoon player in all aspects. Once that happens, you pretty much have to get out of that rabbit hole. It's pretty tough."

On May 3, 2003, the Expos acquired Vitiello from the San Francisco Giants in exchange for Ben Washburn. Vitiello, in a part-time role, had a solid season, hitting .342 with three homers and 13 RBI.

When I chatted with Joe Sr. about his son's Expos experience, he asked, "Do people remember the Expos?"

He then commented on Expos manager Frank Robinson's use of his son.

"Frank Robinson, he had his boys he played, players he was friendly with," said Joe Sr., a former Massachusetts state trooper. "That was the story of his career. My son was in the merry go-round. They get labelled."

When I posted on April 11, 2023 that Vitiello was celebrating his birthday, someone commented, "What a weird stretch (.342 average) to end his career."

Another man commented, "Today's teams would sign him in a flash."

The Expos signed him to a minor-league contract in April 2004 but he never made the team. By early 2005, he had packed it in his career.

Chapter 38

Segui scion of fine royalty

As the son of a former major leaguer, Diego Segui, David Segui knew what his lifestyle would be down the road when he played for the Expos and other teams.

Diego pitched 12 seasons and was travelling all the time, not seeing his family that much.

Diego pitched in 639 big-league games, producing a record of 92-111. He was the only player to appear in a uniform for both of Seattle's major-league franchises: the Pilots and the Mariners.

He was the first reliever after 59-year-old Satchell Paige fired three innings in his last major-league appearance Sept. 20, 1965.

Prior to arriving in the United States from his native Cuba, Diego threw as a kid against Fidel Castro, who was a pretty decent ball player.

Diego mastered the forkball for many years and mesmerized batters with the pitch's intricacies but he lost some of his lustre and the pitch lost some of its lustre when a Vic Davalillo liner dinged him on the knuckle of his right hand. He continued to pitch for a while but he was never quite the same after that.

"I grew up in that lifestyle, that was the normal lifestyle, travelling," David told me. "I personally watched it up front and personal. It was not a glamourous life. It's a grind, there's a lot of sacrifice, especially with the family. You need discipline.

"I was so grateful to my father. As much as he was away, he called pretty much every day to talk to me and my brothers (Danny, Diego Jr. and sister Diana) and my mom. He didn't make a lot of money in those days. He'd play winter ball in Venezuela, Puerto Rico and Mexico – he had to do that to pay the bills.

"Once I started playing, after I had kids, it makes you appreciate it more, the sacrifices that are made. My dad prepared me for my playing career. Being around the game every day (with him), you learned a lot just by watching – the glove work, the foot work, bat work. That prepared me for my playing career."

Prior to the start of the 1974 season, Diego married a Kansas gal, Emily Sauceda, who had Mexican roots, growing up in Argentine, a predominantly Spanish neigbourhood. It was a very industrial, mid-town municipality from really old 1880s and 1890s located near the river across from Kansas City, Missouri.

David was born in 1966 so it wasn't long after this that he began appearing in clubhouses and on the field before games with his dad when

Papa pitched for Oakland, the Pilots, St. Louis and the Red Sox.

"I liked all those guys. Reggie Jackson, Rollie Fingers, Sal Bando, Campy (Campaneris). Those guys were fantastic. I didn't realize they were superstars, celebrities or famous people – just later on," Segui told me. "You thought it was a normal life. You didn't realize it was so special. Then you'd get older and our friends would make a big deal out of it.

"I loved Roberto Clemente, Frank Howard. When I was a kid, Frank was so big. He was a giant, he could hit home runs. I was fortunate that when I played for the Mets, Frank was one of my coaches. He was a great man.

"You try to pretend to be those players and develop. I wouldn't trade that for anything. People don't realize the daily grind every single day, how much work is required to stay sharp.

"I had a bat in my hands when I was two years old. Funny part, my dad was more like mom. Mom would throw batting practice because dad was gone. Our skills were developed by my mom and my brothers playing ball in the backyard.

"My mother was the teacher," he said. "She was the one who took us out and she'd throw batting practice, literally throw batting practice. She'd throw the balls, hit balls. She was there on a daily basis."

One headline years ago said

Mom's fungos helped shape Segui

Emily had several sisters who were Franciscan nuns but she chose to be a mother. She's bilingual and if you heard her talk back and forth between English and Spanish, you'd never know she was of Spanish heritage, said Chris Henchek, a friend of the family from Overland, Kansas.

Diego spoke no English when he came to America but now he's very good at it. He's the godfather of Henchek's son Eddie and Danny Tartabull Jr. Henchek recalls the many times he, David and Diego would go into Diego's old barn and engage in BP, hitting balls against bales of hay and old mattresses taken from the trash.

"Between his mother and father, David learned how to be a person. Mrs. Segui taught him a lot in the baseball area. She taught him how to act. She was phenomenal," Henchek said.

"She grew up with brothers who could play. She was brought up with her brothers so she had to keep up with the brothers. David's mother was definitely a baseball parent. You don't hear anything out of her but she gets her point across.

"Emily is the driving force behind David and so is his brother Danny. The whole family is so storied. David was always driven. A lot of kids struggle through life but David didn't," Henchek added.

Segui attended Louisiana Tech and Kansas City Community College in Kansas and was signed for the Orioles by scout Ray Crone, who at one time scouted for the Expos and played Triple-A ball for the Toronto Maple Leafs.

Segui plied his trade with Baltimore until he was traded to the Mets near the end of spring training in 1994 following the signing of Rafael Palmeiro. Segui had hit 10 homers and drove in 66 runs while batting

Expos**ion**

Segui family photo
Former Expo David Segui, top left, poses with brothers Diego Jr. and Daniel and sister Diana with their parents Diego and Emily.

.273 with Baltimore in 1994 and then the Os went for experience.

"Palmeiro signed as a free agent and that made me expendable," Segui said. "The Orioles talked about sending me to Triple-A. I said I'm not going back to Triple-A. They did me a favour and traded me to the Mets."

In Flushing Meadows, Segui spent the entire 1994 season with the Mets with less stellar numbers of 10 homers, 43 RBI and a .241 BA. He began the 1995 season with the Mets and then something nice happened. He was traded to the Expos for Reid Cornelius on June 8 and his career just blossomed.

"It's a business. It's a game but it's a business," Segui told me of the trade to Montreal. "I was hitting well over .300 (.329) with the Mets. I was platooning. They asked me to play outfield.

"Cliff Floyd (Expos) broke his wrist. They needed a first baseman right away. It was a great thing to happen in my career. I loved playing for Felipe. He was like an uncle. I'd known him since I was a kid (when Diego and Felipe played for Oakland). They were a great bunch of guys in Montreal. It was an opportunity to play every day. All Felipe wanted was for you to be on time and play hard."

Until I looked online, I hadn't realize Segui was such a tremendous first baseman, good with the glove, scooping balls out of the dirt and taking base hits away from opposing hitters.

During his time with the Expos in 1995, his fielding percentage was .997. He sure was underrated and underappreciated and overlooked in the overall scheme of things in all of his time in the majors.

Following the 1995 season, Segui was signed by the Expos to a two-year deal worth $3.1-million.

Segui was a huge part of the miracle that took place in 1996 when the Expos challenged for the NL East for a good portion of the season before they ran out of gas to finish at 88-74.

He batted .286 with 11 homers and 58 RBI and equally as important was what he was doing around first and the second half of double plays. Handling 1,041 chances, Segui committed only six errors and his fielding percentage was .993. He showed he was an all-round, solid player.

"We couldn't catch Atlanta in 1996. It was a learning experience for a lot of guys," Segui said, as he explained how a better than average team can do wonders when they all come together.

"You don't have to be a superstar. We didn't have a roster of superstars. You go out and compete every day at the highest level. That was Felipe and the coaching staff. We were very close. We all believed in each other."

In 1997, the Expos slumped in general but Segui continued to excel with 21 homers, 68 RBI and a .307 average. His fielding percentage remained excellent at .995 based on only six errors in 1,129 chances. Pretty gall-darn good, if you ask me.

In one game, on May 16, Segui was a key cog in the biggest comeback in Expos history. The Expos fought back from a 11-2 hole after three innings to win 14-13, making their way against old pitching friend Kirk Rueter.

Segui went 4-for-6 with an RBI, three runs, a homer and the game-winning RBI in the bottom of the ninth inning. The Expos had tied the game in the eighth inning and then Segui delivered the walk-off hit, scoring Mike Lansing.

Following the 1997 season, Segui wasn't re-signed by Montreal so he inked a deal with the Mariners, his dad's old team. The deal was for $2.35-million which was about $800,000 more than what he earned in 1997.

"I knew they were not going to sign me," Segui said of his departure from Montreal. "I knew it was a pattern. They didn't pay their players. They let them go and they'd go and play somewhere else. If you're going to make some money, they let you go somewhere else.

"I loved the city. I loved Montreal – the culture, the arts, food, restaurants, they talk to you on the subway. People were so good to me. I really enjoyed it," Segui said. "Montreal is the most loving city I've played in and lived in. Seattle was fun, Cleveland, Baltimore. There was something special about Montreal. I went to Texas – it was okay. Toronto is the not the same as the United States. I'd just been traded from Seattle – it didn't make sense. I didn't feel like I was in Toronto. I didn't find it like home. I was only there a short time. It doesn't compare to Montreal."

Thank you, David, for the great chat.

Chapter 39

Terry Francona, Stan Hough and Milton Bradley

Back in 1981, Stan Hough remembers playing Double-A ball against Terry Francona, a hotshot Expos prospect with the Memphis Chicks.

20 years later in 2001, Hough saw Francona in street clothes at NBT Bank Stadium in Syracuse, N.Y. as a scout for the Cleveland Indians. Hough was managing the Expos Triple-A club, the Ottawa Lynx, and they were playing the Syracuse SkyChiefs, the Toronto Blue Jays' affiliate.

Although Hough doesn't quite know the exact date of Francona's presence at the game, he figures it was 10 days prior to the annual July 31 trade deadline.

"Terry Francona had just been let go (end of 2000 season) by the Phillies as manager," Hough recalled. "He had been hired as a special assistant to the president (John Hart) of the Cleveland Indians. He was the only person up in the stands behind home plate. I thought at the time he's here to watch Milton.

"We were having batting practice that day and I went up to Milton Bradley and said, "That's Terry Francona up there. Go up there and talk to him. Cleveland's not going to pick up Kenny Lofton's option and they might like you.' I actually told him Francona was there to see him," Hough was telling me about a priceless story.

"Milton said, 'Really? Really!' He didn't understand where I was going with that. I had to explain to him the situation with Cleveland and Kenny Lofton with him. So Milton goes up there and talks to Francona."

Bradley made his pitch to Francona to be traded to the Indians and very likely in return, Francona conducted an interview with Bradley.

"This is exactly how it all went down," Hough said. "He went to the backstop and called Francona down and they talked until BP was over. He talked to him all through batting practice. We had to go up and get him out of there so we could put a uniform on him to play the game. I didn't talk to Terry at all."

Lofton had played for the Indians on two different stints totalling nine seasons sandwiched around one season with the Atlanta Braves in 1997. Hough had read in a newspaper Lofton was slated to earn $7.5-million in 2002, meaning Bradley would be a much cheaper replacement.

"Lofton was hitting roughly .260 with three home runs. He was older as well," Hough recalled. "I thought he would be let go the next year because his numbers weren't good enough to warrant them picking up that option.

"I was under orders from Montreal to play Milton so they could trade him. Milton was sent to me for good. He was not going to be called back to Montreal for any reason. I told Milton that. I said, 'I'm playing you to trade you.' Evidently, Milton had upset management and/or the owner (Jeffrey Loria) by way of his awful behaviour. I'm not exactly sure why.

"I was made aware his conduct was less than acceptable with the Montreal Expos. What I remember – I was told they didn't care if he hit a home run every time up, he wasn't coming back to Montreal."

Bradley was a hugely talented but mercurial player taken by the Expos in the second round of the MLB draft in 1996. He did some silly and stupid things to upset Expos GM Jim Beattie – and Loria.

Bradley had only played parts of the 2000 and 2001 seasons with Montreal but he was compared to the likes of Vlad Guerrero, Andre Dawson and many others. He was oozing in talent. Oozing. But his bad temper, really bad temper, outweighed any positives he had to offer.

"I added it all up with respect to Milton's situation and told Milton they were there to watch him," Hough added. "I'm not sure who Terry was watching but I made Milton believe he was looking at him. It was all psychology. It worked.

"I didn't tell anyone in the news media about it. I was asked to play him to trade him by Jim Beattie. That is how I got in touch with the Indians. I just put 2 + 2 together and decided that trick might work and it did," Hough said, laughing.

Francona reported back to Hart about this rendez-vous with Bradley and on July 31, Bradley was dealt to the Indians by the Expos in exchange for pitcher Zack Day.

How about that for a story? Priceless indeed.

In notes from the 2002 Expos media guide talking about highlights from the 2001 season, the club rubbed salt into Bradley's wounds and rightly so by saying, "The Expos give up on outspoken young outfielder Milton Bradley, trading him to the Indians for pitching prospect Zack Day."

Bradley's time with Hough and the Lynx was not without controversy.

"There was a time in Ottawa when Milton skied a pop up over second. If he had caught it somewhere else on the bat, it would have been a home run," Hough explained. "So, he stood there at home plate and starting taking his batting gloves off. I told Dan McKinley to go out and take his place in the lineup.

"Carl Pavano was close to me and he said, 'What are you doing?' I told him, 'Wait a minute. You stay out of it.' I took Milton aside in the dugout and I said, 'Sit down and relax. Are you too tired to run? You should be running that ball out as you should be. We're trying to get you traded but if you pull that stuff again, I'm going to take you out of the game.' I told him he had to play hard.

"I was given free rein to remove him from a ball game, if he wasn't hustling. Milton had the tools offensively and defensively. He was a force to be reckoned with. He was a special talent but, in my opinion, socially awkward."

Exposion

Canadian Baseball HOF
Milton Bradley

Hough recalls later on in his career when the Kansas City Royals called him in Waco, Texas, where he lives, to gather his thoughts about Bradley for a possible free-agent signing. Hough's opinions were negative and he was honest.

"I was on a speaker phone. I told the Royals Bradley had a special talent," Hough said. "Water runs in his veins but he was extremely immature. I didn't recommend they sign him."

Bradley's career never did go anywhere. It went sideways.

Following that trade of Bradley to Cleveland, Francona finished that season as a sidekick to Hart and then took on one-season roles as a coach with the Texas Rangers and Oakland Athletics before embarking on a spectacular career as a manager with the Red Sox and Indians.

Later on this decade, Francona will be elected into Cooperstown. He appears to be finished as a manager but you might see him in a team's front office.

That story about him, Hough and Bradley sure was a dandy one.

Chapter 40

The sneaky John Patterson narrative

The Expos lost John Patterson the first time but they got him back at a cheaper rate.

In one of the weirdest draft scenarios in Expos' franchise history, the club selected the highly touted pitcher in the first round and fifth overall in the June, 1996 draft out of West Orange-Stark high school in Texas and then lost him on a technicality.

The Expos apparently sent him a contract offer to sign. The only problem is, the contract was not printed on official team letterhead. Unreal. Can you imagine? At least, that's what I was told. There also were other extenuating circumstances.

The commissioner's office ruled the transaction null and void and Patterson was granted free agency. He signed with the Arizona Diamondbacks, who had been awarded an expansion franchise but would not start playing until 1998.

Patterson signed with the Diamondbacks for $6.075-million. Pretty good coin. It wasn't the type of money the Expos could really afford anyway. No way. Where in their limited funds and small payroll could they find that much money to pay a high draft pick?

It wouldn't have surprised me if Patterson had decided also that he didn't want to play in Montreal.

I wonder if the Expos were quite happy they didn't have to pay that signing bonus. Heading into the draft, the Expos sure loved what they saw in Patterson.

"I remember. I saw him twice that year. He was quite a prospect in Beaumont," recalled then Expos scouting director Jim Fleming. "He had quite an arm."

That's when Fleming began to explain what happened when the club lost the negotiation rights to Patterson. It appears teams were blindsided by agents for certain high picks like Patterson, Matt White and Travis Lee. Fleming and scout Eddie Haas went to Patterson's house before the draft happened.

"There were five kids in that draft they were trying to sneak into free agency," Fleming said. "It was kind of a loophole. There was a document that needed to be signed. We were not aware of it. I don't remember all the details.

"We tried to go in the house to see him and his father and try to get a feel for the player, especially if he was a high school kid, to see how attached there were (to being drafted) and that there would be no surprises after you draft him. The agents were waiting for the draft to happen. They wouldn't let us in the house because they didn't want us to sign that document. There was nothing we could do."

As for that Wikipedia report that said something about the Expos offer being sent on no Expos' letterhead, Fleming said, "I don't remember all the details. There was a loophole. There were procedures."

In a normal draft, Fleming and his staff were prepared to offer Patterson such and such amount of money and there could be some negotiation but it never came to pass. The Expos were prepared to offer much less than what Patterson received in free agency.

What should have been only the Expos negotiating with Patterson, they lost the rights to him and Patterson was open to offers from the other 29 teams.

"We wouldn't have even come closer to that figure," Fleming said of the $6-million amount. "They were free agents and it runs the cost way up."

According to a document I received, Patterson, White and Lee, all first-round picks that year, "filed requests with the MLB executive council to be declared free agents under MLR 4(e)."

The Hendricks Bros, based in Texas, represented Patterson, Scott Boras handled Lee.

I asked somebody what is MLR 4(e)? This was the answer:

"Rule 4(D),(E) revokes a club's Negotiation Right to a draft pick and sets the draft pick free to sign with other Clubs, if the Club fails to tender the draft pick an executed Uniform Player contract within a certain time."

The "certain time" was within a week or 10 days, although the exact number of days is unclear. This whole saga dragged on long after the June draft ended.

So then this is what happened. Close to 3½ months following the draft, a ruling was made Sept. 24, 1996 by Bill Murray of the commissioner's office:

"After reviewing submissions from the players and the respective clubs, the executive council has voided the negotiation rights of the three clubs with respect to these three players.

"All clubs are advised that each of these players may be signed to a major-league contract by any Major League Club, beginning at noon Eastern time on Monday, September 30, 1996."

Oddly enough, Kris Benson, the first pick overall, decided to stick with the Pirates and signed a $2-million bonus, perhaps not knowing about the loophole. No. 2 pick Lee signed for $10.2-million with Tampa Bay. No. 3 Braden Looper had no complaint with the process and received an unknown amount from the Cardinals.

No. 4 pick Billy Koch received $1.45-million from the Blue Jays. Then came Patterson. So I'm guessing the Expos would have offered maybe $1.25-million.

With the help of the Hendricks Bros, Patterson lucked out on the free-agent market. He signed on Nov. 7 after being courted by a number of teams. Because Patterson signed so late, he was unable to play Instructional league ball in Arizona that fall.

I sent an email to Patterson and left a phone message for him but he never replied. In my research April 17, 2023, I stumbled upon an article written about him in a Texas newspaper called the Katy Krail Weekly. In that story, Patterson revealed the whole saga about him not signing with Montreal.

"It looked like I was either going to be the first overall pick with Pittsburgh or the sixth overall pick of the Detroit Tigers," Patterson told the Katy newspaper. "We really hadn't heard much from Montreal. It was a little bit of a surprise, but I was super excited. I had just gotten drafted fifth overall and was excited that I got to live a dream that I had since I was nine years old."

Patterson claimed Montreal was slow in trying to sign him.

"I visited the team, Felipe Alou was the manager and I watched the players take batting practice," Patterson said. "Montreal made me one offer and basically said 'That was it!' "

At one point, Patterson had considered playing in college and perhaps going back into the draft. He had also signed a letter of intent to go to Louisiana State University.

"But I just wanted to play professional baseball," Patterson told the paper.

During negotiations, Patterson said he was flanked by his father Doug, who played eight years in the Baltimore Orioles' minor league organization, and a team from Hendricks Sports Management.

When the Expos' contract offer was not to Patterson's liking, the "unthinkable happened", the newspaper said.

"Call it, in baseball terms, an E-10," the anonymous writer said.

"Did you ever receive an official letter from Montreal?" Patterson's agent asked. "One that said they drafted you fifth overall and offered you this amount of money?" Patterson couldn't remember so he had his dad browse through a bunch of papers. Supposedly, papa Patterson found paperwork not on official letterhead, which apparently is a violation of the terms of contract negotiations.

"Do we file a complaint?" Patterson thought. "It was a pretty big risk." As is stated above in this story, the commissioner's office granted Patterson free agency before he ever fired a pitch in anger in professional baseball.

"We started getting offers almost immediately from everybody that were triple or quadruple what Montreal had offered," Patterson told the paper.

Patterson said he had visits with the Yankees and Tampa Bay Devil Rays but decided on the Diamondbacks.

He was elated with his $6-million contract but admitted to the Katy newspaper he saw jealousy in the eyes of some fellow minor leaguers.

"I felt somewhat guilty because I had so much money and other guys were struggling," Patterson said. "I would take the guys out to dinner, but it is something you really can't escape from. I even felt a little bit from the coaching staff. I started to have trust issues. It was affecting my personality and I began putting pressure on myself."

Exposion

His first round of pro ball in 1997 was disappointing. He was 1-9 with South Bend, Indiana in the Midwest league. Oddly enough, his ERA was very commendable at 3.23 in 78 innings and 18 starts.

In 1998, Patterson was posted to High Point in California. He was 8-7 with a 2.83 ERA. In 1999, he split time in Double-A in El Paso, Tex. and Triple-A in Tucson, sporting an overall 9-11 record.

Also in 1999, he managed to be involved in another project: he had a 1-0 record with a 1.39 ERA and 12 strikeouts in 13 innings for Team USA at the 1999 Pan American Games played in Winnipeg.

"It was the most fun I have ever had playing baseball," Patterson told the paper about the Winnipeg tournament.

It was in the Arizona organization that Patterson met up with Eric Knott, who eventually played for the Expos, just like Patterson. How ironic.

For over 25 years, Patterson and Knott have been best friends and live close to each other in Prosper, Texas. How about that? Knott was born in Illinois, attended college in Florida and with no connection to Texas, decided to move to Texas to be close to Patterson.

"Patty and I played at every level in the minor leagues with Arizona," Knott told me. "Long time friend. Lives down the road."

Pretty neat stuff. I've always admired people who met young in baseball and remained close afterward. In the case of Patterson and Knott, it's very much similar to the great friendship between former Expos Cliff Floyd and Rondell White, who live on the same street in Davie, Florida after they met in the early 1990s.

Patterson finally made his big-league debut July 20, 2002 but he didn't pan out with Arizona. In an ironic twist, he was dealt to the Expos for Randy Choate on March 27, 2004. Choate had spent all of spring training with the Expos but never got to play for them. How weird is that? And the Expos got Patterson at a salary very reasonable because he was a pre-arbitration player. After getting squeezed out of getting Patterson in 1996, the Expos re-acquired him so to speak.

Patterson was 4-7 with the Expos in their final season with an ERA of 5.03. He made 19 appearances, all starts.

He's part of some interesting Expos trivia: he was the last starting pitcher in franchise history, doing so on Oct. 3, 2003 at Shea Stadium. He was grateful to manager Frank Robinson for his time in Montreal that season and getting the ball for the final game.

"When I got to Montreal, I learned more about Frank's career, his accomplishments and all of the adversity he had to overcome," Patterson said. "Turns out that Frank was a great person. I loved Frank. It takes a little bit to get to know him. But Frank was the one manager I ever had that I felt truly cared about me. He wanted you to do well. He could have been self-absorbed, but he wasn't."

Patterson followed Robinson and the Expos to Washington and was outstanding in 2006 with a 9-7 mark and a neat 3.13 ERA in 198.1 innings. Due to injuries and depression/mental health issues which he revealed in his book Perspective Perception Perseverance, he was out of baseball before he reached age 30.

The sneaky John Patterson narrative

As Fleming looks back, drafting Patterson out of high school meant you never know how a player like him may fare out.

"If you draft 20 guys and sign three or four, you've done well. It takes some luck. You're betting on the future," Fleming said.

Patterson had earned many look-sees in the 1990s from scouts after head-turning stints at West Orange high, an institution of maybe 1,100 students, some of whom took auto-body and woodworking courses to develop a skill or a craft.

Patterson wanted more constructive employment so he pursued baseball. He committed to Louisiana State University until he was drafted. He went directly into pro ball.

Canadian Baseball HOF
John Patterson

"I think John had the change up of the 1990s," said his high school coach Dan Hooks. "It had that type of slip. He had a two-seam fastball and a four-seamer. He could bring it.

"The work ethic was there. He never agreed with all my decisions but he did everything I asked him to do. He was our greatest athlete. There's one game he pitched and there were 60 scouts there to see him and Joe Lawrence.

"I wasn't surprised he was drafted. I was surprised by who (Montreal) he was drafted by," Hooks said.

Chapter 41

Ad in Baseball Weekly paper stoked DeHart

From the famous, laid-back, midwest city of Topeka, Kansas that has spawned Expos such as Ross Grimsley and Mike Torrez and actresses like Annette Bening, Rick DeHart thrived on determination, resilience and positivity to keep going in the face of adversity.

The end result was that he earned a spot in the annals of the major leagues with the Expos without benefit of an invitation to spring training. He was called up to the majors and had never been on the 25-man roster.

His story is a good-feel energizer. It's the kind of story I love.

"When I signed with the Expos, I didn't get any money, just a glove and cleats and a jacket that was too small," DeHart told me. "I wasn't a big kid. I was never fast or big enough. I grew up in baseball with a ball and glove in my hand. Me and my brother would throw tennis balls against the wall.

"Every morning, we'd get up and the first thing, we're throwing and pitching and hitting against each other in games. Morning till night. It was only in my senior year at Seaman high school that we started a baseball team. It was a 10-game season, a trial, in 1986."

The team was called the Topeka Stars, a Babe Ruth team. Coach was Frank Magee, probably one of the biggest coaches in the state of Kansas.

"Rick would have people tell him that he couldn't do it. They said, 'Hang it up.' He's a great role model because he had people telling him he couldn't make it," Magee told me. "He had not matured yet (body wise at Seaman). He was skinny. He didn't throw real hard. He had movement. His arm was nice and relaxed. You see guys not throwing anything and looks like they have nothing but Rick, it would just shoot out of his hand. He had a nice, loose upper body."

It was Magee, who helped nurture and promote DeHart, helping him as much as he could. He would drive DeHart around to draft-combines tryouts. Nobody took him. Prospective teams thought he wasn't fast enough, wasn't big enough.

In his draft year of 1986, DeHart wasn't selected. He was disappointed but he just kept plugging away. There had to be somebody interested in a southpaw. That was his mindset. He continued to pitch while getting some education at Washburn University. It was a NAIT school in Topeka.

"Rick was told over and over and over again he couldn't do it," Magee said.

He didn't grow up until he went to Fort Scott Community College two hours from home where that pencil-thin frame "started to grow up", as Magee phrased it.

Then came some unexpected turn of events, thanks to a newspaper owned by USA Today no longer in existence. It was March of 1992.

"Baseball was still in my blood," DeHart said. "There was a paper called Baseball Weekly. Every Monday I'd get off work and go to the grocery store and get Baseball Weekly. They had a lot of articles and then at the back of the paper, they had ads, selling equipment and stuff like that.

"I noticed an ad talking about an umpiring school. I said to myself, 'Maybe that's my calling.' Then right below that was an ad saying people were needed for a new league in Taiwan. It gave a phone number to call. Randy Kierce was the guy running it. It was going to be a three-day tryout."

So with the blessing of his parents, DeHart packed his bags with clothes and magazines and got on a Greyhound bus that took him to Fort Lauderdale. Next day, he shows up at a complex with 150 others from professionals to high schoolers at an open tryout – directed not really at Taiwan but for an independent league.

"Make a long story short, I got in there, I got on the mound and I pitched," DeHart said. "I threw over the backstop. There was a screen behind home plate. Some people were saying, 'Hold it, this kid is too wild.' But I settled down and I ended up striking out three guys on nine pitches. I must have been good on the radar gun.

"A scout for the Montreal Expos, Randy Kierce, came up to me and said, 'How bad do you want to go to Taiwan?' "

Kierce picks up the story by observing DeHart was a "lefty and throwing pretty hard". Kierce proceeded to tell DeHart he wanted to arrange something different for him that day.

"Rick didn't understand what was going on. He was kind of upset at the beginning. I didn't want him to throw for the independent teams," Kierce told me. "It turned out to be his advantage.

"I wasn't running the camp. I let organizations run tryout camps there at the Play Ball Baseball Academy. I had been doing all national scouting for the Expos. I saw Rick warming up in the bullpen. We took him up to West Palm Beach."

DeHart said he was just a "kid from the midwest" being given an opportunity by the Expos in the minor leagues 30 minutes north of Fort Lauderdale.

"Randy took me to the minor-league camp in Lantana and dropped me off at the Marriott hotel. I was thrown into a hotel. I didn't have a hotel room, There was no room," DeHart said.

"Some of the rooms had three guys staying in them and they were pissed off. They were so mad at me because they put me in their room. I had to sleep in the lobby a couple of nights. Spring training was off and running already.

"Nobody is talking to me. Players were saying, 'What is he doing here?' Nobody wanted to play catch with me. There were other left-handers there. We were all in competition. They were all kind of against me. I was one of the most hated guys.

"I was a left-hander who showed up out of nowhere. I was in Montreal camp for a few days before anyone paid attention to me. I finally walked up to the office and told them I wanted to go home. I told them I was on a Greyound bus for three days."

Whoever he talked to him, told him he would get to pitch that day.

"It was an intrasquad game and the first three batters were Cliff Floyd, Shane Andrews, and I can't remember the other guy – I ended up striking out all three of them," DeHart said.

Kierce and a few others watching him couldn't believe what DeHart was doing, striking out three guys and agreed something had to be done to sign him.

"In two days, they gave me a contract, no signing bonus, nothing to bargain," DeHart told me. "They gave me cleats, a glove and a jacket that was too small but I felt like a million dollars – all because of an ad in the newspaper."

Crazy, crazy good stuff happened to DeHart after all the grief he had gone through. According to Baseball Almanac, the Expos signed DeHart on March 24, a terrific birthday present because he turned 20 on March 21.

Said Kierce: "I like to tell the story that the first guy I signed was Rick DeHart, a left-hander, and the last guy I signed was Rick van den Hurk, a right-hander, for the Marlins. He now runs the Dutch baseball federation."

So DeHart pitched in West Palm, Harrisburg, Ottawa and then one day in 1997, while he was with the Ottawa Lynx in Columbus, Ohio playing against the Clippers, he got the shock of his life. After five years bouncing around with different minor-league teams, he got the chance of a lifetime.

He was in the Lynx clubhouse and teammate Geoff Blum handed him his latest cheque. He was making no more than $1,200 a month and he opened up the cheque to see that it was only $300 after paying so many taxes in Canada.

DeHart was pissed. He threw the cheque into his locker and started yelling.

"I can't make any money doing this," he muttered to himself, Blum and anyone else within hearing distance. He wasn't on the Expos' 40-man roster and he had thought of going to Japan but Kierce told him to hang on. Hanging on paid off.

What raised DeHart's eyebrows during and after the first game was that he was not used in the first game of a doubleheader against the Clippers, who he said were "full of left handed hitters and I'm a lefty." He added "I was the only lefty in the bullpen." He wondered why he wasn't called in to pitch or warm up in the bullpen. He thought, oh, maybe they were just saving him for the nightcap.

After the first game, he got a tap on the shoulder in the clubhouse from manager Pat Kelly and pitching coach Bo McLaughlin. He figured they had bad news for him.

"I was yelling and throwing things. I figured I was being let go," DeHart told me. "I could understand. I wasn't making any money."

Kelly and McLaughlin directed him into the manager's office and he sat down on a chair. He wasn't being let go but was told he was to report to Philadelphia to meet the Expos. He was going to the big leagues finally. He was kept out of the first game because the Lynx didn't want him to get hurt since he was going to the big show.

"My body went limp. I thought it was a pipe dream. Oh my god," DeHart said. "Pat and Bo had tears in their eyes because they knew the trials and tribulations of playing in the minor leagues. Lee Smith had retired or was told to retire and they would have to release him to make a spot on the 25-man roster. He was one of the best closers in baseball.

"I couldn't even afford my own car in the minor leagues – and I got a plane ticket to meet the Expos in Philadelphia. I left early in the morning and got there early in the afternoon.

"I got a phone call from Ugueth Urbina. There was Mark Grudzielanek and Pedro Martinez was the biggest star – they were there when I got to the hotel. They were in the lobby. We were going for lunch. I had a lot of buddies, guys I had played with in the minors.

"I played winter ball with (Vladdy) Guerrero. I was blown away. I knew Urbina. I used to watch Pedro and watch him dominate. When I saw him face to face, God, he's small. He's one of the nicest guys in baseball. Here I am a nobody and he treated me so nice."

DeHart travelled with some of the players to the ballpark from downtown and he gets into the clubhouse, noticing very quickly about what he's going to be wearing and the feel of his new clothing.

"When I put on the uniform, it felt like pyjamas. 100% cotton uniforms. They were so light, so comfortable. It was something you'd wear to bed," DeHart said, gushing. "They were so different than the minor-league uniforms.

"I had no cleats so Jamey Carroll gave me a pair of old cleats to wear in the game. I'm from a small Midwestern town where they'd never been more 1,000 at a game and here I am pitching before 20,000. Different lifestyle, bigger hotels, bigger cities. I was happy just to be in Triple-A. Triple-A is the farthest I thought I would get."

DeHart was the fourth of four Expos pitchers that night and the Phillies would eventually win 6-0. DeHart replaced Jose Paniagua in the ninth inning. The date was July 15, 1997.

"They threw me right into the game," he said. "It was old Veterans Stadium. I was sitting in the bullpen. In front of the bullpen was plexiglass. I couldn't see the plexiglass because of bubble gum and dirt. I got the call to come in. I was nervous. I opened up the bullpen door to go on the field and I was looking at the Jumbotron and I'm saying, 'Don't trip, don't trip.' My legs were shaking. I was trying to be an umpire and I get called up to the big leagues. I signed for a pair of spikes and a glove. There was no money invested in me. It blew me away.

"There were men on first and second with one out when I came in. Rico Brogna was the first batter I faced. Brogna hits a ball to Mike Lansing at second and he throws to Grudzielanek at the bag. Grudz caught the ball and thought there were two out and started jogging to the dugout."

DeHart should have been out of the inning with a double play if not for Grudzielanek's guffaw. Instead, there were runners at first and third with two out. Then, perhaps nervous, DeHart threw a wild pitch and walked Mike Lieberthal.

Kevin Blocker drove home two runs with a double before DeHart fanned Curt Schilling on a called strike for "my first major-league strikeout."

DeHart was sent back to Ottawa exactly one month after he was called up and then he returned as a September call-up. It was on Sept. 28 when DeHart really turned heads in the fifth inning when he replaced Paniagua, the same guy he replaced in his debut.

Yep, he inherited three runners and stranded them all by striking out Lenny Watkins, Jon Nunnally and Chris Stynes.

"It was the last game of the season. We were losing against the Reds. I came in with the bases loaded and nobody out. I struck out the side. I got a standing ovation," DeHart said. "Felipe said, 'You did an awesome job. You proved us wrong.'"

Shortly after the season ended, DeHart reported for winter-ball duty in the Dominican Republic. In parts of the next two seasons, he pitched a little bit for the Expos, proud to have made the team out of spring training in 1998 at "my first big-league camp."

Then he was sold to Hiroshima Toyo Carp in Japan on June 11, 1999.

"I was heartbroken to leave Montreal. I always wanted to stay with the Expos," he said. "I came up with them. Two months into the season, my agent said the Japanese team was very interested in me. The team had to buy out my contract for $300,000. Montreal got a deal out of it."

On Dec. 17, 1999, he was signed as a free agent by the Dodgers and cherished the time meeting Dodgers greats Sandy Koufax and Tommy Lasorda but he sat out all of the 2000 season due to a long recovery from Tommy John surgery.

He finished out his short career in the big leagues by playing for the Royals in Kansas City, Missouri, just across the river from Topeka.

"I loved Montreal. I loved Ottawa. I hold Montreal dear to my heart. Olympic Stadium – I stared at the stadium. It was the most beautiful thing in my life. It was like the seventh wonder of the world. You'd see it on TV and on posters. I felt perfect with Montreal," DeHart said. "I remember we had a meeting in the clubhouse in 1999 and they didn't know if they'd have a team next year.

"My most prized possession is a team photo on the night Felipe Alou was honoured. There was a painting given to Felipe. The photo was taken in the middle of the field by second base. I'll take that photo to the grave with me," he said, laughing.

DeHart hung around long enough to qualify for a MLB pension and since the age of 50, he has been taking advantage of it. He wasn't aware of such a pension until Lorenzo Bundy in the Expos organization told him about it.

He thought he only got paid for the games he pitched in but the way it works, you get paid if you are on the 25-man roster, even if you do not appear in a game. He could just pitch on the side in the bullpen, sit in the dugout and you get service time.

"It ain't much – $1,000 a month for throwing a baseball," he said, chuckling.

Since 2016, he has been working at a juvenile-corrections facility in Topeka where he works as a quasi gym teacher with kids, who've been into drugs, gangs, violent crime or have had a bad family life. He also does some public speaking and tells people how he got to the big leagues.

"I try to bring something to kids' lives," he said.

Somewhere in those speeches, he's mentioning that ad in Baseball Weekly.

Thanks, Rick, for this wonderful story. I have to admit it's my favourite chapter in this book.

"Danny, thank you from the bottom of my heart for taking the time to do this," DeHart said.

Canadian Baseball HOF
Rick DeHart

Photo courtesy Rick DeHart

This is a partial team photo Rick DeHart is most proud to have in his possession. It was a night in 1999 when manager Felipe Alou was honoured prior to a game in Montreal. Top row, left to right: Vladimir Guerrero, Felipe Alou, Bobby Henley, Dustin Hermanson (30) and Rick DeHart. Front row: Anthony Telford, Chris Widger and Shane Andrews.

Chapter 42

The ups and downs of Hideki Irabu

In his brief, unsuccessful venture with the Expos, the late Hideki Irabu found some peace and solace when he met 2001 teammate Fernando Tatis.

What I didn't know until June 20, 2023 was that Irabu had secured a special bond with Tatis in 2001 due to scenarios that had developed in their lives. Both had spent a fair amount of their time on earth trying to find their respective fathers, who had vanished for a long time.

Expos fan and Japanese Buddhish monk Hiroo Toyooka, who I featured in one of my earlier books and speaks/writes pretty decent English, tipped me off about this fascinating story on that day in June while I looked at my emails in the middle of the night. I was immediately intrigued and fascinated. Thank you, Hiroo, for this revelation.

I did know Irabu was born to an American GI meteorologist Steven Thompson, who was stationed in the U.S. Air Force on the Japanese island of Okinawa. While in Japan, he dated a Japanese lady, Kazue, who gave birth to Hideki on May 5, 1969. His birthplace is listed as Hirara in Japan and he was raised in lower-class Osaka, according to writer Robert Whiting.

"I know Irabu was friends with Fernando Tatis when he was in Montreal," Toyooka said. "Tatis' father, a baseball player, was separated during his childhood. Tatis had set goals for his MLB success to find his father. Same with Irabu – his father had been in Vietnam before his birth."

According to at least one online report, Thompson did meet his son and Kazue shortly after his birth but disappeared and father and son didn't meet again for close to 30 years when Hideki pitched for the Yankees. Their reunion was cordial, but they never continued to see each other much afterward.

"Tatis was in a similar situation after his father Fernando Sr. vanished when he was a young man," Toyooka told me. "Father and son did meet many years later. It seems that there was a deep symmetry between Irabu and Tatis."

Tatis, the Expo, was born in 1975 but his dad left the household when he was four in 1979. For 20 years, they didn't see other until 1999. A story in the New York Times by Murray Chass talking about the search for the father resulted in a reunion.

I tried getting a hold of Tatis through his agent Gary Goodman but there was no reply. I talked with Goodman, and he suggested sending

The ups and downs of Hideki Irabu

McCord Museum collection
Hideki Irabu, left, struck up a friendship with Fernando Tatis, the guy in the middle.

him an email about Tatis. A photo I have in this chapter shows Irabu smiling with Tatis to his left in the Expos' dugout.

Another guy I would have like to have chatted with about Irabu was Tim Raines, who was Irabu's teammate for two seasons with the Yankees and part of the 2001 season with Montreal.

From what I could see in my research is that there had been no prior mention of the Irabu-Tatis friendship until Toyooka told me.

Irabu was a loner for the most part during his time with the Expos and I was told he was not close to anyone on the team in his two seasons there, other than Tatis and likely Raines.

"The Expos had high hopes for him, but it didn't work out. He had some injuries," Irabu's agent Don Nomura told me in 2023 in a brief phone interview. I wanted Nomura to tell me more, but he declined to talk anymore down the road.

For sure, the Expos had "high hopes" for Irabu because he was a Japanese institution, he was a quasi-star with the Yankees, who won the

Explosion

World Series in both 1998 and 1999. Oddly, Irabu only pitched in one post-season game in 1998-99. He appeared in one game of the 1999 ALDS against the Red Sox, and it was a bad outing – he allowed 13 hits and eight runs in only 4.2 innings.

In one of those regular-season games, Irabu pitched in Montreal against the Expos and singled up the middle. In another bat, on an attempted bunt as I saw online, he put his bat way up over his head on a ball and made contact and the ball bounded out to short. He made it to first on an E6.

Seeing the potential Irabu had and the fact that he did win two World Series rings, the Expos acquired him as a Christmas present on Dec. 22, 1999 in exchange for Jake Westbrook and two PTBNL: Ted Lilly and Christian Parker.

Expos owner Jeffrey Loria orchestrated the trade because he's from New York and loved the Yankees and would have seen Irabu pitch at Yankee Stadium. Loria had taken over principal ownership of the Expos not long prior to that.

Two days earlier, Loria had signed Australian lefty Graeme Lloyd to a ridiculously high free-agent contract – three years for $9-million – as if the Expos could afford him. It was Loria trying to be Jerry Jones or Charlie Finley.

From what I have read, Irabu's approval was needed for a trade to Montreal and Loria was so eager to get him that he agreed to restructure the option year in his contract for 2001. The Expos guaranteed $2.5 million of the $4 million salary and provided for more of it to be guaranteed incrementally depending on the number of innings he pitched.

"We're not doing this for the short term," Loria told reporters. "We're interested in improving the starting rotation and he'll be one of the top three starters. He's a tremendous addition to this rotation. We're looking to bring in quality players. Hideki's got one of the meanest split-fingers I've ever seen."

And he had a mean fastball that sometimes got near 100 mph.

Nomura told reporters at the time Irabu was "somewhat surprised" by the trade, "but he's happy with the deal we cut with Montreal. He's happy that he's wanted up there. Jeff Loria certainly was a big thing. He really supports Hideki."

Yankees GM Brian Cashman put it this way: "Maybe he gets a chance to start fresh, in a new country with a new team. In New York, it's a tough situation. It's not for everybody. I'm not saying it wasn't for Hideki. But playing elsewhere can be easier for some players. That might be the case with Hideki."

Irabu never did get to show much what he was made of with Montreal. He did show some promise in his first month with the team in April of 2000. He got banged around in his debut on April 4 when he lasted all of two innings in a 10-4 loss that saw him give up a homer to Devon White. But he righted himself in his second start April 9, working seven innings and allowing just one run and seven hits to the Padres as the Expos won 2-1.

That was the kind of Irabu the Expos were hoping he'd be in the course of his tenure with the team. His forkball was working nicely, and his jellyfish pitch jammed batters inside and made their hands sting.

Irabu held the Phillies to two runs in six innings of work on April 16 and when he left the game, Montreal led 4-2 but the bullpen fared poorly, and the Phillies won.

On May 3, 2000 at Coors Field in Denver, he lasted all of two innings, allowing eight earned runs, as the Rockies rocked the Expos 16-7. Expos pitchers gave up 24 hits, which broke the previous record of 23 set in a loss June 29, 1971.

In 2001, Irabu pitched in his last game for the Expos on June 13 against his old Yankees buddies, faring poorly. He gave up five runs in 5.2 innings at Yankee Stadium, including a solo homer to Jorge Posada. The Yankees won 9-3. Less than a week later on June 19, Irabu was placed on the DL with a right-elbow strain, retroactive to June 14. From there on, it was rehabbing and spending time with the Ottawa Lynx.

In his only other outing with the Expos in 2001, Irabu was somewhat brilliant. On June 6, just a week before the bad outing against the Yankees, during a matinee on a Wednesday before only 5,102 at the Big O, he worked six solid innings. Today, they would call it a quality start. He allowed seven hits and two runs but most impressively, he fanned nine batters as the Expos lost 2-0 to the Braves.

Aside from his elbow problems, Irabu also encountered knee woes with the Expos. More often than not, he was on the DL. He was 2-7 with a 6.69 ERA in 14 starts over two seasons. He could wing it. Aside from that elbow surgery, Irabu also underwent arthroscopic surgery on his right knee under the auspices of Expos surgeon Dr. Larry Coughlin a few months before the elbow job.

Over the long haul, Irabu didn't have much luck with the Expos. He was injured too much. Medical staff and some other people didn't have much use for him.

"He was a real jerk. I didn't like him," Expos trainer McClain told me. "I did not care for Irabu at all."

Expos bullpen coordinator Pierre Arsenault would often be Irabu's battery mate prior to his starts in warming him up with long toss and then short toss out and full-blown pitching near the outfield wall and in the bullpen, but Arsenault wasn't the least bit complimentary.

"I did catch Hideki but that's about it. No relationship there whatsoever," Arsenault said. "He was a loner who would be on his phone every free minute he had – while smoking cigarettes," Arsenault said. "Hard to remember things about a person when you had zero interaction with that person."

Off the field, Irabu was his own worst enemy. He loved to drink, he loved to smoke. Those libations worked against him, especially the suds and the hard liquor. His last night with the Expos' organization was a doozy.

On Aug. 29, 2001, on a Wednesday night, Irabu was with the Lynx, while they were on a road trip to Buffalo to play the Bisons.

According to an Expos' media guide, Irabu was with the Lynx while recovering from a strain to his right elbow and had been placed on the

Exposion

60-day disabled list.

So that night, Irabu got sloshed and out of control at a bar and according to Japan's Kyodo News Service, he had to be hospitalized the day of a scheduled rehab start.

A few of the Lynx players let it be known to team manager Stan Hough what happened. So, the morning of the 30th, when the all-nighter ended, Lynx manager Stan Hough called Expos GM Jim Beattie and told him what happened. Beattie immediately suspended Irabu "seven days without pay for violating terms of his contract."

Until I initially advised Hough of the Japanese story, Hough wanted to be diplomatic about what Irabu did that night.

"I have to be careful. Let's put it this way – he missed curfew. I could tell you the real story, but I want it to be private. I don't want to be dipping people in the grease," Hough told me in May of 2023.

Hough then agreed to talk in much more detail when I told him about the Kyodo News story.

When the seven-day suspension was up Sept. 6, the Expos parted ways with Irabu and gave him his "unconditional release."

When I talked with Hough on June 3, 2023, he gave me previously unpublished details about Irabu's episode in Buffalo.

"Irabu was taken by ambulance to Buffalo General Hospital. I think that was the name of the hospital," Hough said. "I got a call around 3 a.m. from our trainer (Sean Bearer) letting me know he was taken to the hospital. I assume Sean got a call from the hospital. We got up, gathered some clothes for Irabu and went to the hospital.

"When we got there, the attendant took us to the emergency room where Irabu was. He was being fed by intravenous injection. The doctor came in and told me he was so profoundly drunk and would not release him until mid-morning or after.

"So we left and went back to the hotel. I spoke with Carl Pavano and Brian Schneider. They told me Hideki was okay to walk back to the hotel and that Hideki called the ambulance himself because he wanted to get sober faster via the intravenous injection of fluids back into his body."

When I looked into the matter of intravenous injection online, I was curious. I read that patients with acute alcohol intoxication are brought to the emergency department for evaluation and treatment. That's how it was with Irabu.

What I found out is that it's not out of the ordinary for medical professionals to administer someone like Irabu an intravenous injection of normal saline in the hopes that the saline will cause a dilution effect on the level of alcohol – thus, helping patients to get sober quicker and therefore having a shorter length of stay in the ED. Crazy stuff.

One study showed that 73-87% of American emergency medicine physicians use intravenous fluids to treat alcohol intoxication. I would think Irabu was so accustomed to these treatments because he was drank so much. Crazy, huh? A bar was Irabu's lair.

You might assume Irabu would have consumed the Japanese delicacy sake or one of many beers popular in Japan and in many parts around the world: Sapporo Premium, Asahi Super Dry, Kirin Light and Suntory.

I've tried Sapporo and it's not bad.

I was told Irabu drank a lot of beer that night, but he also was heavy into hard liquor, straight up in shooters.

"It is my recollection that he had roughly 20-25 shots of straight vodka," Hough revealed. "My information came from Carl Pavano and Brian Schneider, who were at the same bar with Hideki. Pavano and Schneider tried to talk him out of going to the hospital. He should have listened to them.

"The next day, he was supposed to pitch," Hough said. "When I went to him to talk about it (in the clubhouse), he was shaking like a leaf on a tree in a strong wind."

The "next day" was actually the day the binge ended – a few hours later when Hough approached Irabu, who was completely hungover. This was pure alcoholic poisoning. It was scary.

"Yes, this is where my angst was really high," Hough said. "I was concerned that he might take a line drive off of his head and be severely hurt. I didn't want him to get hurt. Also, I couldn't fake it or hide it. I had to tell the truth to Beattie. That was the only option I was left with."

Hough went back into the coaches' office at Pilot Field and called Beattie in Montreal. Hough told Beattie what had gone down and "told him I didn't feel comfortable sending him out to pitch" that night.

"Beattie called back about 30 minutes later and told me not to pitch him at all until further notice," Hough said. "I didn't want to see him get hurt. He was in that bad of shape physically (250 pounds or so)

"In the meantime, I got a call from his agent(Nomura) in California. He gave me a pretty hard time. He was venting on me, and I knew it. The guy was talking down to me and very condescending. I told him he had no say in this matter and if he wanted to air laundry – to call Jim Beattie. I hung up the phone and went about my business. This is all I know about that incident. I have not embellished it at all."

The story Hough gave me was shocking. The drinking bout in Buffalo was only the tip of the iceberg with Irabu and his time with the Expos. The details of the fiasco in Buffalo have never been revealed and what has never been published until now is that Irabu was often a drunk in bars while in the employ of the Expos.

What I learned is that Irabu habitually beat up his interpreter, a young Japanese man. It was not George Rose, who also handled Irabu's translations while he pitched for the Yankees.

Not once, not twice, but three times Irabu administered beatings on his interpreter while he was out on the town in various cities, according to McClain. Hough said Irabu didn't have an interpreter when the pitcher was with Ottawa.

"He came to me to treat his cuts and abrasions," McClain told me about the interpreter. "He said this was the third time Irabu hit him. I don't know what city it was. He came in early the next day and got his stuff, as he was heading home. He didn't ask for help in the other situations. After each one, he would not talk about the marks on his face.

"The guy (interpreter) quit after the third time. I told Beattie why he left. He came to us all cut up. We were lucky he didn't sue the player and the club for damages. They didn't publicize it for obvious reasons. He beat him up outside the bar in the parking lot before they took a cab to the hotel."

McClain said that when the interpreter quit, it was shortly after he hurt his elbow and then had surgery. According to notes I see about his 2000 stint with the Expos, Irabu injured his elbow during a game July 27 against the Mets. He was put on the disabled list the following day before undergoing arthroscopic surgery Aug. 15 to remove five loose bones and a bone spur in his right elbow. The surgery was done by the famous elbow pioneer Dr, James Andrews in Birmingham, Alabama.

Beattie, at the time of Irabu's release, told reporters he was disappointed with what transpired but it was better for the team. Beattie said he went to the Expos' clubhouse to sendIrabuoff while he was packing his stuff to leave Montreal. By then, the pitcher's nameplate was taken down and his locker emptied.

"I wished him luck. He's a talented guy who can do things other people can't," Beattie told the Gazette. "We thought about our options concerning Irabu during his suspension and we didn't think he was going to be able to help us that much. It's a risk that we can't take. We think the best thing was to go ahead and release him. We can't afford to spend a couple million dollars on someone who might not be there to help us.

"We're disappointed about the way things happened and it's time to move on. If he gets healthy and demonstrates that he wants to pitch, he has the talent to do it in the major leagues. Not being healthy is tough, and he hasn't been healthy very much."

Hough actually didn't think that badly of Irabu while he threw for Ottawa.

"He didn't do that bad. He was 1-2," Hough said. "By the way, Danny, Hideki was a good guy. "I did not have any axe to grind with Hideki. I liked the guy.

"I had two players that were different -- Hideki Irabu and Milton Bradley. Some of these guys wanted to go by their own rules but I had to tell them, 'I don't change my rules for anybody.'There were things I couldn't put out there (to the media) because he (Irabu) was hurt.

"Coaching in the minors – it's such a revolving door. I told the players that if you work harder and maybe we can win a championship and that also benefits me. I want to be an advocate, not an adversary. That was at a time when the Expos were falling apart."

That's right. Months later, the Expos were sold by Loria to Major League Baseball, Loria acquired the Florida Marlins while Marlins owner John Henry swooped in to purchase his beloved Boston Red Sox.

Hough, a baseball lifer from Waco, Texas, had joined the Expos' organization after spending two seasons as manager of the Yankees' Class-A Greensboro Bats in the South Atlantic League. He had previously worked in Canada as a pitching coach in Surrey, British Columbia, where my brother Bernard lives, for the Glaciers of the independent Western league.

"I love baseball, and this is an outstanding opportunity," Houghsaid when he was hired. "To go to Ottawa is like a feather in the cap."

The ups and downs of Hideki Irabu

Getting back to Irabu – we all know what happened to Irabu on July 27, 2011. He was found hanged, a victim of suicide at his home at 2212 Via Velardo in the wealthy neighbourhood of Rancho Palos Verdes near Los Angeles.

Sad and tragic. Like that night in Buffalo, he was found with a lot of alcohol in his blood content, about 0.23 and there was a half-empty bottle of anti-depressants and some anxiety pills. His wife and his kids had left him some time before that.

You sure don't like to see this happen, especially when it's a former Expo.

Koji Hiromatsu, a friend of the "decedent", a term used by the LA County Sheriff's department to ID a deceased person, entered Irabu's house through a sliding back door. He became "hysterical" and he called another friend.

They also ran into acquaintance Mary Felicerlicht on the street, and she said, "What's wrong?"

"Hiromatsu tried to explain (to her) what happened, but he was in shock, crying and scared at seeing his friend (Irabu)," the sheriff's department's report said. "He stated the unknown female (Felicerlicht) called 911.

Once the officers made their way into the building, they could smell the odor of a decaying body.

"We saw a rope tied aroundIrabu's neck hanging around the door tied to the doorknob," the report said.

Irabu was IDed by his California licence plate number, which showed a police-blotter account of DUI: alcohol and drug offences.

"He had a history of depression for the past year due to a pending divorce and financial problems as a result of it," said the autopsy report I obtained. "His wife and kids are reportedly living in another country. On 7/23/2011, he was at either a baseball practice or a game when he told another friend that he was "tired of all this" and "I don't want to live anymore."

In the police report, Mitsuak Yoshino was briefly detained by police, pending an investigation but he eventually was released.

"Matsuak stated Irabu was going through a divorce and was very depressed," the police report said. "He stated Irabu had been depressed for one year."

The autopsy report indicated he had a beard and moustache, which he never wore while with the Yankees, Expos and Rangers.There was a tattoo of a skull on his left chest and a tattoo on his back.

"Rigor mortis was resolved, and livor mortis was fixed," the report said.

Suicide among Japanese people is considered by some to be accepted. It is a rather common cause of death for Japanese people who live there or abroad. In the case of Irabu, it was California, his adopted country.

When Thompson, his biological father, heard about his passing, he openly wept on the balcony of where he lived.

Irabu should be remembered as a trailblazing pioneer in baseball because he improved Japanese-American relations in the sport. His request or demand to be traded from the Padres to the Yankees in May of 1997 was met.

The Padres had signed a working agreement with the Chiba Lotte Marines, permitting San Diego exclusive signing rights for Irabu. Nomura and Irabu had told people he wanted only to sign with the Yankees, the glamorous, back-page tabloid team. The Padres and Marines never consulted Irabu about this deal and San Diego signed him.

The MLBPA sided with Irabu but MLB's executive council stepped in to say the Padres hadn't violated any existing rule and said the Padres legally held the rights to Irabu. For several months, Irabu considered his options and finally in May, the Padres relented and traded him to the Bronx Bombers.

What resulted following the trade was a posting system agreement between MLB and the Nippon. This posting agreement meant MLB teams were obligated to make offers to acquire a Japanese player.

The Expos had success with reclamation projects such as Dennis Martinez, Pascual Perez, Tim Burke, Otis Nixon and Oil Can Boyd but much less so with Gilberto Reyes and Irabu.

Irabu had his faults, and he had an unfortunate ending but he was an Expo. We should remember that. He was part of the Expos' legacy. This chapter is an acknowledgment to him.

Carl Pavano, Vladdy and Marcel Hubert

At an Expos caravan, way back in the day, about the year 2000, Vladdy Guerrero and Carl Pavano were on the scene with duties usually becoming of Expos players during the winter to promote the team heading into the next season.

Marcel Hubert, a former minor-league player, Sherbrooke, Québec native and one-time roommate of Kent Tekulve, had come to his roots in Montreal and turned up at one of the stops the caravan made.

Hubert was making every effort to get an autograph form Guerrero, whose reputation was as a tough autograph. He was distant when it came to giving out autographs. It was a chore for Guerrero, especially if he was not being paid.

"It was Vieux (Old) Montreal," Hubert was saying in early 2023. "I knew I would get Guerrero. I waited outside two hours -30 degrees. It was one of the coldest days I have ever endured. My car started.

"My girlfriend told me Guerrero and the Expos would be at the shopping centre. I am driving fast to Vieux Montreal because I know I will get a Guerrero jersey. Eventually, I'm going to Vlad only."

Then Hubert found out Guerrero was living up to his reputation of being a tough ask.

"Problem is he said he don't want to sign. I lift up my arm and I'm ready to KO him," Hubert recollected. "Pavano was between me and Vlad. Pavano said to Vlad, 'You speak Spanish. Marcel speaks French. Oh god, I'm the only one who speaks English.' Still today, I laugh so much. Pavano was great."

On the road or at home, Guerrero sometimes made up a homemade sign which stated No Sign in his flawed English near the dugout.

We heard Guerrero on April 21, 2023 the night before Expos Fest signed autographs at a table for four consecutive hours and didn't move, never took a break, never went to the washroom. But I'm sure he was paid huge bucks to sign.

Chapter 43

Schneider was a leader in many ways

He was a warrior.
He was a solid hitter, he had reasonable power, he could handle pitchers, he framed pitches eloquently and boy, could he throw out runners.
That was Brian Schneider.
Schneider worked his ass off to be a very competent catcher in the major leagues. Nothing came easy for him. He wasn't a star, but he was better than average.
He even caught a ceremonial first pitch from former President George W. Bush.
He was born in Jacksonville but got grew up in Northampton, Pennsylvania where his military-service father Peter was posted.
In high school, his uncle Mike was the coach, and he was an all-state basketball player, having fun and winning championships every year. He grew up around sports.
Then one day June 1, 1995, he was thrown for a loop when the Expos selected him in the fourth round out of Northampton.
"I was surprised. I was shocked," Schneider told me in May 2023. "I had no idea. I had just finished high school. I was obviously proud. I was concentrating on college ball."
That's right. Schneider had signed a letter of intent to play at Central Florida University in the fall of 1995. But the Expos appeared in the picture and Schneider slowly changed his tune.
My goal was to finish high school and go to college but honestly, playing in the big leagues – the Expos were taking a chance on me and giving me the opportunity to go professionally. It was not an easy decision. It was kinda cool, getting drafted. I wanted to play. I didn't want to take a chance at not getting drafted later."
In the end, Schneider, rather than risk not getting interest from clubs in another draft year, agreed to terms two days following the draft with the Expos and scout Jim Gabella. The circumstances regarding his contract were very interesting, as Schneider explained.
"There were negotiations on the phone. Jim had come to some of my games. He saw me prior to the draft. He talked to my parents. I had a number I wanted to sign for. $60,000. It was very reasonable. I was playing a game and had one more at-bat and then I took myself out of the game."
Schneider decided in the middle of a game to agree to terms with the Expos. Kind of a neat story. He took himself out of the game so he

wouldn't get hurt and screw up the deal. Ironically on the same day, the Expos drafted Michael Barrett, an infielder who was converted to a catcher.

"I want to say I saw him play three times," Gabella told me of Schneider. "What really intrigued me was that he was also a basketball player – it showed me he was athletic. He had the athleticism, the work ethic and the makeup. He could hit, a left-handed hitting catcher, who could use the whole field to hit. He received and blocked well."

Ironically, Gabella became Schneider's manager when he played in the Gulf Coast rookie league in West Palm Beach.

"That was kinda cool. He was my first coach in pro ball in West Palm Beach," Schneider said.

Canadian Baseball HOF
Brian Schneider

As his pro career progressed, Schneider made stops in Delmarva-Cape Fear, North Carolina, Harrisburg, Pennsylvania and Ottawa. It was in Cape Fear in his second round of duty in 1997 that his bat started to come around. He hit four homers and drove in 49 runs.

Then on May 24, 2000, a series of events transpired that would change Schneider's life forever. During the Expos'deflating 18-0 loss to the Giants at Pacific Bell Park in San Francisco that afternoon, catcher Chris Widger got hurt.

In the fifth inning, Widger was replaced by Lenny Webster. By the next day, May 25, Widger hadn't improved so he was placed on the 15-day disabled list with a "left hand contusion."

That move prompted general manager Jim Beattie to make some corresponding moves as I looked at notes from a 2001 media guide which gave details of team transactions from 2000. As baseball jargon goes, Beattie "selected the contract" of long-time veteran receiver Charlie O'Brien, who had been playing Double-A ball in Harrisburg, Penn., trying to extend his career.

And then Beattie had some awfully good news for Schneider, who was playing Triple-A in Ottawa.

"I was at my apartment just outside Ottawa. I got a call late that night because the team was in San Diego. Chris Widger got hurt," Schneider said. "I was told I was getting called up. It was my manager Jeff Cox who called. After some one-liners, Jeff said, 'You're getting your chance. You're getting called up.' It was definitely emotional. It's more of a shock when it settles in.

"When I hung up, I called my parents. We broke down in tears. It was pretty emotional – definitely. You can hear the emotions of your dad and mother crying. It was the culmination of a lot of sweat and tears, bumps and bruises.

"I flew out the next morning. I flew all the way across North American from the northeast to the southwest. It was a long flight."

Schneider arrived in the clubhouse from the airport for a night game against the Padres. O'Brien started the game and then Schneider entered the game in the eighth inning for his official major-league debut in a double switch. Schneider was pencilled in to replace infielder Felipe Lira and Wilton Guerrero replaced O'Brien on the scorecard.

In the top of the ninth in his first plate appearance, Schneider flied to left.

"I had to borrow Charlie O'Brien's blue spikes," Schneider said. "I'd come with all black catcher's gear (from Ottawa)."

As Schneider looked around in his new surroundings, he saw a different tune than in the minors.

"It was nerve wracking, absolutely," he said. "The sheer size of these guys. They're older guys and mature. I grew up admiring (Padres) Bret Boone and Gwynny. It was pretty cool. Spring training is one thing and I'm glad Felipe gave me a chance in the game. It got some of the nerves out of the way.

Ironically less than a month later, O'Brien was released, never to play another game in the majors, Schneider was optioned to Ottawa and Webster was reinstated from the disabled list to share duties with Widger.

Schneider spent most of the 2001 season in Ottawa with some time in Montreal as the third catcher behind Randy Knorr and No. 1 Barrett. He then became an Expos' roster player in the final three seasons of the franchise. In 2002, he appeared in 73 games behind Barrett and then slowly got more playing time with 108 games in 2003 and then he was the full-time receiver in 2004.

"When I got called up, I was young. I had a lot to prove," Schneider said. "Catching everyday was a relief. I had to show them I could be an everyday player, not a backup. Michael Barrett was a good friend of mine. We were both young and playing for playing time."

What Schneider established very quickly was an inordinate ability to throw runners out trying to steal. He was uncanny with that strong arm of his. As a part-timer in 2001, he eliminated 50% of base stealers, 43% in 2002, 53% in 2003 and 50% in 2004. Baseball Reference, in producing stats for Schneider's, boldfaced the 53% and 50%.

"In Double-A, my manager Doug Sisson was very hard on the catchers. I learned a lot from catching coach Bob Natal. He took me under his wing," Schneider said as he explained his success after taking throws from the pitcher.

"When push comes to shove, you give credit to your pitching coach and your pitchers. It's not just me, it's the pitchers, the manager and the pitching coach. The pitchers gave me a chance by being quick to the plate because they know I have a good, accurate arm. If the pitchers are quick, I had a good chance to throw out runners."

Aside from handling pitchers so good and throwing out runners, Schneider also improved at the plate. His best output was in 2004 for solid numbers of 12 homers, 49 RBI and a .257 batting average.

Exposion

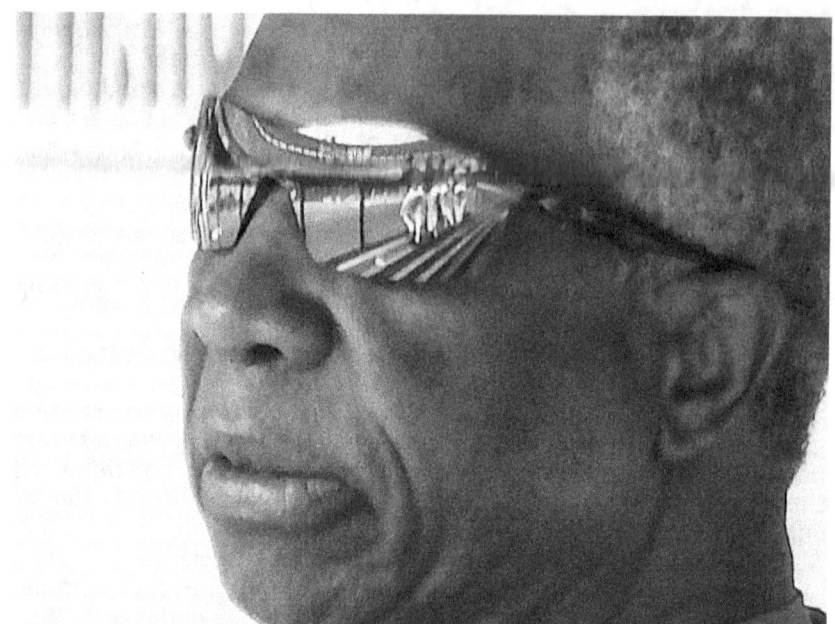

Joe Gromelski photo
Frank Robinson was admired a lot by Brian Schneider

"I had good offensive numbers coming out of high school and finally at 21, I finally started to mature and put on more weight," Schneider said. "I got stronger, and I was capable of hitting home runs. I would lose a lot of at-bats to put up some good numbers. I was going from hitting third, fourth or fifth to seventh or the eighth hole or the pitcher's spot."

One chapter in a book by Barry Svrluga of the Washington Post really struck me about the underdog status of Schneider. Svrluga alluded to the value and importance of a leader like Schneider on a team. The book was called The Grind: Inside Baseball's Endless Season.

"He (Svrluga) did a good job. It's an article you want to be proud of, that I was the type of player I was," Schneider said. "I never wanted to take myself out of the lineup. I wanted to be a leader for the pitchers, doing all my homework. I'm glad I could help the pitchers and give them information," Schneider said.

When it came to 2004 and the swan song of the Expos, Schneider was front and centre in passing info on about the imminent departure of the team to his team in his role as the union player representative.

The games played in Puerto Rico in 2003 and 2004 were taxing on the players and their families, who were hardly excited about this scenario, other than it was a way to explore Puerto Rico as a travel destination. Major League Baseball and commissioner Bud Selig wanted the games in Puerto Rico as an avenue of producing more ticket sales, compared to the inadequate fan support in Montreal.

"It was very hard with home games not anywhere near home. It was far away. It was hot and we had long flights. MLB was going to do what they wanted to do. They were trying to create more revenue, how to make it better," Schneider said. "They flew the families down and we got extra meal money going to Puerto Rico."

Schneider had grown to admire manager Frank Robinson, although the skipper left him out of the lineup for both the final game in Montreal Sept. 29 and the final game ever in New York Oct. 3. He didn't see action in either game as Robinson chose to employ mostly part-time players, some minor leaguers, a strategy which upset many of the veterans and the media.

"Absolutely," Schneider said when I asked him about wanting to play those final crucial games so important in franchise history. "Thinking back, I can't put any blame on him (Robinson). I wasn't hurt. It was tough not to play that last game (in Montreal), whether you are not healthy and hurt.

"Some players didn't like Frank, and some did. Frank was the best. He was awesome – just coming from me. You had to take advantage of Frank's keen mind and personality. He was very hard on people. Some people took it personally. You want a coach to be hard on you. I didn't take it as a negative.

"I'd go into his office, and he'd give me crap. He'd say, 'What do you want? Get out of here.' Then you'd sit for an hour and a half before he'd be done talking with me.

"I wanted to prove to him I could play hard and play the game correct. He motivated me. He was teaching me. He wanted me to be successful. Even when was no longer in baseball, we texted on the phone. I was honoured to know him as a person."

When Robinson died Feb. 7, 2019 at the age of 83, Schneider said it was "hard for me" and he made a point of attending his funeral in the Los Angeles area.

"It meant the world to me," he said of going to the funeral. "His daughter reached out to me. Him and I had a great relationship. I miss Frank all the time. He taught me how to play the game hard."

On Twitter, Schneider wrote about Robinson this way upon hearing of his passing: "So honored to not just have known you, Frank, as a great man, manager, person, and human being, but who I truly called a good friend and someone who I honestly played as hard as I could for."

What was most disconcerting for the players was the pre-game stuff going on Sept. 29. Team president Tony Tavares announced that day at a news conference that yes, indeed, the Expos were moving to Washington.

It had finally sunk in – after years of talk and rumours that the club was moving, Nos Amours were finally heading out of town.

"100%, it was not fun," Schneider said. "I remember walking with some of the players into the front office, the ticket offices – everyone was in tears. It took a heavy toll on us. We were tearing up because we were leaving Montreal and going to Washington.

"People were losing their jobs, they were losing their team. It was very hard. Nothing easy. It had to do with the people and their livelihoods and their careers. Yes, that was different. It was the last game – it had way more meaning than the one in New York. It's one of my career highlights. I took a clip, and I was waving and saying goodbye."

In Washington, one of Schneider's most memorable moments was Opening Day April 14, 2005. Baseball was back in town for the first time since the 1971 season when the Senators were relocated to Texas to become the Rangers.

There were 600 national media on hand to write about the game. The Washington Post even assigned a reporter to write about this excessive media conflab. Schneider was the Opening Day catcher and he caught starter and Expos teammate Livan Hernandez, who to this day, is Schneider's friend along with Barrett, T.J. Tucker and Brad Wilkerson.

Schneider and Hernandez were in Québec for an Expos Fest celebrity softball tour in August 2023.

What Schneider remembers most is catching the First Pitch from one of the most famous politicians in the world: George W. Bush. Can you imagine the honour of this, but can you imagine the butterflies Schneider felt!

Bush threw a ball that was used in the Senators last game in 1971. That's what I read online.

"I was pretty nervous," Schneider said of his time with Bush. "I spent some time with him underneath in the cages. He was literally asking me questions. I had a pretty good time with the president.

"We were in the dugout. The team was announced on the third-base side, and we were getting ready for the national anthem. The president said, 'Look left – a wall of cameras taking pictures.'"

It wasn't just the president, but baseball was back in America's national capital, and it was on national television.

"I stepped onto the field for the first pitch, and I remember the press, the president and the pictures. There was fireworks. It was crazy, the security," Schneider said.

As we winded down our interview, I had to ask Schneider where he got the nickname Hoops. I figured it had something to do with basketball and that was true – but he had another story to tell.

"That came from my dad. Burt Reynolds was a stunt man in Hooper, who'd jump off rocks and cliffs and do dumb things – and he played basketball," Schneider said. "My dad started calling me Hoopster and Hoops."

Following his playing career, Schneider has been coaching for many years using his expertise as a catching coach with various organizations.

Based on what he saw in Montreal when he was with the Expos, does Schneider see hope for another franchise?

"Absolutely, I see hope, but not only do I see hope, but I think it will happen," he told me. "They want to expand to 32 teams and my prediction is that Montreal will be one team. I played there – guys loved to play there. The teams visiting there loved Montreal. It's a totally different city with the architecture and the buildings and the mountains and good fans."

Thank you, Brian, for the great chat.

Chapter 44

Chavez solid in 2003 and 2004

The story goes that the Colorado Rockies lost interest in Venezuelan prospect Endy Chavez due to his slight stature of 5-foot-11 and 170 pounds.

The Mets signed him but after a series of deals where he was placed on waivers several times, not just by the Mets but the Kansas City Royals and Detroit Tigers, he ended up with the Expos.

That streak with the Expos was memorable because he got to play full-time as a leadoff hitter and play centre field for Montreal in 2003 and 2004.

When I got a hold of him, he declared his love for the Expos.

"I got to the Expos in 2002 and I started with the Triple-A Ottawa Lynx. I played most of the season over there. I was called up with maybe two or three weeks left in the regular season," Chavez said. "It was a great feeling getting called up. It was awesome.

"I won the batting title in the International league. I made the all-star team. It was a pretty good year."

Chavez's .343 average was something to behold with Ottawa. He appeared in 103 games for the Lynx, hitting four homers and driving in 41 runs and collecting a 15-game hitting streak. With Montreal as a callup, Chavez hit .296 with a homer and nine RBI and was voted Expos player of the month for September.

His performance with Ottawa and a solid spring training in 2003 prompted GM Omar Minaya and manager Frank Robinson to make him their everyday centre fielder. Chavez helped the Expos to a near playoff spot in 2003 but when MLB wouldn't allow Minaya to call up players from Ottawa, the Expos faded near the end of the season.

"I had a lot of hits and threw out a lot of runners (eight). I was very accurate with my throws but I wasn't like Vlad Guerrero," he said, laughing. "Frank Robinson – it wasn't easy. He was a tough guy. As a rookie, I wanted him to be happy with the way I played."

Chavez hit five homers, drove in 47 runs and batted .251

Then came 2004 and what turned out to be the final spring training for the Expos. He received bad news when Robinson decided Chavez was starting the season in Triple-A in another Canadian city, Edmonton. It was hard to believe this when he had enjoyed such a great season in 2003.

"They sent me down. They said my numbers weren't good enough to make the team," Chavez said. "After 18-19 days, they called me up

Exposion

again."

With Edmonton, he hit .344 in 14 games. That was the impetus for the Expos to call him up. He finished that season with 32 stolen bases, five homers, 34 RBI and a .277 average.

"We played those games in Puerto Rico in 2003 and 2004 because they knew already they wanted to move the team. It was pretty hard emotionally," Chavez said. "I'm so blessed to be part of Expos history and the last game the Expos ever played.

Courtesy Endy Chavez
Endy Chavez

"I was the last out in the last game in New York. A photographer sent me a picture, telling me I was the last batter for the Expos. I have that picture. I don't remember too much about that game. It was so long ago."

As for the highlight of his career, Chavez quickly thought of a game against the Reds in Montreal and he's playing centre. Who is at the plate? Junior Griffey. The date was May 30, 2004.

The oddity of this game is that Robinson had starting pitcher Tomo Okha hitting in the eighth spot with second baseman Jamey Carroll batting ninth in an attempt to create more offence. Can you imagine?

Anyway, back to Chavez and Junior.

"Griffey hit a ball and I thought it was gone. I jumped and caught the ball. It was the third out," Chavez said. "He looked at me and said, 'Nice catch.'"

Here's Chavez chasing down a fly just like Junior would to rob somebody of extra bases. Highlight-reel variety. And that's not the end of the story. In the Retrosheet note on the play, it merely stated Griffey "flied to centre" but maybe there could have been a notation about a crazy catch.

"The next inning, I come up to hit and I hit the ball to centre field and I hit it out. Junior was playing centre," Chavez said. "I ran the bases and he saw me later and he turned and said to me, 'Hey, hit the ball on the ground.' He was laughing. He was very gracious."

There was another highlight for Chavez with the Expos. He was facing hard-throwing lefty Dontrelle Willis of the Marlins, somebody who could hit the gun at 100 m.p.h. Almost scary. Don't know what kind of heat Willis was throwing Chavez but Chavez connected.

"There were men on first and second and we were losing by one run," Chavez said. "I tried to put the bunt down but I got to two strikes. I was so mad I couldn't bunt. I hit a two-run triple. It puts us ahead and we won the game. I remember the third baseman for the Marlins – Mike Lowell – he told me, 'If you put the bunt down, we win the game.' "

Chavez went on to accumulate over 10 years of service time, just qualifying him for the MLB pension.

Nice job, Endy.

Diaz caught the last home game and final game

It was a bizarre decision by manager Frank Robinson when he made up the lineup for the final Expos home game and the last Expos game, period, in 2004.

One of the lucky recipients was Einar Diaz, who was pencilled in to catch those two games. He was a part-time, journeyman catcher.

In his wisdom, Robinson decided to go with part-time players or September call-ups.

"I was very happy to play the last game of the franchise, the Montreal Expos," Diaz told me. "Major League Baseball had tried to get an owner. The team was there a long time and now, they have nothing.

"It was tough for the fans. At the last game in New York, Frank told me, 'Have a nice time. You're playing today, the last game of the season.' I remember John Patterson was the starting pitcher."

Diaz said Robinson, for the most part, never talked to him all season. When he got traded to Montreal at the end of spring training in 2004, Robinson told him he was going to be the back-up catcher behind Brian Schneider. For six months, Robinson never struck up a conversation with Diaz.

"I never spoke to him," Diaz said, laughing.

Diaz appeared in 55 games, hit .224 with a homers and 12 RBI.

Diaz was 10 years old when he began playing baseball in his native Panama.

He said him and his friends would play with no helmets. There would be pitchers and catchers, throwing balls and shagging flies.

"My manager was my mentor. He told me to go to the United States for a tryout," he told me.

So he did. That was in the early 1990s. He went to Cleveland where he worked out with 10 other prospects. He was a third baseman/shortstop at the time.

"I signed with Cleveland for $10,000," Diaz said. "The second year in the minors, I got hurt and had surgery on my left hand.

"I really enjoyed my time with the Indians' organization but the best time was when I came to the big leagues," he said. "I was very happy. When you're in the minors, the goal is to play in the majors.

"I had a few good moments and the special moment was one good game against Seattle. We won 15-14 and I had two hits in four at-bats."

Diaz managed to spend seven seasons in the Cleveland organization but the 2001 season was spent in its entirety in the majors, where he enjoyed his most production campaign. He appeared in 134 games, hitting four homers and driving in 56 runs, while batting a solid .277. Not bad for a small guy, 5-foot-10 and weighing about 165 pounds.

That season and the one he spent with the Expos will stick in his mind forever.

Chapter 45

Livan Hernandez delivered the goods

Livan Hernandez was an inning-eater in his two seasons with the Expos in 2003 and 2004.

He was a workhorse, continuing the success he had in three seasons with the San Francisco Giants prior to a spring training trade involving four players on March 24, 2003.

The Expos sure were getting mighty good quality in Hernandez. He was San Francisco's Game 7 pitcher in the 2002 World Series for manager Felipe Alou.

The Giants lost the World Series as Hernandez lasted all of two innings, giving up all four runs as the Angels won their first World Series with a 4-1 win.

Expos general manager Omar Minaya still liked the idea of Hernandez in the starting rotation and went for the jugular and got Hernandez for next to nothing.

With the Expos owned by Major League Baseball, Hernandez's salary of $3.835-million seemed a bit high but Minaya convinced his bosses at MLB to accept the deal. Hernandez was in the option year of a four-year deal he had signed with the Giants prior to the 2000 season.

Hernandez was certainly the plum in the deal. The Giants also sent Edwards Guzman and cash to Montreal in exchange for relative unknowns Jim Brower and PTBNL Matt Blank. This was a lopsided deal in favour of the Expos.

Hernandez had produced records of 17-11, 13-15 and 12-16 with the Giants and a half season of 3-3 after he was acquired from the Marlins during the 1999 season.

Not sure what Giants GM Brian Sabean was thinking. I sent him an email but I got no answer. Funny thing is, the Giants won 100 games in 2003 without Hernandez in the picture. They lost only 61 games. They qualified easily for the playoffs but were knocked out in the NL West playoff series.

"I don't remember this being about a contract but I know the Giants were keen to promote a couple of younger pitchers so it certainly could have been money-related," recalled long-time Giants beat writer Ray Ratto. "I just don't remember the Giants being tight with a buck back then because they were selling out every game and were still riding the Bonds gravy train."

Minaya could see the Expos had the potential to be good in 2003 and this deal was a shocker, considering Hernandez was a quality pitcher for

Livan Hernandez delivered the goods

more than three seasons with San Francisco.

The Cuban was downright excellent in 2003 when the Expos went on a surprise run to challenge for the NL East before they faded.

Hernandez took the ball every five days and posted a 15-10 record with an excellent ERA of 3.20. He fired a National League-leading eight complete games. Crazy, a rarity in baseball for many years. He struck out 178 batters. He went deep in games, saving the bullpen on many occasions. Montreal was 6-2 when he went the distance.

He allowed three or fewer runs on 10 occasions in 2023 but came away with a loss or a no-decision.

In this trivia item, Hernandez trumped the total of 20 teams with his eight complete games. Remarkable. Stunning, too, was his stamina and ability to throw a lot of innings as a larger version of Alek Manoah.

"Turned in what he self described as the finest season of his career," the Expos media guide from 2004 said about Hernandez's 2003 campaign.

Hernandez was 6-4 with a 4.19 ERA through the first half of the season but he rebounded to go 9-4 with a 2.42 ERA in the final three months. He had worked to get better by getting some advice from pitching coach Randy St. Claire in tweaking his arm angle.

Whatever happened, Hernadez 's slow hook curve was working better and better. This slop pitch sometimes went under the radar – under 60 m.p.h. but it got him plenty of Strike 3 calls. It was his out pitch.

Battters were mesmerized and fooled. They'd be looking for something in the 80s or 90s but the curve would be 20 mp.h. or less and batters would be swinging wildly and crazy without so much as connecting.

He threw 3,927 pitches, hit 50 batters and allowed 27 home runs.

Hernandez was a bulldog the following season on a less talented Expos team that went 68-95, their final in Montreal. He won 11 and lost 15 but took the ball regularly again, working a major-leading leading 255 innings with nine complete games.

In one special game in Puerto Rico on July 2, 2004, Hernandez was outstanding. He went the distance as the Expos beat their Canadian buddies, the Blue Jays, 2-0 before 8,220 fans. He struck out five, walked one, getting help from a pair of RBI hits by Tony Batista.

Just days prior to that in Toronto on June 27, Hernandez was the winning pitcher as the Expos beat the Jays 9-4, going seven innings. It might have been the only time a Montreal pitcher beat the Jays twice within five days.

Hernandez was getting on in years when he was with Montreal but his work ethic was something to behold. He was an older veteran, who set a great example for younger gunslingers such as Tony Armas Jr.

"Livo, for me, was one of the best, not because he was my teammate. It was more on how he went about his business – every bullpen and every game," Armas told me. "I think he threw some long bullpens when some things weren't working. He was a guy that played with any hitter's mind."

Especially with that slop curve.

Armas distinctly remembers one game in which Hernandez really

Exposion

played with a "hitter's mind." That mind belonged to big Mo Vaughan of the Mets. The date was April 12, 2003 as I found out on Retrosheet in a game that saw Hernandez as the winner. Vaughn was known for putting fear in opposing pitchers but on this particular occasion, he was fooled by Hernandez and struck out.

Hernandez's slow-mo pitch was a high arching fling similar to a slo-pitch softball throw.

"I remember he threw Mo a 3-2 pitch in Puerto Rico. In my mind, it was a curveball and he got big Mo really good," Armas said. "Wow, it was a good pitch. Yes, man, he threw Mo Vaughn an eupheus pitch. I think like it was the slowest one he ever threw. 50-50 mph."

In baseball jargon, as Armas put it, Vaughn "broke his bat" on the pitch. It's a technical term used to describe how fooled a batter is on a pitch or several pitches.

"All due respect, wow, that's a great pitch. Mo was down on the ground for awhile. I think he hurt his knee, something like that. He was down for awhile after that. That pitch was slow," Armas said.

"It was really slow, not much velocity. He had good deception when he threw it. Hitters had trouble picking up the pitch. It was tough. It was fun watching him. "

What happened was that in his follow through while striking out on the Hernandez slop pitch, Vaughn got hurt and while he finished that game, he had to leave the following game the next day due to a "knee injury". Armas had come close by saying "he missed the rest of the series."

For the seventh consecutive season in 2004, Hernandez started more than 30 games. By the time he had finished his career, he had started at least 30 games in 13 consecutive seasons.

When you think of Expos highlights from 2003 and 2004, you would often look at Hernandez. When the Expos were supposedly ready to leave town and be transferred somewhere, Hernandez shut down the noise and nonsense and pitched in stellar fashion.

"It was fun talking to him and learning from him. He was a guy who threw 96-97 in his prime and dominated with different velocity on every pitch with such great hitters, maybe 83-84," Armas said.

The training staff discovered he required very rarely needed treatment. He was never on the disabled list with the Expos.

"He was a great guy with a great rubber arm. He was a delight," Expos trainer Ron McClain said.

When Hernandez followed the Expos to Washington, it was he who threw the first pitch before 45,596 fans on April 1, 2005 at old RFK to welcome baseball back to that city in 34 years.

His battery mate for four consecutive seasons, two with the Expos and 1½ with the Nationals, was Brian Schneider.

Heranndez played for both the Cuban national junior and senior squads on the Isla de la Juventud, an island governed by the central government in Havana. Like the Russians in hockey for many years, Hernandez and the Cubans were full-time baseball players. That's all they did. That's why they were powerhouses on the diamond like those

Russians on the ice.

Hernandez was one of the top prospects in the world when he was a junior. He was 2-0 with a startling 0.00 ERA at the 1992 world youth championship in Monterrey, New Mexico.

In information I plucked from an Expos media guide, Hernandez was outstanding at the 1993 world youth tournament in Windsor, Ontario, located across the river from Detroit. He went 2-0 with a 1.59 ERA and fanned 21 batters as Cuba won the championship. Hernandez shut down the U.S. in the final as Cuba won 5-1.

"Hernandez wore No. 26," recalled Windsor tournament chairman Bernie Soulliere, one of Canada's finest baseball men, not only in Windsor but at the provincial level, the national level with Baseball Canada and internationally.

The Cubans, because the Castro government wouldn't allow any of their people to leave the country for America, kept close watch on their players so they wouldn't defect. Hernandez, who was billeted at the University of Windsor with his teammates, was tempted to leave Windsor on his own and he must have been envious when his teammate Alberto Castillo, a fellow pitcher, did walk away during that event. Castillo had a lacklustre career in the majors with the Orioles.

You mean, Hernandez was a top-of-the-line amateur pitcher. He wanted to seek fame in the major leagues and not be stuck in Cuba, making poor money under a rigid, archaic system of governance.

He played the 1994-95 season as a national member of the adult team and finally decided to defect at the world championship held in Monterrey, where he had played in 1992.

Hernandez finished his MLB career with a 177-165 record, making him one of the best Cuban-born pitchers in MLB history along with Luis Tiant and Camilo Pascual. He pitched more than 200 innings for eight consecutive seasons.

Expos fans were happy to have him around for two seasons.

Chapter 46

The drama behind the last home game

Why so late in the 2004 season did MLB pull the plug on the Expos?

Could there not have been more notice time given, maybe several months, considering the franchise was already on death row for a few seasons?

On the night of Sept. 28, 2004, a Tuesday, at about 10:15 p.m., the truth was finally starting to settle in. There were radio reports the Expos would be moved to Washington following the season finale on Oct. 3. It felt like a fait accompli.

The Expos had just finished playing a game at home, losing 5-1 to the Marlins with only 5,416 in the stands, if that.

The heads-up from the rumour/news was less than a day for Expos management, players, fans and the like to get ready for the good-bye of the Expos at their last home game, the next day, Sept. 29.

Expos executive vice-president of business affairs Claude Delorme had settled into his office chair after the night game of the 28th, knowing the 2005 schedule had already been put out, meaning Montreal was on it.

"Are you hearing the rumours," somebody then asked Delorme as he settled into his chair.

"We heard those rumours every frickin' day," Delorme told me in 2023. "That night, the news was on a few sports stations and then there was more on the 11 o'clock news. When I left that night, there was not just a rumour – there was the possibility the team would no longer be in Montreal.

"It was crazy. I can tell you – I came into work on the 29th at about 6 a.m. I tracked down president Tony Tavares to tell him about the report on the radio. Tony had-had no discussions with Major League Baseball. I said, 'Tony, are you hearing anything of this?' He told me, 'Chances are good a team will be back in Montreal.' I told him, 'With all due respect, I've heard that story year after year.'

"I called Pat Courtney, the public relations man at Major League Baseball. I knew him from the World Baseball Classic in Miami. Pat said, 'It's a rumour like everything else. It's typical of everything we have to deal with it. If this is true, let me make a call.' Pat called me back and said,' Claude, it's true. Bud Selig is having a conference call with all the owners at 8:05 a.m. to vote and agree to the move and there will be a press conference at 11 a.m. in Washington.'"

What notice time is that?

The drama behind the last home game

"I think the pieces probably fell together. If you are doing it (relocation) for 2005, you needed time to set up, to integrate into Washington," Delorme explained. "Whether it was coincidence, baseball was always late in their decision making. It didn't really surprise me. I can tell you – Tony, myself, Frank Robinson would have known about the news. It was leaked. I just know it was coming from various sources."

As the radio folks kept pushing the rumours of the Expos' demise, the office was deluged with requests from media and fans. Delorme and other key figures had to concede the news, yes, was true.

Delorme told me that prior to this unfortunate, sad news about the death of the Expos, there had been only, what maybe 10,000-12,000 tickets, if that, sold for the last home game. With the finality of the news coming to fruition, fans quickly realized that this was it. It was game over for the franchise so they wanted their souvenir ticket for the final game and send the Expos off in person.

Courtesy Claude Delorme
Claude Delorme with Halle Berry who threw out the first pitch at an Expos game

Heading into the final game before the shocking news finally came, Montrealers were more or less expecting the Expos would return for 2005. That's why only about 10,000+ tickets were sold before the they began selling like hotcakes.

And it was magical but sad. Manager Frank Robinson told a reporter later that day he was surprised to see the upper deck full of fans. Where were these fans in the last few seasons of the franchise?

"Scalpers came flying in to the park and they were very emotional", Delorme said.

"We called it day-of-game tickets sold day of game, the walk-up sales. We had to open up all of the concessions. People could buy their tickets online. We sold 23,500 tickets that day, morning through to game time to bring the game total up to about 35,000.

"People wanted their collectibles (tickets and memorabilia)," Delorme said. "We'd barely sold over 10,000 the day before.That game, we were honouring the 1994 team. That was our promo for the last day."

After the game, a lot of tears were shed, Jacques Doucet was crying. Claude Raymond was crying. Brad Wilkerson was crying. Tons of fans were crying as they lingered around after the game. Very few fans were leaving quickly to go home. They wanted to absorb and take in the sadness and the finality.

Delorme admits he didn't get emotional that day because of his duties. It was only until December he truly grasped the toll the Expos' exit did on his emotional state.

"Danny, to this day, it was so hard. I didn't have time to get emotional. I was just trying to get to the finish line. We had staffing issues (with the big crowd). We had to change our entire programming," he said. "We had set out to honour the 1994 team but we had to realign to put highlights of the history of the club on the scoreboard. We were doing a lot of interviews," he said.

It wasn't Tavares, who was left to do the essential work to deal with the exit of the Expos. It was Delorme, a bilingual native of Sudbury, Ontario, who at the end was responsible for all business components for the Expos: public relations, corporate sales, ticket sales, operations, ticket office, retail, concessions. In addition, he oversaw the coordination of the 22 games played in Puerto Rico in both 2003 and 2004.

"I wrote a lot of reports. MLB was asking the team to travel more. Puerto Rico is not their (Expos) home. We had 59 games in Montreal, 22 in Puerto Rico," Delorme said. "We played those games to maximize the value of the franchise. A lot of ground-breaking work for the Puerto Rican games was done by New York. Tony and myself put together financial statements.

"There were rumours every year about the Expos leaving. Jeffrey Loria moved to Florida. That's where I came in. I had a transition plan. A lot of options (cities) were considered. We were looking at Portland, Vegas, Washington."

Delorme was indeed an extraordinary figure, an unsung hero. He was so respected and had a lot of clout in the running of the Expos on and off the field. He may not have been a household name like Tavares, Minaya and Robinson and assistant GM Tony Siegle but he held immense responsibilities.

"It probably wasn't until over the holidays, Dec. 29, when I had time to grieve," Delorme said. "I'd spent 23 years there. It was craziness. I thought of what we had accomplished in very difficult circumstances."

Yet, that was not the end for Delorme in his role with the Expos, at least not for a few months. Something I didn't know until I talked with him on July 11, 2023 was that he went to the Expos' office once a week until late April of 2005 to close out whatever had to be done, the final tasks associated with the Expos.

He had unofficially left the Expos' employ in February, 2005 and departed to Florida to work for the Marlins four days a week to work on the team's new stadium project but stayed on with the Expos for a few months to tie up loose ends.

It was either the Monday or the Friday of each week that he flew to Montreal from Miami and worked at Olympic Stadium, all by himself in what was left of the Expos' office.

"I remember the last time I was there. I think it was the last Friday or Monday of April. I was alone in the office. I came to leave the office. It

The drama behind the last home game

was 6 p.m. I shut the lights off," Delorme said. "I mean this was going to be the last time I'd be leaving the premises at Olympic Stadium. It's over. This is it. The team had been transferred.

"It was definitely more emotional than the last day. It was more emotional at that time. Part of my life is left behind. I would have never have left Montreal if baseball continued there. I would have stayed there forever."

While he was working his one day a week on behalf of the Expos, he was working another four days each week with the Marlins, who had been trying to pry him away from the Expos long before the final season. Loria and Samson wanted him in south Florida to help the team get a new stadium.

"I was working with three teams: the Expos, the people in Washington and the Marlins," he said, somewhat wryly. "In February of 2005, I went to Washington to meet all the staff there. Tony Tavares was co-ordinating with me from Washington as he was getting ready for the Nationals first season in Washington.

"Jeffrey Loria and (step-son) David Samson (Marlins) came after me many times. They wanted me to be a middle man. I told them I would much rather stay for the continuity. I felt with my family I wanted to stay. I explained that to him (Loria) several times. They said, 'It's time for you to come.' I told them, 'As long as the team is in Montreal, I will stay.'

"Jeffrey always wanted to own a team. Once he arrived, his understanding and expectations of the market of what he witnessed – he turned the page on Montreal," Delorme said.

Not long after the Loria regime started operating in place of the Claude Brochu consortium, Delorme had begun to assemble a binder of information in the event the team was sold. This binder contained hundreds of pages of notes written by Delorme and it contained 50,000 words.

This was how smart Delorme was. He wasn't waiting for anyone to do something at the last minute.

When Loria and Samson saw this binder, they were very impressed. No wonder they wanted Delorme to come with them to Florida when they took over the Marlins prior to the 2002 season.

"I put together a proposal for Jeffrey and David. It was a pretty lengthy document, if ever the team was sold," Delorme said. "We'd use it as a benchmark. When they made the announcement to move the team, I updated my binder and used it as a template to close out operations, severance packages, disposition of assets – it was a full, pretty extensive binder and it took a good six months after Sept. 29 to close out operations.

"When we were closing out, I shared my binder and provided a copy to Bob DuPuy and John McHale Jr. at MLB," Delorme said. "I openly shared that document about what laid ahead. We had 45 employees who were extremely dedicated, extremely loyal. They did receive severance and several years of consulting services for job search."

On Nov. 29, as I found out through research of newspaper files, 3-4

Exposion

transport trucks left 4141 Pierre-de Coubertin Ave. at Olympic Stadium for either Washington and New York with Expos' goods. Sad. A lot of files and furniture, that were in good condition, were "dispositioned" to Washington on multiple trucks, according to a document I read.

"The last truck left Olympic Stadium on Friday, Feb. 11, 2005," Delorme said.

Player contracts of existing players and other baseball info, in general, were shipped to New York and MLB offices. Info about players not on the roster and alumni also was delivered to MLB. Photos were sent to the McCord Museum in Montreal and the Canadian Baseball Hall of Fame in St. Marys, Ontario.

The Expos' seasonal staff was let go between Oct.15 and Oct. 30. It represented approximately 25 people.

"In terms of the full-time staff of 45, we had reduced the staff to 15 people by Dec. 3, 2004 and 10 people by Christmas," Delorme said. "The team store officially closed on Dec. 18, 2004. All items had been sold by that date. We were down to five employees by Feb.11, 2005. Some accounting, payroll personnel, Tony and myself."

Delorme also brought up something I had only vaguely remembered: he said one-time Expos managing general partner Claude Brochu was close in the late 1990s to selling the team to a group in Charlotte, North Carolina – or at least he expressed interest in doing so.

"Claude knew Charlotte would have been a good location for the team. There were discussions. He saw Charlotte as a top market at the time," Delorme said. "He thought the sponsorship support would be great and there was a lot of growth taking place there."

One of the last deeds for Delorme at work for the Expos was selling the rights to the impish character, Youppi. He received many offers. This is all new information as far as I know, in terms of different options facing Delorme.

"A casino in the U.S. wanted to buy it (Youppi) for $1-million," Delorme said. "It was not the money. We wanted to make it a brand that we would identify with. We agreed to sell it to the Canadiens for significantly lower than the million dollars."

As he looked back, Delorme talked about all the memories and the players and personalities he met. He's proud to be in one photo with Halle Berry, who threw out the first pitch at several Expos games.

"My favourite player was Gary Carter. I always admired how well he connected with the fans, He was very approachable and very accessible. I always admired he had the skillset. He had pure talent," Delorme said.

Another key figure in the dying days of the Expos and for some time afterward was Monique Chibok, a fireplug, who was an executive assistant to the various team presidents going back close to a quarter of a century.

She was single, never married, and thrived in prosperity despite being born with a degenerative hip. She had attended a crippled children's school for nine years. She didn't let the disability bother her as she walked around with a noticeable limp.

She was a true Montrealer, through and through.

Chibok would often pitch in to help people like Marcia Schnaar and Sina Gabrelli find apartments for players. Sept. 29, 2004 was a sad day for sure.

"It was a difficult day going around the office," Chibok said. "I had a broken heart. I was there for 25 years. The stadium was just down the street from where I lived. Whenever I have to take the Metro (subway) and go by station Pie 1X (Pee Noof in French), it brings back memories. I gave a lot of myself. There were long days and long hours."

Chibok helped Delorme to keep the office glue attached until it was no longer possible, having to deal with sad employees who were losing their jobs.

"I was involved in so many situations. I attended ownership meetings all over the place," Chibok said. "I was more of an administrator than I was a baseball fanatic. I went to the games in Puerto Rico. I touched a lot of things. I loved what I was doing or I wouldn't have lasted 24 years. I was a very loyal person."

Chibok was the conduit with the team presidents and members of the various consortiums. Sometimes, she would have to say no to someone asking to speak with one of the presidents. It wasn't always easy. She had to sit back and listen to minority shareholders expressing frustration with either Brochu or Loria because Brochu and Loria called all the shots with the title of managing general partner.

Chibok would run into "sometimes very difficult situations when certain people don't agree with certain decisions."

Employees would come to her to see if she knew of any impending layoffs near the end of the franchise. She had to pretend she didn't know.

****

Monique Giroux has gone into hibernation and gone underground.

Many people who knew her don't know where she is. She has gone into hiding but wherever she is, thank you, for all you did through the 36 seasons the Expos operated.

She never looked for attention. She doesn't look for attention now. She never wanted any publicity. She operated in obscurity behind Rich Griffin, the better known member of the Expos' media-relations department.

Giroux made me laugh, she made me smile. She boasted a genuine, down-to-earth personality.

She was such a nice lady to deal with as a member of the media way back when.She just went about her business, mostly on the French side of the media, fashioning media relations, looking after media credentials and writing in French the annual team guide handed out to the media and sold to fans.

"It's been a great life. This is the only full time job I had. I have very good memories," she said in an interview late in 2004 with the Hometown Cable Network based in Champlain, New York. "I'm very thankful for baseball and all the Montreal people who ran the company here. I came in as an assistant and I was mainly doing releases in French.

"I evolved from an assistant to public relations and media services. I was in college for three or four years. When I graduated, I was looking for a serious job. Larry Chiasson was the one who hired me. He was a wonderful guy.

"It was in the second year of Olympic Stadium that he got sick with leuke-

Exposion

Courtesy Elias Makos

Monique Giroux, middle, with media-relations assistants Elias Makos, right, and Matt Charbonneau.

mia. That happened in mid season. When he died, it was a real shock. Richard Griffin and I were promoted after the departure of Larry. I guess we did such a good job that they kept us."

Giroux told the network she was approached about going to Washington to continue her job but she said no.

"I said, 'No, my roots are here. It's been enough.' From the very beginning, I said no," she said in the interview. She also said she had no plans to write a book – it was just something she had no interest in pursuing.

In the interview, she talked about arriving at work each day about 9:30 a.m. for a night game and getting home at 1 or 2 the next morning.

"There were long days. It was part of the job. If you're working for a baseball team, it's like working in entertainment," she said.

Like many who are asked about their favourite memory while on the job, Giroux said, "I think the 1994 squad was very special – the team being away ahead of the Braves. We had great crowds and we were getting ready for the playoffs. In August, we started planning for the playoffs."

Then the strike came Aug. 12.

Giroux remarked in the interview that at that time, the Canadian dollar was worth only 63 cents on the U.S., placing a "huge burden on Canadian teams."

Giroux finished the final season with help from John Dever, Elias Makos and Matt Charbonneau.

* From Giroux, we move on to give credit to P.J. Loyello, who was replacing a legend so to speak when he took over as the main media-relations guy with the Expos following the departure of Griffin to the Toronto Star. Griff had been with the Expos since 1973 and decided he want to do something different after 22 years.

That was in February of 1995 at a time when baseball was in limbo, in a flux, in a really bad space, a terrible spot. The strike was still on.

"I got a call from the Expos," Loyello said. "They said, 'Would you be interested?' I had been director of baseball operations in Ottawa. My first two years were in PR. I went in on a Tuesday to see Richard Morency and Claude Brochu. On the Thursday, I was on a plane to spring training.

"I was excited, not only because it was a major-league team, but I grew up in Dollard-des-Ormeau (Montreal suburb). It was truly surreal," he said. "I knew the history of the franchise so it helped. I wasn't parachuted into it. It helped knowing the history of the franchise."

Loyello wasn't going in stone cold, though, because he had been employed in a similar role with the Expos' Triple-A team in Ottawa, the Lynx.

He was completely bilingual and knew the ins and outs of dealing with the media and compiling game notes and media guides.

"I had huge shoes to full. I had a start in the strike year of 1994," Loyello told me. "When the strike was on, media from Montreal would come to Ottawa for the Lynx games. Dave Van Horne and Ken Singleton came.

Loyello talked about how Vlad Guerrero "came up and made the impact. Pedro won the Cy Young award in 1997 (17-8) when the team was well below .500. He was very dominating and he was getting little or no help from the offence.

"Jim Fleming (scouting director) did a great job with the draft. With low revenue, the team did a really good job of bringing in players. Low revenue was reflected in our payroll. We couldn't afford to make a mistake."

Loyello doesn't think Montreal has much of a chance in getting a team back.

"It looks like other teams have moved ahead of Montreal," he said. "The city has fallen behind in the race. To build a new park is very expensive. To get an expansion team will take a lot of money."

Michaud raised hell as minority rep

Pierre Michaud was a thorn in the side of Claude Brochu and Jeffrey Loria.

He raised hell many times over the way the Expos were operated for 10 years but he could do little about it because he represented a limited partner group (Provigo grocery-store company owned by Loblaw group) in a consortium operated by the managing general partner, whether it was Brochu or Loria.

Michaud's true/bad values were set out in a 2023 book by Loria called From the Front Row: Revelations of a major-league owner and art dealer.

Loria revealed Michaud's anti-semetic views, recalling that Michaud went up to him prior to an Expos' game in the club's executive suite and asked Loria if he would sell back shares to the limited partners at their "original percentage." Loria said no.

That's when Michaud went on a rant against Loria, who is a New Yorker and is Jewish.

"We don't like Americans. And by the way, we don't like Jews," Michaud reportedly said to Loria.

I asked Brochu what he thought Michaud would think of what Loria revealed in the book.

"Danny, he is so arrogant and narcissistic. I'm sure he's not fazed at all," Brochu replied.

Can you imagine a big wheel with a brand-name Quebec company like Provigo engaging in anti-Jewish sentiments?

Dan Ziniuk, a freelance writer from Ottawa, Ontario, recalled having an interview with wealthy businessman Martin Stone of upstate New York in 1994 when Stone was thinking of becoming a minority investor in the Brochu-run consortium.

"At the time, Stone owned the then AAA Phoenix team but summered in Lake Placid, NY. He had a meeting with Brochu and the then local owners and was shocked by one of them being openly anti-semitic. I can now only assume that it was Pierre Michaud ," Ziniuk told me.

"If this was in the USA, then the Business section of the newspapers would pursue it and turn it into a business story rather than a baseball story. As we learn more of what went on behind the scenes, the more the whole story seems more and more tragic." What is interesting is that Michaud has apparently scrubbed most of anything written about him off the internet. I was unable to get a hold of him, even through Loblaw head office, but I sure tried to get his side of the story.

Chapter 47

Bob DuPuy, contraction, Loria's sale and the end

I've always been intrigued by the ploy Major League Baseball pulled off Nov. 6, 2001.

It must have been talked about for months, the issue of contraction.

The contraction ruling called for the Expos and Minnesota Twins to be eliminated. Even the Marlins and Tampa Bay Rays, who are still not drawing many flies these days, were mentioned as teams to be doused.

Nothing ever came of this embarrassing situation. Expos players, officials and fans wondered what they were going to do. Were the players going to be free agents immediately? Pretty weird scenario. It was certainly an ominous sign that most owners of all the other MLB clubs, mostly based in the U.S. – and acting commissioner Bud Selig didn't give a sweet fuck about Montreal as a viable franchise.

"It makes no sense for Major League Baseball to be in markets that generate insufficient local revenues to justify the investment in the franchise," Selig said at the time for the need to eliminate the Expos and Twins. "The teams to be contracted have a long record of failing to generate enough revenues to operate a viable major league franchise."

Almost 23 years later, the Rays and Marlins could still be considered endangered species. The Twins are still in existence on solid ground.

Only two months following the contraction meeting, there was the puzzling, three-way transaction of Jan. 16, 2002 that saw despised Jeffrey Loria sell the Expos to MLB. In return, Loria acquired the Marlins while Marlins owner John Henry swooped in to buy the Red Sox.

"Oh, that's something that just happened," Selig told me several years ago when I asked him about the three-way deal. He just didn't want to talk about it much.

In his 2023 book From the Front Row, Loria makes reference to contraction. He still owned the Expos and was at a meeting and stood up to voice his dissent. That was at a meeting in May of 2000 when contraction first began trending.

"At that meeting with all 30 owners present, I read a statement declaring that, as an owner of the Expos, I had no wish to exit baseball and I didn't find the proposed solution equitable but I was more than willing to collaborate to find a mutually beneficial solution," Loria wrote in his book. "Potentially, the easiest one, moving the Expos to another geographic market, was not feasible, since that would result in too great a financial windfall for me as a new owner."

Sounds like a crock of shit to me – Loria trying to say such crap "about too great a financial windfall." He wanted money more than anything.

In that paragraph, Loria acknowledged this: "In Montreal, only minimal sponsorship revenue was available, the free ticket requests were substantial and both the current and long-term situation were not sustainable. It became clear to me that contraction was partly a negotiating ploy by the league."

As for that free ticket scenario, I remember members of the media, for example, getting free ducats if we wanted them for friends and relatives. That was in the late 1980s and early-to-mid 1990s.

Selig's chief aide, Bob DuPuy, was an instrumental engine in the final years of the Expos since he did all the work Selig wanted done. DuPuy, whose surname is French, was officially known as the president and chief operating officer of Major League Baseball.

I'm glad I was able to get him to talk, at least by email. For years, this talk of the Expos' dying days/months/years has been all hush-hush. Nobody wanted to say anything much to piss off Montreal fans.

DuPuy presented ideas to team owners and representatives and the commissioner's office. He was part and parcel to anything and everything that went on in baseball off the field. He served one year in Vietnam and who knows he may have ran into Bill Campbell, the only known Expos player to serve in the Vietnam conflict.

DuPuy did the leg work for Selig but doesn't get praised or criticized in public for what happened. When something happened, it was Selig, not DuPuy, who spoke to the media.

DuPuy merely banked on his experience as a lawyer with Milwaukee-based Foley and Lardner firm which to this day, mainly revolves around the buying, selling and restructuring of sports franchises. This category he specializes in is called Sports Industry. No wonder he had a good handle on the inner workings of franchises.

DuPuy knew the sports business. He suggested contraction be done and he was part and parcel to the three-way, three-city transaction. I bet if baseball does somehow return to Montreal, he will be involved in some way.

As much as people despise Loria and his step-son David Samson, you can agree he did ask his limited partners to pitch in and pay players and other expenses but they declined cash calls so Loria ended up as the majority shareholder of the franchise

In 2023, DuPuy agreed with Selig.

"The Expos' problems were not a secret. Everyone was brainstorming about how to turn the industry economics around, and contraction was merely one of the options that were being considered," DuPuy told me. "As you know, the players and management were at that point beginning their discussion of a new CBA which was reached in August 2002. If you look at that agreement, I believe there was a provision in it about the consideration of contraction.

"The Expos were always on the list as a possible candidate given their history and the inability to get a new ballpark. A significant amount of time was spent on reviewing possible candidates for contraction.

"John Henry wanted to buy a team other than the Marlins. There was

Explosion

a discussion of the Angels, and he then turned his attention to the Red Sox and partnered with Tom Werner to do so. Since the Marlins were then available, Jeffrey expressed an interest, given the difficulty he was having in Montreal."

In his book, Loria wrote that "a group of us met often with Bob DuPuy" in an attempt to somehow resolve the situation in Montreal by way of selling the franchise to the powers that be in New York City.

"Bob was, and remains, a brilliant, well-organized executive and a special human being," Loria wrote."We discussed the creative potential of an unusual and novel three-way franchise trade, which to my knowledge had never been done before in baseball or in any other sport," Loria said in the book. "I would agree to sell the Expos back to Major League Baseball and it would control the team's destiny and do with the team as it saw fit."

The three-way deal finally was consummated on Feb. 15, 2002 just when spring training began. Loria was no longer involved with the Expos and the general consensus was: good riddance. I've always considered Loria a shyster but I do realize he was a shrewd businessman, who took over the majority shares in the team after the limited partners declined cash calls.

So in the three years the Expos were owned by MLB, local businesses and companies and corporations were given every chance to make a bid to buy the club back. Nobody came forth. It was sad.

When it became apparent nobody was interested, Selig struck a committee that would look at alternate sites outside Canada. I believe this is the first time anyone has actually mentioned this committee was in existence and who was on the committee. Not sure though.

"There was a committee formed that included White Sox owner Jerry Reinsdorf, me, John McHale Jr., Wendy Selig-Prieb, Corey Busch and Tom Ostertag that I recall that looked at various venues including Northern Virginia, Washington, Charlotte, Portland, San Antonio, Mexico City and/or Monterrey and the Southeast triangle in Virginia," DuPuy told me. "There may have been others. Locating to Washington or Northern Virginia required discussions with the Baltimore Orioles since the team was moving into their territory."

What I found ironic about this committee is that Expos legend John McHale Sr.'s son John was a member of the committee. Not that I'm trying to criticize John Jr. but it was odd he was on a committee that was trying to relocate his dad's franchise.

McHale Jr. had enormous amounts of experience, having been involved in high-end roles with the Colorado Rockies, Detroit Tigers and Tampa Bay Rays before he joined the MLB staff. Selig-Prieb was a Brewers' big wig and Bud's daughter, Busch was a former Giants executive tabbed by Selig as an outside consultant to lend his expertise in "market evaluation" and Ostertag was MLB's general counsel and a vice-president.

McHale said he was "fully retired", except for some work he does for Manfred, and due to other issues, declined to talk about the Expos' situation.

"In light of all that, I pass on any comment and defer you to the Commissioner's Office. Best of luck on your project," McHale tdold me.

On Sept. 29, 2004, Selig officially announced that the Expos were being moved to Washington and DuPuy was part of the MLB crew that came to Montreal for the final home game that night to express condolences to all involved. He made his way into the Expos' clubhouse.

DuPuy was Selig's representative at the game. I can't imagine Selig would have wanted to show up because he would've been booed out of the stadium. His reputation had been smeared after he was forced to announce the cancellation of the 1994 season, thus robbing the Expos of going to the playoffs.

"I was at the final game on September 29 and addressed the players and thanked them for their patience and their effort," DuPuy told me. "The playing of games in Puerto Rico and the uncertainty over the future of the franchise was difficult for everyone.

"It was certainly a sad day for the city and the history of the franchise but represented a new beginning in Washington. The team of course was sold in 2006 to the current owners.

"We tried very hard to keep the Expos in Montreal with their history, the history of the Canadiens and Alouettes but we could not get public or private support to build a new ballpark which was necessary," DuPuy continued. "I have been away from the sport now for almost 13 years, but I think Montreal is a wonderful city with a proud baseball tradition. But there needs to be the local wherewithal to get it (new-team scenario) done."

Busch told me the committee "needed a thorough investigation of the various criteria baseball would look at" so he spent a lot of time on the ground in various markets in gauge any city's interest in taking on the Expos.

Busch said he talked to the people involved in each city, taking into consideration the "population, the distance to the ballpark, the media markets, sponsorships, all those things that make up the elements of a great baseball market."

In the end, Busch said, Washington and Northern Virginia offered the "two best options" to take over Montreal's team.

"They were two well organized groups that were working with us to try to be the best markets for the Expos," Busch said. "There was some interest on the part of Charlotte, a real interest in Portland, Austin, Texas, Nashville, Indianapolis and – Las Vegas was particularly interested. San Jose was really interested – and Orlando, Florida. We did a lot of work by phone, interacting with cities.

"Montreal – there were a couple of issues. Olympic Stadium was just a terrible venue for a major-league team. And I knew something about terrible teams when I was with the Giants. Candlestick Park was just as bad as Olympic Stadium. It was very clear, looking at the situation, that the Expos did not have stability. At the time when the decision was made, it was pretty clear those answers weren't there in Montreal.

"I think it's fair – I can tell you we were really diligent in our work. I've known Bud Selig since 1979-80. The last thing Bud Selig wanted was to see a team leave its territory. He hated it. As a Braves fan, he was devastated when the Braves left Milwaukee (1964) and he helped bring a team back there."

Busch admitted the committee had recommended Washington long before Sept. 29.

"The committee had the authority to make the decision, the recommendation being made not far in advance before the announcement," Busch said.

Ostertag, understandably, was reluctant to give me any information about the inner workings of the committee and said he was not of any liberty to tell me how far in advance the committee and MLB had known the Expos were going to Washington.

Was it days, weeks or months? Why all of a sudden on the day of the last home game did MLB decide to make the announcement? 20 years later, out of confidentiality and privacy, Ostertag took the fifth amendment.

Courtesy The Score Network
Expos fan Katie Hynes sheds tears while being interviewed by Ryan Paton during the last home game of the Expos

"So much of what I know about the subject is, unfortunately, privileged and/or confidential because I was the MLB's general counsel at the time," Ostertag told me. "Getting into facts or our work in any detail is different – if it relates to our internal work or thought processes or anything that could be privileged or confidential, I'm afraid I just cannot help. I trust you understand."

When I Googled Ostertag to find out any information about him, I noticed he had posted something fascinating about the Expos' scenario on the website of his former employer, Sidley Austin LLP:

"The biggest – and longest – challenge I had at MLB was the relocation process for the Montreal Expos to Washington, D.C. Never had MLB bought a team for ourselves, run a team ourselves, relocated a team ourselves, sold a team ourselves and negotiated a new ballpark for ourselves. There were no precedents lying around the office for any aspect of what was required."

"My comments to Sidley were carefully chosen to be general, well-known publicly or my opinion about the matter," Ostertag told me.

When I sent Selig a letter to his residence in Milwaukee seeking comment about the Expos, especially the decision made on the morning of Sept. 29, I never heard back. He has been good to talk with me on other occasions in the past but not this time.

I'm sure he's fed up with talking about this portfolio.

Chapter 48

Who from the Blue Jays voted to contract the Expos?

Yes, who was it? The million-dollar question I've been trying to answer for this book.

Who was the Blue Jays official who voted yes to vote for contraction of the Expos on Nov. 6, 2001?

Paul Godfrey wants to make it clear he wasn't the Blue Jays representative who voted on behalf of the team to contract the Expos and Minnesota Twins. He was the president of the Jays from 2001-2008.

There have been a lot of hard feelings over the years among Expos fans after it was revealed the Jays voted to eliminate the Expos. I get this negative feedback all the time on Twitter (X) and Facebook when the Jays come up in conversation.

It's part of the hate fest many Montreal fans have for Toronto and the city. Even the rest of Canada doesn't have much use for Toronto, whether it's the city, the Leafs, the Jays, Raptors, Argonauts, you name it.

Some of those people mistakenly blame Paul Beeston but he was working in the commissioner's office in between two stints as Jays' president. When I talked to Beeston in late 2023, he didn't want to get into any talk of who with the Jays cast that vote. He probably knows.

Godfrey doesn't recall being present at such a meeting on the above date when even the Florida Marlins and Tampa Bay Rays were being looked at as elimination franchises.

"I was at every meeting. I was definitely at the various meetings. Every meeting, I was a spokesman," Godfrey told me in September of 2023. "We were all over the place for meetings, even one in Arizona where the commissioner had a home. No way I would register a vote against the Expos. I would never have voted in favour of eliminating the Expos.

"I remember that. I think that was the deal discussed behind closed doors. I tried my very best to work behind the scenes to work on and better help the Expos. Problem is that they wanted a team in Washington desperately. It's the nation's capital. I know that."

If such a meeting to eliminate the Expos was held behind "closed doors" outside of an actual owners meeting, was the late Ted Rogers, the head of Rogers Communications, the person who voted to eliminate the Expos? Was it Rogers, without Godfrey being present, who cast the vote on behalf of Toronto against Montreal?

The million-dollar question.

When I asked publicist Pat Courtney of the commissioner's office

Exposion

who the Jays representative was that day, there was no reply.

Allan Chapin, who was chairman of the Blue Jays during the time when the Interbrew beer conglomerate owned the ball team, said he wasn't at the meeting.

"By then, Ted was in charge, not us," Chapin told me. "Paul Beeston probably knows. He's always been in the thick of everything. Paul Godfrey should know. Maybe he can't say anything."

Said Beeston, "I don't want to get involved in any of that stuff. That just causes problems. It's privileged information."

I believe Godfrey when he thinks some matters were settled out of reach of the owners meetings, that decisions could have been made by other owner reps in private discussions.

"Bud Selig was the commissioner and he knew how to handle things and get what he wanted. I'm almost sure he wanted to shrink the league. He wanted to get down to 24-26 teams. I'm almost sure of that," Godfrey said. "I can assure you the vote was basically done with the support of the commissioner. Just like the NHL, the NBA, they're all controlled by the commissioner. When I was the super mayor of Metro Toronto, anything I wanted I could get done."

"I was very disappointed when Montreal was moved to Washington. It left a sour taste in my mouth. I even spoke to the Expos' people. I remember all that. It was all the American people (team owners) who seemed to be gung ho at the time they were moved.

"It was the Expos who came first. They broke the ice to bring a team to Canada. We were able to use them to get the Blue Jays with the support of Howard Webster, Labatt's and the Canadian Imperial Bank of Commerce."

As for the possibility of a team returning to Montreal, Godfrey was cautiously optimistic.

"I think it's possible a team will end up three. You would have to have an enterprise person who loves baseball, who can funnel the interest and drive the interest the Bronfman family had," Godfrey said. "You would have to have ownership that is prepared to do things to make it a long-term thing. Who knows what can happen. No. 2 – you have to have the province to build a facility that would at least match the revamped Rogers Centre in Toronto.

"You know what, there are so many people in Canada that could financially buy a team. There's great pride in being the owner of a baseball team. There are a lot of multi-millionaires. There shouldn't be a problem getting someone with financial clout. A team now is worth a billion dollars. I think the Expos and Blue Jays would definitely have a drawing card for people in Canada.

"You know attendance was very, very poor (in Montreal). Attendance is very important. You need an ownership that is prepared to do things to make it long-term."

Beeston, like Godfrey, is gung-ho and hoping Montreal gets another team. He was one of the first employees the Blue Jays hired in 1976 and had two different stints as Blue Jays president sandwiched around a tour of duty as deputy commissioner.

Who from the Blue Jays voted to contract the Expos?

"I'm not speaking on behalf of Rogers or the Blue Jays or the commissioner's office but in my opinion, I believe it is unequivocally good for Montreal to get another team. It would be great for baseball in Canada," Beeston told me. "Absolutely. The answer is yes. Montreal would be a great city. It would be good for commerce.

"When the Expos were winning in 1981, I was there. There was happiness. There was just the mood, a feel of good will in the entire stadium. There was this love of the game. Montreal has history, Jackie Robinson, Roberto Clemente. They were two icons of the game. They transcended centuries. People forget Clemente played in Montreal.

"I grew up in Welland, Ontario and my father used to take me over to Detroit to see the Tigers play. Everybody was an Expos fan when they first came in. It was fun and dancing and John Boccabella. I was a proud Canadian. We claimed all those guys. The Expos were ours.

"Hopefully, they can get a new stadium. That is the key. You could never play at Olympic Stadium. There are too many impediments against it. It's important. I know when we moved two kilometers to the east to downtown (SkyDome) from Exhibition Stadium, it made a huge difference."

Loving the Expos in West Virginia

"When I was a young, young, young kid, my first little T-ball team was the Expos, because they all had MLB team names, and because I was (and still am!) a full team girl, I started asking for Expos' posters and baseball cards and pennants and all of that stuff. The Dairy Queen would always do the summer helmets and I would ask for the Expos one. My aunt had a satellite dish, so I would get to see MLB games from all over the country, which was a big deal in the 1980s, and I also grew up with Pittsburgh TV stations and TBS on cable, so I saw a lot of Pirates and Braves growing up, too. I moved to DC for work in 2008, and my co-workers would ask "Want to go to a Nationals game this weekend?" and my answer was "No, I do not want to go see the Expos that you people stole." My husband's favorite Expo is Larry Walker, for sure. I think mine is Gary Carter, but definitely hard to pick. Could go with Vlad, Andre Dawson ... there was that time Pete Rose was an Expo."

— Jacque Jo Bland, director of communications for the West Virginia Senate.

Chapter 49

Olympic Stadium bullshit

They want to fix the roof and technical ring at Olympic Stadium in Montreal. Oh no.

They want to spend millions and millions to fix it up – again.

That news came in the summer of 2023. The saga of this complex facility in east-end Montreal is mind boggling. For years, the retractable roof would never work.

On Sept. 13, 1991, a portion of the side of the stadium fell apart, causing the Expos to play home games for the remainder of the season on the road.

All this stadium nonsense began in the 1970s when contractors were getting paid many, many times for each load of dirt, shit, concrete and whatever to build the bloody place. It's been a money pit ever since.

The technical ring is what Darryl Strawberry, Dave Kingman (foul ball) and Henry Rodriguez hit with monstrous shots.

"This is a new development, a whole new dimension, to replace the roof and ring. It will cost hundreds of millions of dollars," said Jeremy Filosa, a seasoned, eloquent reporter with Cogeco's Montreal radio station 98.5. "They should keep it superficial. This is my opinion – this is where we should draw the line. This is a massive one. I really don't think they should go ahead with it. This is something they should have done a long time ago.

"They're trying to kill two birds with one stone. The technical ring – they might as well take it apart. I'm no engineer but you could get rid of it instead of replacing it. It needs to be replaced to tell you the truth. The roof caved in – in January of 1999. It's almost 25 years ago. The roof core is no longer functional. Nobody believes anything they say or do until they actually work on it.

"They spend $50-million per year for the upkeep of Olympic Stadium. That's privileged information," Filosa revealed. "Desjardins has offices there in the stadium tower and I know some sports federations operate inside the stadium. They don't have a full-time (sports-team) tenant."

What has unnerved some people also was the decision by the Olympic Installations Board to annihilate baseball enthusiasts by converting Olympic Stadium into a football-only facility like what was done years ago at BC Place Stadium in Vancouver.

The football-only scenario for all intents and purposes eliminates the idea of having baseball games there in the near future. The move was done in part because the Blue Jays exhibition games stopped being played there in 2019 and you have to remember, too, that the CFL's Montreal Alouettes have their facilities there and conduct practices there.

So to clarify this situation, I asked someone in the know.

Can baseball games still be played at Olympic Stadium after the recent renovations?

"It can be done, if the opportunity is enticing," said Cedric Essiminy, a media-relations specialist with the Olympic Installations Board.

I got the same kind of an answer from the BC Place complex in Vancouver.

"While we are not currently exploring any opportunities to apply for a Major League Baseball franchise at BC Place, we are open to the possibility of welcoming baseball to our stadium in some capacity," said Jenny McKenzie, senior manager of marketing and communications at BC Place.

In other words, both Montreal and Vancouver could do something to convert to baseball but I'm assuming the cost would be very significant.

With the advent of possible renovations, it has been determined by some people, including me, that this venture will be a detriment to anyone wanting to bid for an expansion franchise. Why? Because the Big O would not be available as a temporary field to use before a new team moved into a stadium downtown.

Filosa made a lot of sense when he pinpointed that three of the city's major sports facilities are not up to snuff and he's talking about Olympic Stadium, Saputo Stadium, home of the MLS's CF Montreal and McGill Stadium, which plays host to the CFL's Montreal Alouettes.

"We have a soccer stadium that is not adequate. They have to have something better than that if Lionel Messi comes here," Filosa told me. "For sure, Saputo Stadium is not up to MLS standards. We have a football stadium for the Alouettes that is 100 years old. The facilities are far from ideal in both cases.'

And then there's bullshit Olympic Stadium.

"When the split-season idea with Tampa was turned down, Stephen Bronfman basically pulled out. We know Rob Manfred has a plan for expansion and I mean, logistically, how could you not look at the biggest market in Montreal?" Filosa argued.

"We won't get a sniff – there's Nashville, Charlotte, Portland – there's simply not much confidence in stuff getting done in Montreal. We lost the Expos and Nordiques. We are light years behind. It puts us behind the eight ball. One thing I can tell you – there was a group including Bronfman and Lino Saputo Jr. that were willing to offer to buy Olympic Stadium and do whatever they saw fit. Nothing worked out.

"Surprisingly, to tell you the truth, they invested quite a bit of money to host Blue Jays exhibition games every year, that by the end of the last visit in 2019, MLB gave Olympic Stadium a stamp of approval for regular-season games. They had invested quite a bit of money to make sure Olympic Stadium was up to par for MLB regular-season games."

In September of 2023, months after I had interviewed Filosa, he re-

Exposion

ported that higher-ups at MLB in New York told him they thought highly of Montreal as an expansion franchise but that the Big O was a no-go.

His report received a lot of play online and got a lot of Expos fans in a tizzy, a positive one, at least for the time being. What else would MLB people tell Filosa – that they didn't want a new franchise in Montreal?

On another matter, what I understand is that the bullpens were sold.

What I found interesting is that the maintenance crew at Olympic Stadium uses a crane to dig up the pitcher's mound and eventually placed somewhere in a room.

"That's what I was told," said John Harkness, who knows a thing or so about what is going on in the ancient facility.

Then there's the case of the missing lockers in the Expos clubhouse or did they go missing?

People I am familiar told me in early 2023 that the Expos clubhouse was dismantled and purists like 1970s batboy Danny Plamondon were disheartened. Some of these people had actually gone into the clubhouse located not far from the Expos clubhouse on the first-base side to discover the cubicles gone. All they saw was walls.

"They're taking the Expos history and glory away," Plamondon said.

Was it possible the OIB took away the stalls/cubicles and then brought them back – freshly painted in dark blue – when people complained to me? No idea. It's all a mystery.

Essiminy showed me a photo and a video of the cubicles. I believe the people who told me about the missing lockers and I believe Essiminy. So there.

CP rep on old board still hopeful

Joshua Fireman knew the ins and outs of a consortium that ruled the Expos.

Freeman sat on the board for a famous railway company, Canadian Pacific.

"I represented CP Limited during the awful Loria years and was forced to watch the team I love fall into the wrong hands," Fireman told me. "My feelings about that era and the individuals involved are not fit to print.

"A full relocation of a team is likely our only hope, whether it is Tampa or another borderline franchise. I'm assuming expansion will go to a U.S. city where the expansion fee will be massive. This brings us to the issue of MLB itself. Relocation requires an admission of failure that does not appear to be in the cards with current leadership.

"This second factor, then, might be thought of as the X factor: A long-term, renewed political mission that likely only succeeds with the next commissioner. The players' union also needs to be politicked and brought onside, as will key owners (Rogers). With Stephen Bronfman withdrawing, this leads to the third factor: local ownership.

"I am loath to play the one-man saviour card, but my experience in the late 1990s showed me that a collection of equal owners is a model that cannot succeed. Minority owners can absolutely be a part of a model but the Expos will need a deep-pocketed local majority owner. Perhaps someone (Pierre Peladeau?) who controls a media network, internet pipes, and mobile networks - and who purchased the (football) Alouettes.

"The bottom line is: Sports need to be firmly attached to broadcast rights and viewed as a programming asset to succeed today. All fingers point to Peladeau as the most attractive candidate."

Chapter 50

Tribute to coaches the last three years

Jerry Morales had been out of Major League Baseball as a coach for a long time when he got a surprise call from the Expos in February of 2002.

The team was under new management, new ownership. The club was now owned by Major League Baseball. Weird situation for sure.

On the phone with Morales was new Expos general manager Omar Minaya, who was working in unison with president Tony Tavares, skipper Frank Robinson and vice-president of business operations Claude Delorme.

Morales was in his native Puerto Rico when Minaya's call came. Morales had been coaching a Puerto Rican team in the Caribbean World Series in Venezuela and then from there, he was going back to amateur baseball.

Morales, a former MLB player, told me had not coached in the major leagues since the mid-1980s.

"They were wondering if I was interested in coaching with the Expos because at the time, they belonged to the major leagues," Morales was telling me. "Frank Robinson was to be the manager and they had to make a staff. I was pretty excited. I thought I would not go back to the United States in the major leagues. I thought I would never go back.

"I thought I would give it a shot. I wasn't doing anything. I accepted a job to work for them as the first-base coach and the outfield coach."

The official date of hiring was Feb. 19, a week after Robinson was appointed. Joining Morales on the coaching staff for that season were Wendel Kim, Manny Acta, Dick Pole, Tom McGraw and Québec-born Expos hero Claude Raymond.

Morales, Kim, Acta, McGraw and Raymond were also kept for the 2003 and 2004 seasons in a three-year run of employment by the Expos. There were some changes made to the coaching staff the last two seasons but those five stayed. Nice. Raymond was more or less an eye in the sky at home games.

The others felt like kings – plane trips, 4-star hotels, delicious food, buffet grub in the clubhouse and more service time and money added to their pensions.

I love humanizing coaches and part-time players because they are underestimated or undervalued so that's why I am paying tribute to Morales and these coaches.

"I remember watching Vladdy (Guerrero). He was a great player,"

Exposion

Morales said. "People loved Vladdy, great ball player, good outfielder, very good arm, very good hitter. Even though he didn't know the language (English) or couldn't speak the language, he was the leader of the team. He took over."

It was a bit of a treat for Morales to go to his home country of Puerto Rico when the Expos played a number of games in both 2003 and 2004 and yet at the same time, it was taxing for him, players and families to be away so long from Montreal and their residences.

"I remember a road trip one time in 2004. We left Montreal and played over there in Puerto Rico. We were away for 28 days. That was bad, tough. The all-star game was in Atlanta," Morales said, explaining that the club stayed around in the U.S. to continue the season after the all-star break in Atlanta."

Morales made a point of mentioning that on top of the aggravation of having to play home games in Puerto Rico that one game scheduled for Montreal on Aug. 9 was rescheduled to be played in San Francisco on Aug. 18 with Montreal the home team. Pretty weird.

Morales didn't say it but the rescheduling of the game was just another headache and a way of MLB creating havoc for the Expos, another way to piss the team off in its final season.

According to online info I obtained, the game was redone as a result of discussions among the Expos, Giants, MLB and the MLBPA. The proposed game Aug. 9 supposedly "created difficult travel conditions for the Giants" was one explanation I saw. The Giants had finished a series in Chicago and then went on to Pittsburgh.

"The final year was pretty tough. It was a tough situation we went through, " Morales said. "The final home game was really sad for the fans. The people were disappointed. That was a sad situation. So many people went through that organization. There would be no baseball in Canada.

"In New York for the final game, that was sad because they knew there wasn't going to be baseball in Canada the next year when the team moved to Washington."

Minaya asked Morales if he wanted to go to Washington but he had to turn the offer down because his wife became sick with something that wasn't very pleasant.

"She was diagnosed with some kind of lupus. I told Frank and Omar that I would stay with my wife," Morales said.

Some of his fellow coaches went to Washington. Raymond, for one, wasn't invited.

Any chances baseball will return to Montreal? I asked Morales.

"I don't know because of the situation with the fans. Opening Day, they packed the stadium. After that, hardly any fans."

Thank you, Jerry, for your time.

Tribute to coaches the last three years

Batista was a slugging maestro in 2004

If you love to travel, have you done an all-inclusive vacation to the famous tourist town of Puerto Plata in the Dominican Republic?

Millions of people from around the world including my wife and I have visited that city over the years. You either go there or Punta Cana in the Dominican for all the sun, food and drink you can handle.

Puerto Plata is where 2004 Expos player Leocadio Francisco (Tony) Batista was born. It's not a baseball hotbed in the Dominican, though, compared to San Pedro de Macoris, Santo Domingo, Santiago and San Cristobal.

In looking at Dominican hometowns for major leaguers over the years, I never ran across many from Puerto Plata. With more research, I see there is a list of 10 Puerto Platans, including Nelson Cruz and Nelson Liriano and controversy-filled Wander Franco.

Batista was Montreal's third baseman and slugger maestro in the club's final season. He only batted .241 but he drilled 32 homers and drove in 110 runs. He added 30 doubles and a career-best 10 sacrifice flies, which was seven more than his nearest teammate. I was impressed by the sac-flies statistic – he hit in the clutch.

Some people have complained about Batista's negative WAR that season but I don't pay much attention to WAR. He was a solid presence at the plate – with that unorthodox batting stance that captured the imagination of many, including Gar Ryness, the cult hero Batting Stance Guy.

Chapter 51

Robbie Hart's 'biblical' documentary

Robbie Hart is going all out in his new tribute to the Expos.

The Montreal filmmaker is directing and producing a major documentary on the departed but not forgotten franchise titled 'Nos Amours - The Saga of The Montreal Expos.'

"It will be released in the spring of 2024 at festivals and cinemas across Canada. Broadcasters like CRAVE, RDS and TSN will follow up in late September 2024 to coincide with the 20th anniversary of the last Expos game played in Montreal," Hart said in an interview. "The 90-minute documentary will be the singular and definitive film on the Expos.

"It follows the 10-year journey (2012-2022) to resurrect the team and bring baseball back to Montreal while in parallel telling the biblical story and exploring key moments, players and protagonists since 1969. It's loaded with everybody. Nos Amours is a love affair for the ages. A film that unravels the unique, profound relationship that can exist between a city, a team and fans."

Hart's film features Charles and Stephen Bronfman, Warren Cromartie, the 1981 and 1994 teams, cartoonist Terry (Aislin) Mosher, magician Alain Choquette, superfan Katie Hynes, journalist Philippe Cantin, rapper Annakin Slayd of Expos Nation and Pierre Boivin of the Bronfman-run company Claridge Inc.

The film was shot over 10 years and includes archives from Hart's original Expos documentary released in 2002

Hart has conducted private, in-house screenings with a number of people, including Stephen Bronfman. Other than that, he has kept the film out of circulation, for privacy and confidentiality reasons until it officially airs in late spring of 2024. I did have a private Vimeo look at the film. Nicely done, Robbie.

When I asked Hart if this documentary is a "follow up" to his first documentary, he replied, "it's much more than a follow up."

Hart is the narrator of the film which includes a segment on the split-season scenario promoted by Stephen Bronfman in conjunction with Tampa Bay, a concept that was quashed by MLB in January of 2022.

Bronfman had a special committee that was all ears on the Tampa Bay project. I knew William Jegher was one of the committee members but there were two others involved I wasn't aware of: Boivin and lawyer Richard Epstein.

They called themselves the Fearless Four, a moniker they had kept

Robbie Hart's 'biblical' documentary

Courtesy Robbie Hart

Filmmaker Robbie Hart, in black, poses with a group that called themselves the Fearless Four, who put a lot of time and effort into the split-season, twin-sister concept with Tampa Bay. MLB and its owners quashed the idea in January of 2022. Hart spends considerable time on that portfolio in his documentary on the Expos. Left to right are Richard Epstein, Stephen Bronfman, William Jegher and Pierre Boivin

secret until Hart sent me photos of the group. This group worked on the Tampa Bay portfolio for several years before it met its demise.

Bronfman's actual partners with money included Mitch Garber and Alain Bouchard but the Fearless Four put together the nuts and bolts of the split-season concept.

This documentary puts to pasture any thoughts of a similar production by Francesco Giannini of Montreal and Christopher Blow of London, Ont. They told me in March of 2023 they were in talks with investors to obtain money to shoot the film about Nos Amours.

"We are not working on the same project as Robbie Hart," Giannini told me in an interview. "We tried to reach out to them and they never responded to us. Would of been nice to collaborate, but you know how Darwinism goes."

Hart said he had heard from the Giannini/Blow camp but said he had no interest in merging with them. Hart had his ducks in order years ago, long before Giannini and Blow came along.

It would not have made much sense for Giannini and Blow to duplicate what Hart was doing and try to bring it out in 2024.

Attraction Images of Montreal has also told me the company is developing a major documentary series project on the Expos to be released likely in the next several years but not 2024.

"This series will be broadcast on a major international platform," said Nancy Audet, a journalist and author with Attraction Images. "The series will focus on the sale of the team and its departure from Montreal. We want to know what happened behind the scenes."

Exposion

Courtesy Terry (Aislin) Mosher

Famous Expos broadcaster Rodger Brulotte poses with the cover of an upcoming Expos book being produced by prolific Terry (Aislin) Mosher (inset). The book will be released at Expos Fest in April of 2024.

Stairs held out for more money

On Jan. 17, 2024, the 35th anniversary of the Expos' $15,000 signing of Canadian Matt Stairs on Jan. 17, 1989, I chatted with a guy who helped set up the contract for Expos scout Bill MacKenzie.

His name: Bill Saunders, who knew Stairs all the way through minor baseball in Fredericton, New Brunswick.

About 10 months before the signing, MacKenzie was in New Brunswick running a tryout camp and Stairs was there and so was Saunders, who has been prominent in ball in that province for decades.

"Bill has some roots down here so he brought his mother and dropped her off at my house," Saunders recalled. "We had the tryout camp and Bill went away with no contract signed. Then later that year, Bill was making a sweep across Canada, rounding guys up for the best prospects for tryouts from B.C. to Newfoundland.

"Bill said to bring Matt to Olympic Stadium in Montreal for a tryout camp. I drove there with Matt, my wife, and a friend of mine, Kelvin Hoyt. There were about 20 guys there. Bill was running the camp and he asked me to throw Matt batting practice. I'm like a kid in a candy store – I'm saying it's the closest I'll ever get to the majors. I was excited as hell."

Again, like that tryout in N.B., this tryout at the Big O resulted in no contract for Stairs. Then MacKenzie calls Saunders some time later to tell him he was couriering a contract to him and he asked Saunders to try and get Stairs to sign him.

They had gathered in Marysville, N.B. at the office of Bob Kenny, a friend of Saunders. Saunders whispered in Stairs' ear not to sign. The offer was $10,000. Saunders said he would call other teams and see what type of money Stairs was actually worth in the days when there was no MLB draft.

"I wasn't going to tell Bill I was calling around to see if I could get more money from other teams," Saunders said. "A guy from the Yankees said they didn't have enough working visas for Canadians. We couldn't get any bites from other teams (to sign Stairs)."

Then all of sudden, MacKenzie couriered another contract from Ottawa. This time, MacKenzie supposedly offered $15,000. That's the amount MacKenzie told me close to 20 years ago. But Saunders told me the contract says $12,500. Stairs signed.

At this meeting, again in Kenny's office, Saunders, Stairs, his mother Jean, his then girlfriend, and at the request of Matt, his best friend Rob Kelly, were on hand. Sadly, Kelly died in a helicopter crash later in life.

Look at the career Stairs had. Not much time with the Expos but he carved out a solid career with other teams, including the Blue Jays, thanks in part to Saunders and MacKenzie.

Epilogue

The Nashville Stars, the Portland Baseball Project and Big League Utah are ahead of the game in wanting an expansion or relocated team.

As we went to press with this book, Montreal and Charlotte, two other cities mentioned as favourites, had no official group put together.

This doesn't mean Stephen Bronfman of Montreal or some other individual will not consolidate a group to consider an expansion proposal when commissioner Rob Manfred calls for bids, hopefully in 2024.

Bronfman has never publicly said since January of 2022 he's not in favour of a franchise playing 162 games but Mitch Garber, one of his partners, told me that number of games in one season is too much.

What it comes down to is that it's very, very expensive to operate a team playing from April-October. Plus, there is the issue of the money required to build a new stadium, the expansion fee, etc.

Years ago, I would often say Tampa Bay owner Stuart Sternberg would sell his franchise to Bronfman long before the Rays lease ends at Tropicana Field in 2027. I no longer hold that view. Sternberg loves being a major-league owner.

I have been told Bronfman does want to be involved with an expansion-team application but it's all speculation.

I've also learned Sternberg and Bronfman meet socially often in New York. They thought they had a deal with MLB regarding the twin-city, split-season concept but it was turned down in January of 2022. Thank God.

Tampa Bay appears to be staying in that area as a result of an announcement in September of 2023 and MLB owners approved the transfer of Oakland to Las Vegas.

Question is: would Montreal and its fans all over support the team consistently over the long haul a second time around?

I point to a headline on a 2023 Travel section story in the Toronto Star which stated

Montreal has it all. Chic, Modern, Cool.

Montreal has architecture and vibrancy and Old Montreal but it hasn't had a major-league baseball team for 20 years.

At this point, the prospects of Montreal getting an expansion team are bleak. It would be nice if somebody proved me wrong.

Appreciation to individuals and organizations

Sherry Gallagher
Dawna Dearing
Robert Di Palma
Tibob du Longueuil
Don Rice
Kevin Glew
Bob Elliott
Rory Costello
Philippe Grenier
Rich Griffin
Russ Hansen
Stéphane Harvey
Joe Gromelski
Terry (Aislin) Mosher
Don Nomura

Burton Peck
Dariush Ramezani
Robert Whiting
National Baseball Hall of Fame
Canadian Baseball Hall of Fame
Canadian Baseball Network
Archives of City of Montreal
National Archives of Québec
Griff's The Pitch Podcast
Montreal Gazette
Montreal Star
La Presse in Montreal
Le Journal de Montréal
New York Times
Washington Post
Southwest Voice in Québec

Sporting News
Canadian Press
Associated Press
Home Town Cable Network
LA County police department
Retrosheet
Baseball Reference
Baseball Almanac
Pinterest
Wikipedia
Twitter
Facebook
SABR Bio Project
Expos Fest

Interviews

Tony Armas Jr.
Pierre Arsenault
Nancy Audet
Bernie Beckman
Paul Beeston
Dennis Blair
Tom Brady Sr.
Corey Busch
Allan Chapin
Endy Chavez
Monique Chibok
Dr. John Cisna
Murray Cook
Warren Cromartie
Fernando Cuza
Claude Delorme
Pat Daugherty
Kris Doorey
Bob DuPuy
Cedric Essiminy
Michael Farber
Jeremy Filosa
Joshua Fireman
Jim Fleming
Jim Gabella
Wayne Garrett
Bob Gebhard
Paul Godfrey
Roberto Greco
Philippe Grenier
Marc Griffin
Tom Grieve

Marquis Grissom
John Harkness
Robbie Hart
Chris Henchek
Dan Hooks
Stan Hough
John Hughes
Maxwell Kates
Randy Kierce
Bob LaMonte
Bill Lee
Eric Knott
Jeanine L'Ecuyer
PJ Loyello
Frank Magee
Kevin Malone
Oreste Marrero
Danielle Martin
Ron McClain
John McHale Jr.
Andy McGaffigan
Jenny McKenzie
Denis McSween
Pierre Miquelon
Jerry Morales
Jose Morales
Eric Niskanen
Dan Norman
Don Nomura
Rick Nye
Larry Jaster
Tom Ostertag

Dave Parker
Larry Parrish
Danny Plamondon
Ray Ratto
Mike Raymond
Buck Rodgers
Nelson Santovenia
Bill Saunders
Brian Schneider
David Segui
Bob Scotti
Ron Shapiro
Lee Anne Simons
Chris Smith
Randy Smith
Bernie Souliere
Corey Stackhouse
Don Stanhouse
Michael Teevan
Henry Tran
Ken Turner
Alain Usereau
Jerry Van Velden
Joe Vitiello Sr.
David Wainhouse
Connie Sparma Walenick
Paul Warfield
Gary Ward
Gary Waslewski
Lenny Webster
Floyd Wicker
Dan Ziniuk

Courtesy Terry (Aislin) Mosher
Brad Wilkerson has been called The Last Expo who followed the team to Washington for 2005

Courtesy Terry (Aislin) Mosher
This cartoon was fashioned shortly after the Expos moved to Washington

www.ingramcontent.com/pod-product-compliance
Lightning Source LLC
Chambersburg PA
CBHW072150070526
44585CB00015B/1081